AF830779

Trade, Investment and the Environment

During the financial year 1998–9 the Energy and Environmental Programme was supported by generous contributions of finance and technical advice from the following organizations:

Amerada Hess
BG
Blue Circle Industries
British Nuclear Fuels
British Petroleum
Eastern Electricity
ENI
Enron
Esso/Exxon
LASMO
Mitsubishi Fuels
Mobil Services
Osaka Gas
PowerGen
Ruhrgas
Saudi Aramco
Shell
Statoil
Texaco
Tokyo Electric Power
Veba Oil

Sponsorship for the conference 'Trade, Investment and the Environment' was received from:

The Guardian
UK Department for International Development
UK Department for Trade and Industry
ICI
International Centre for Trade and Sustainable Development
World Wide Fund For Nature (WWF)

Trade, Investment and the Environment

Proceedings of the Royal Institute of
International Affairs conference
Chatham House, London, October 1998

Edited by Halina Ward
and Duncan Brack

THE ROYAL INSTITUTE OF
INTERNATIONAL AFFAIRS
Energy and Environmental Programme

earthscan
from Routledge

First published in the UK in 2000 by
Royal Institute of International Affairs, 10 St James's Square, London, SW1Y 4LE
(Charity Registration No 208 223)
and
Earthscan

For a full list of Earthscan publications please contact:
Earthscan
2 Park Square, Milton Park, Abingdon, Oxon OX14 4RN
711 Third Avenue, New York, NY, 10017, USA

First issued in hardback 2017

Earthscan is an imprint of the Taylor & Francis Group, an informa business

Copyright © Royal Institute of International Affairs, 2000. Published by Taylor & Francis.

All rights reserved. No part of this book may be reprinted or reproduced or utilised in any form or by any electronic, mechanical, or other means, now known or hereafter invented, including photocopying and recording, or in any information storage or retrieval system, without permission in writing from the publishers.

Notices:
Practitioners and researchers must always rely on their own experience and knowledge in evaluating and using any information, methods, compounds, or experiments described herein. In using such information or methods they should be mindful of their own safety and the safety of others, including parties for whom they have a professional responsibility.

Product or corporate names may be trademarks or registered trademarks, and are used only for identification and explanation without intent to infringe.

A catalogue record for this book is available from the British Library

ISBN 13: 978-1-138-42387-9 (hbk)
ISBN 13: 978-1-85383-628-2 (pbk)

Typesetting by Composition & Design Services, Minsk, Belarus
Cover design by Yvonne Booth

Contents

Preface and acknowledgments

The present volume of papers presents a snapshot of what may, with hindsight, come to be viewed as a turning point in the ongoing debate on the relationship between trade, investment and the environment.

It is a companion volume to a collection of papers edited by Duncan Brack, entitled *Trade and Environment: Conflict or Compatibility?* (RIIA/Earthscan, 1998), but it can also be read alone by newcomers to the area or by policy-makers seeking an enjoyable and readable introduction to the main issues and their possible solutions.

Both volumes were based on RIIA conferences, but, in contrast to the earlier volume, this book features a wider range of issues and a greater depth of debate (largely because this second conference was twice as long as the first). In particular, the topic of international investment, as well as trade, is covered here. Increasingly, and significantly, the flow of economic activity across national frontiers includes the movement of capital for investment as well as that of goods and services for sale. The ever more fraught progress of the negotiations around the OECD's proposed Multilateral Agreement on Investment (MAI) during 1998 made it clear that, although the trade–environment and investment–environment debates are not the same, they are very closely interlinked.

The Chatham House conference on which this book is based took place in late October 1998, just a fortnight after two defining moments: the final collapse of the MAI, and the World Trade Organization Appellate Body's report on the *Shrimp/Turtle* dispute. These critical events are reflected in some of the key questions that the authors return to again and again in their papers. What are the implications of the Appellate Body report, in a dispute that focused on a trade embargo applied in the name of the conservation of endangered species, for any future reform of the World Trade Organization – is it evolutionary or potentially revolutionary? What lessons does the failed MAI offer negotiators of trade and investment liberalization in the future? Did the environmental dimension feature adequately in each set of discussions?

Many of the papers look forward too. How can options for addressing the relationship between trade, environment and investment be designed so as to move beyond stale adversarial discussions to offer genuinely 'win–win' solutions? The varied aspirations for a 'High Level Meeting' on trade and sustainable development make thought-provoking reading in the light of the WTO Director General's two symposia on trade and environment and trade and development held in March 1999. At the time of going to press, the 1999 Seattle Ministerial Conference of the WTO and the beginning of the next 'Millennium Round' of trade negotiations are drawing ever nearer. It is striking that the ideas put forward in this book on 'environment in the Millennium Round' are as fresh as they were at the time of the Chatham House conference a year ago.

A number of the papers in this volume have been rearranged from the order in which they originally appeared, to reflect the core themes of the authors' ideas and recommendations. Some have been edited, revised or updated by their authors, and a small number of the conference presentations have been omitted from this book to avoid duplication of authors. Additionally, a conference presentation by Michael Grubb on trade issues related to the Climate Change Convention, substantially based as it was on research at Chatham House led by Duncan Brack, has been omitted; the results of that research are being published by RIIA/Earthscan in parallel with this book (Duncan Brack, with Craig Windram and Michael Grubb, *International Trade and Climate Change Policies*).

Part I contains six papers which present a strategic overview of the key issues, the state of the debate and the big issues for the future. They include the three keynote papers from the Chatham House conference: by Renato Ruggiero, at the time the Director-General of the WTO; Brian Wilson MP, then UK minister for trade; and John Gummer MP, former UK secretary of state for the environment. Part II seeks to explore some of the main ideas and positions in the rapidly evolving debate on how to secure 'win–win' solutions: how can solutions be devised that offer everyone, including the environment, more than traditional competitive bargaining? Part III contains a series of papers that focus on how to resolve some of the more technical issues as they relate to the rules of the multilateral trading system. After an overview of the issues – one from a developing country perspective and one from a lawyer – separate chapters consider the debates concerning multilateral environmental agreements, process and production methods and conflict resolution in the WTO. Part IV looks at the relationship between investment and sustainable development in two lights: the issues relating to foreign direct investment itself; and lessons from the Multilateral Agreement on Investment. Finally, Part V contains a short note on the discussions at the conference. The audience included Chatham House's normal wide range of participants, drawn from national governments and international organizations, industries, academia and NGOs, from developed and developing countries; and the presentations and discussions reflect a rich variety of backgrounds and perspectives.

The Institute gratefully acknowledges the sponsorship and support of the six conference sponsors: the Guardian; the UK Departments for International Development (DFID) and Trade and Industry (DTI); ICI; the International Centre for Trade and Sustainable Development; and the World Wide Fund For Nature (WWF). Without their support, the conference could not have included such a wide range of participants.

Our sincere thanks are also due to all those who have contributed their time, energy and ideas, both to this book and to the October 1998 Chatham House conference; the speakers and authors themselves; Charles Arden-Clarke, James Cameron, Steve Charnovitz, Caroline Lequesne and Nick Robins for helpful comments on various draft conference agendas; and to colleagues at Chatham House for their vital work in making the conference and this book happen: Philippa Challen, Julia Thomas and the Conference Unit; Nikki Kerrigan, Matt Thomas and Laura Shiver in the Energy and Environmental Programme; and Margaret May and her colleagues in the Publications Department.

September 1999 Halina Ward and Duncan Brack

Contributors

Moses Adigbli, Manager, Ghana Timber Export Development Board's London office; Director of Ghana Timber Supplies Ltd (now working for Gloimpex Ltd)

Charles Arden-Clarke, Head, Trade Policy Unit, World Wide Fund For Nature (WWF) International

David Batt, Head, International Economic Policy Development, Department for International Development (DFID) (now Acting Director, International Division, DFID)

Duncan Brack, Head, Energy and Environmental Programme, Royal Institute of International Affairs (RIIA)

Tom Burke MBE, Visiting Professor, Imperial College; Environmental Policy Adviser, Rio Tinto plc

James Cameron, Director, Foundation for International Environmental Law and Development (FIELD); Associate, Baker and McKenzie

Dr Thomas Cottier, Professor of European and International Economic Law, University of Bern; Director, Institute of European and International Economic Law

Dr Kristian Ehinger, Deputy General Council of Foreign Holdings, Volkswagen AG

Dr Damien Geradin, Associate Professor, University of Liège; Professor, College of Europe, Bruges

John Gummer MP, former Secretary of State for the Environment, UK

Jan Huner, Senior Policy Adviser, Trade and Investment Policy Directorate, Ministry of Economic Affairs, The Netherlands

Dr Veena Jha, Consultant to UN Agencies (currently Project Coordinator, Trade and Environment Projects, UNCTAD c/o UNDP, New Delhi, India)

Nick Mabey, Head, Economics Policy, World Wide Fund For Nature (WWF), UK

Pradeep S. Mehta, Secretary General, Consumer Unity & Trust Society (CUTS), India

Dr Konrad von Moltke, Visiting Professor of Environmental Studies, Free University, Amsterdam

Dr David Owen, Head of Research, VTZ Delphi

Dr Michel Potier, Senior Economist and Head of Economics Division, OECD Environment Directorate

Dr Reinhard Quick, Head, VCI Liaison Office, Brussels, Verband der Chemischen Industrie eV; Chairman, UNICE Working Group on Trade and Environment

Nick Robins, Coordinator, Sustainable Consumption and Trade Initiative, International Institute for Environment and Development (IIED)

Renato Ruggiero, Director-General, World Trade Organization (now Chair, ENI SpA)

Dr Gary P. Sampson, Director, World Trade Organization (currently visiting academic, London School of Economics, London)

Krista Nadakavukaren Schefer, Research Fellow, University of Bern

Dr Magda Shahin, Deputy Assistant Minister of Foreign Affairs and Head of Economics Department, Ministry of Foreign Affairs, Egypt

René Vossenaar, Chief, Trade and Environment Section, International Trade Programme, United Nations Conference on Trade and Development (UNCTAD)

Dr David Wakeford MBE, International Trade Manager, Group Public Affairs, Imperial Chemical Industries plc (ICI)

Halina Ward, Senior Research Fellow, Energy and Environmental Programme, RIIA

Professor David Wheeler, Head, Stakeholder Development, Body Shop International (now Director of Sustainable Development, KPMG)

Brian Wilson MP, Minister of Trade, Department of Trade and Industry (DTI), UK (now Minister of State, the Scottish Office)

Abbreviations and glossary

Agenda 21	The major non-binding policy document that resulted from the UN Conference on Environment and Development (the 'Rio Summit') in 1992. Its implementation is overseen by the UN Commission on Sustainable Development.
Amicus curiae	Literally, a 'friend of the court'; a bystander who provides legal or factual information to an adjudicator (e.g. WTO panels or the Appellate Body) on points on which he or she is unclear or mistaken
Appellate Body	Appeal body within the WTO's dispute settlement system
Basel Convention	1989 Basel Convention on the Control of Transboundary Movements of Hazardous Wastes and their Disposal
Beef Hormones dispute	Dispute between the United States, Canada and the EC over EC regulations restricting sales of beef from cattle treated with certain kinds of hormone
BIAC	Business and Industry Advisory Committee to the OECD. A similar committee, the Trade Union Advisory Committee (TUAC), exists for trade unions
BIT	Bilateral Investment Treaties
CBD	Convention on Biological Diversity
CFCs	Chlorofluorocarbons
Chapeau	Sometimes called a 'headnote'; the introductory part of Article XX of the GATT, which contains requirements that must be met by measures falling within any of its sub-paragraphs
CITES	The 1973 Washington Convention on International Trade in Endangered Species

Codex Alimentarius	The 'food code': an international set of standards, codes of practice, guidelines and recommendations on protection of consumer health and fair practices in the food trade compiled by the Codex Alimentarius Commission of the World Health Organization and the Food and Agriculture Organization
CTE	(WTO) Committee on Trade and the Environment
DANIDA	Danish International Development Administration
DETR	(UK) Department of the Environment, Transport and the Regions
DFID	(UK) Department for International Development
DSU	WTO Understanding on Rules and Procedures Governing the Settlement of Disputes
DTI	(UK) Department for Trade and Industry
EMAS	(EC) Eco-Management and Audit Scheme
EMS	Environmental management system
EST	Environmentally Sound Technology
FDI	Foreign direct investment
FSC	Forest Stewardship Council
GATS	General Agreement on Trade in Services
GATT	General Agreement on Tariffs and Trade
GDP	Gross domestic product
GEF	Global Environment Facility
GMOs	Genetically modified organisms
GSP	Generalized System of Preferences
Havana Charter	The draft Charter of a proposed International Trade Organization (ITO), which was to have been concluded in Havana in 1948, but fell because the US Congress failed to approve it. The GATT was initially intended to have operated under the umbrella of the ITO.
ICC	International Chamber of Commerce
ICJ	International Court of Justice
ICM	Integrated Crop Management

IFC	International Finance Corporation, the private-sector lending arm of the World Bank group of institutions. The IFC finances and provides advice for private-sector ventures and projects in developing countries in partnership with private investors.
IMF	International Monetary Fund, one of the so-called 'Bretton Woods Institutions' alongside the World Bank Group. The IMF exists to promote international monetary cooperation.
IPRs	Intellectual property rights
ISO	International Organization for Standardization
ISO 14000 series	A series of ISO standards concerning environmental management, eco-labelling and related issues
ITTO	International Tropical Timber Organization
LCA	Life cycle analysis
MAI	Multilateral Agreement on Investment
MEA	Multilateral environmental agreement
MFN	Most favoured nation principle of the GATT, which requires that there should be no discrimination between different imported products on the basis of their country of origin
Millennium Round	New round of multilateral trade negotiations due to begin in 1999
Montreal Protocol	1987 Montreal Protocol on Substances that Deplete the Ozone Layer, a protocol to the 1985 Vienna Convention for the Protection of the Ozone Layer. The Protocol controls production and consumption of, and trade in, ozone-depleting substances.
MTS	Multilateral Trading System
NAFTA	North American Free Trade Agreement
National treatment principle	Core GATT principle, which requires that there should be no discrimination between imported and 'like' national products under national rules
NGO	Non-governmental organization

OECD	Organization for Economic Cooperation and Development
Panel	Part of the WTO's dispute settlement system: dispute settlement panels hear cases and issue reports in disputes between WTO Members. In the WTO, panel reports can be rejected by a consensus of WTO members acting as a 'Dispute Settlement Body'. Appeals from panel reports on issues of law can be made to the Appellate Body.
PPMs	Process and production methods
Shrimp/Turtle dispute	WTO dispute between the United States and a number of exporting countries, concerning US restrictions on imports of shrimps from countries not requiring the use of turtle excluder devices
SMEs	Small and medium-sized enterprises
SPS Agreement	Agreement on the Application of Sanitary and Phytosanitary Measures
TBT Agreement	Agreement on Technical Barriers to Trade
TED	Turtle excluder device
TNC	Transnational corporation
TRIPS Agreement	Agreement on Trade-Related Aspects of Intellectual Property Rights
Tuna/Dolphin disputes	Two disputes between the United States and a number of exporting countries, involving US restrictions on imports of yellowfin tuna from countries that did not have regulations similar to those of the USA governing 'incidental' catches of dolphins
UNCED	United Nations Conference on Environment and Development, which took place in Rio de Janeiro in June 1992 and is sometimes known as the 'Earth Summit' or the 'Rio Earth Summit'
UNCSD	United Nations Commission on Sustainable Development, which was established following UNCED

UNCTAD	United Nations Conference on Trade and Development
UNEP	United Nations Environment Programme
UNICE	Union of Industrial and Employers' Confederations of Europe
UNIDO	United Nations Industrial Development Organization
US CAFE standards	US regulations on corporate average fuel economy
WTO	World Trade Organization

Editors' overview

Halina Ward and Duncan Brack

Introduction

The politics of the relationship between trade liberalization, foreign direct investment and environmental protection are as uneasy today as at any time this decade. But the thinking and analytical work on the means of ensuring just how trade, investment and environment can be made mutually supportive have advanced substantially, and there is no shortage of ideas for resolution of the problems. This book is a guide to both the politics and the policies as they were when the conference on Trade, Investment and Environment took place at Chatham House in October 1998.

The 26 papers included in the book explore, from a variety of perspectives, many of the issues in the complex relationship between trade, environment and investment. Our aim in this introduction is to provide a summary of the papers themselves, and to make a few short remarks on the debates surrounding the trade–investment–environment nexus one year on, as the Millennium Round approaches.

There are three basic focuses around which the extraordinarily complex and interlinked issues addressed in these papers centre. First, there is 'protection versus protectionism'. Do powerful trading nations use trade measures as a way of forcing developing countries to adopt essentially their own world-view? Is the trade and environment debate a form of 'eco-colonialism'? From an economic, as well as an environmental, perspective, when does it make sense to link environmental protection objectives to trade policy?

Second is the relationship between foreign direct investment and the environment. Do the activities of transnational corporations tend, on balance, to help or hinder environmental protection? How can transnational corporations most effectively be regulated in order to maximize their potential contribution to sustainable development? And what does this mean for any potential multilateral investment framework?

Third, there is a collection of institutional issues. How far can and should the WTO go in incorporating environmental considerations into its day-to-day thinking before overstepping its proper mandate? Would 'mainstreaming' the environment throughout the WTO and the agreements it oversees somehow challenge this? Would strengthening the role of non-governmental actors in the system be a threat to sovereignty or a recognition of a new 'international civil society'? And is there a need for a new global environmental organization equal in authority to the WTO to act as a counterweight to it, and to address some of the problems that result from the fragmented nature of the existing international environmental regime?

The much-misunderstood phenomenon of globalization overlies each of these themes. What are the most appropriate policy interventions in a globalized economy if environmental protection and social welfare are to be maximized? What system of global governance is needed? The practical challenges involved in defining new roles for all of the actors in the face of the 'globalization phenomenon' come across clearly in this book.

If these three *issues* lie at the heart of the subjects addressed in the papers, four major *events* in the trade and environment and investment and environment calendars also dominate: (1) the WTO Appellate Body report in the *Shrimp/Turtle* case (published in October 1998); (2) the collapse (in the same month) of the negotiations on the draft Multilateral Agreement on Investment; (3) the proposed (as it was then) High Level Meeting on trade and environment or trade and sustainable development (which eventually took place, in a slightly different form, in March 1999); and (4) the potential for the environment to figure as a negotiating item in the Millennium Round of trade negotiations, scheduled to kick off at the Seattle WTO Ministerial in November/December 1999.

Part I A strategic overview of the debate and key issues for the future

Part I is a collection of short papers that aim to set the scene for the remainder of the book by identifying the key strands and strategic issues in the trade–investment–environment debate and some options for the future. The papers do not offer a complete guide to the issues – in particular, they do not incorporate a developing country critique – but none the less, the different cultural starting points of the different protagonists analysing the relationship between liberalization and the environment are clearly apparent. And each of them underlines the need to view globalization as the overarching context within which the trade–investment–environment relationship is set, and to consider the system of global governance that it calls for.

Renato Ruggiero (then WTO Director-General), in a speech originally titled 'A Global System for the Next Fifty Years', focuses on the challenges of globalization. Does it force us to re-examine the global architecture? How should the structure of global governance reflect our increasing interdependence? He calls for a more collective leadership in the international system, with a focus on new, post-Cold War values of consensus and cooperation, to ensure that at the highest political level developing countries and economies in transition are effectively represented.

On the environment and global governance, Mr Ruggiero takes a clear position. The WTO, he claims, is a strong institutional friend and supporter of the environment. None the less, the task of strengthening bridges between trade and environmental policies would be made immeasurably easier if 'we could also create a house for the environment to help focus and coordinate our efforts'. Certainly, arguments about the extent of the WTO's competence on environmental issues, and how far it can go in accommodating environmental concerns have hampered progress in the trade–environment debate. But would the creation of a global environment organization help to address this? Mr Ruggiero points to the social clause debate, an area where there is a 'house for labour' – the International Labour Organization. Here, he says, no progress could have been made without a consensus on the ILO's and the WTO's competence. But that debate is not over. Notwithstanding the conclusion of an ILO Declaration on Fundamental Principles and Rights at work in 1998, suggestions have been made that labour issues should be addressed in the Millennium Round. The 'competence' debate continues in discussions under the WTO's Trade Policy Review

Mechanism and in the ILO itself. Similarly, it is not at all clear that the establishment of a global environment organization would in fact resolve trade–environment clashes unless WTO rules were themselves modified.

Mr Ruggiero's themes are reflected to some extent in *Brian Wilson*'s paper. The then UK Minister for Trade expresses the classical economic perspective that trade liberalization helps to ensure that resources are used efficiently, thereby generating the wealth necessary for development and environmental improvement. It also encourages the spread of clean technology worldwide. He places a strong emphasis on the values of consensus, cooperation and dialogue. He applies this to the WTO itself, with his reassurance that 'there is no way of setting aside the WTO rights of member countries against their will ... Nothing will – or can – change without consensus'. But he also stresses the need for the WTO to shed its reputation for secrecy if dialogue at all levels is to be fully effective.

Gary Sampson addresses the key opportunities and challenges of the 12 months leading up to the Seattle ministerial conference. The key challenge, for him, is to find a way of dealing with civil society criticisms of the WTO without damaging its credibility as the body responsible for the rules of the non-discriminatory trading system and the progressive liberalization of trade in goods and services. He identifies three types of possible initiatives for the 12 months ahead, according to the degree of governmental involvement necessary. First, there are those that can be achieved if there is sufficient informal support for the Director-General or the Secretariat to undertake them; second, there are initiatives that require the collective approval of WTO Members, but not formal rule changes; and finally, there are objectives that can be achieved only through changes in rules.

Like Mr Wilson, *David Wakeford* also asserts in his paper that liberalization of trade and investment creates wealth that leads to higher environmental standards and a move towards sustainability. Since trade and investment liberalization and environmental sustainability are already mutually supportive, this leaves only the questions of the rate at which progress is achieved, and the degree of improvement of environmental performance. For Dr Wakeford, the source of the belief that the WTO will solve environmental problems is the failure to address environmental issues coherently at an international level. Paradoxically, perhaps, he sees the WTO Millennium Round itself as an opportunity to achieve a consensus on the establishment of a World Organization for the Environment. Without this, 'we are like startled rabbits in the light of the WTO'.

Tom Burke also focuses on the 'globalization' theme: 'globalization of responsibility must follow globalization of opportunity'. He assesses the key distinctions between the two 'cultures' of trade and of environment. If the rules associated with each – and, more than that, their modes and habits of operation – are to merge, then looking to WTO case law alone will not be enough: a much better *shared* basis for policy-making in both areas is needed. But WTO dispute settlement procedures will also need to be reformed, in particular to create a more transparent system and to enhance non-governmental access to dispute processes.

What of the role of companies themselves? Here Burke makes an important distinction between different kinds of activities carried out by multinational corporations and their impacts: portfolio investment involves a very different kind of commitment to a host country than an investment that involves 'sinking several billion dollars into a hole in the ground that cannot be moved'. Each calls for a distinct analytical approach.

John Gummer takes up the global governance theme, associating it with the notion that rights and responsibilities should be more closely linked in the multilateral trading system: commercial freedom at the international level should be accompanied by the kinds of protective measures that exist at the national level to protect the vulnerable and the credulous. Yet at the international level, he notes that the environmental bodies and institutions that might provide that kind of protection do not have the same credibility as the WTO. Contrary to Mr Gummer's suggestion, many would see this international mismatch reflected in a lack of proper integration between trade and environment at the *national* level. Indeed, Mr Ruggiero suggested, in discussion at the Chatham House conference, that the proposed WTO High Level Meeting could be viewed in part precisely as an opportunity to 'ease the relationship' between trade and environment at the national level.

Mr Gummer highlights the dilemma that surrounds much international environmental policy-making, in which, while it is in every country's interest to cooperate in tackling challenges such as climate change, it is difficult for individual countries to see the benefits of taking action unless such cooperation is guaranteed. He goes on to argue that 'fairness' has to come to be understood as a matter of practical necessity. Only by understanding what interdependence really means can a system be developed that properly represents a global solution to a global problem.

Part II Towards win–win solutions?

Part II contains a series of papers that contribute to the emerging 'win–win ' debate, the idea that, in addressing trade, environment and investment issues, solutions that bring some benefits to all the players should be favoured. The aspiration has to be a valuable one, not to say politically attractive. But can 'win–win ' in a small number of hand-picked areas resolve much bigger issues of equity in the multilateral trading system? Is there not a need for more wholesale reform, reflected in action both within and outside the WTO; in enhanced technical and financial assistance; in a more inclusive international leadership, of the sort that Mr Ruggiero's paper calls for? The papers in this part of the book illustrate both the potential and the limitations of the 'win–win' approach.

David Batt highlights the British Department for International Development's commitment to integrating a development perspective into trade and environment policy-making, as reflected in the UK Government's 1997 White Paper on Development. (This 'integration' theme is also reflected in the May 1999 UK Sustainable Development Strategy, which devotes a section of the chapter on 'International Cooperation and Development' to a consideration of trade and the environment, and sets out guiding principles on trade and the environment.)

Mr Batt's paper highlights a number of practical initiatives being undertaken by the DFID under three themes: ensuring fair trade rules;

increasing sustainable trade and raising environmental standards in developing countries. Finally, he focuses on a fourth area of activity, namely the 'win–win ' approach, an area that is not drawn out explicitly in the White Paper. The terminology is, he suggests, beguilingly simple, but the reality is that policy changes do not always have simple effects; some changes could produce a mixture of environmental effects, some positive and some negative. In short, there may be a mixture of winners and losers even where the aim is 'win–win'. Mr Batt identifies a need for more research to build up a list of positive 'win–win' examples, so as to begin to pin down the areas that present the strongest possibilities for further 'win–win' options.

Nick Robins does just that. He presents a series of case studies on 'sustainable trade', based on the experiences of producers who have been able to turn new demands in their export markets to their advantage. Effective partnerships along the supply chain, along with product quality, emerge as critical success factors. Conversely, a lack of trust over the motivations and impacts of rising social and environmental demands presents a real barrier to responding positively to those demands.

Supply chain management and the role of procurement policy are attracting increasing policy interest. Mr Robins suggests that corporate supply chain management, driven as it is by a mix of risk management and market creation concerns, can often take place ahead of consumer demand. And, in a conference focusing on the environmental aspects of sustainable development, it is interesting that Mr Robins stresses an apparent convergence of previously parallel initiatives to strengthen the social and environmental dimensions of trade – perhaps signalling a move towards a more integrated consideration of the two aspects.

Moses Adigbli outlines some of the negative impacts of environmental concerns over tropical forest products as they affect the Ghanaian timber sector. His paper demonstrates just how hard it will be to fashion 'win–win' solutions that foster market access and sustainable production unless the huge resource constraints of developing countries are addressed. Tariff concessions alone will not do the job.

Mr Adigbli makes his remarks in a personal capacity. In his view, environmental campaigning can misinform buyers, deliberately generating discrimination against the use of tropical timber. Environmental groups should rely less on boycotts than on assisting the process of change towards better forest management. Their demands, he says, are often insufficiently sensitive to the political and economic constraints that exist in developing countries. One result is a perceptible shift in tropical wood exports away from sensitive markets to less sensitive ones, but another result may also be an 'investment chill': Mr Adigbli notes that capital and skills from investment sources in Britain are 'markedly absent' from the development of Ghana's forest products industry. He concludes by expressing the classic development-versus-environment dilemma: 'If the developed world wants a high level of environmental protection in the developing world, then it should be prepared to pay for it.'

Finally, *David Wheeler* offers a rather different perspective on green consumerism, from the perspective of The Body Shop. His starting point is the limits of voluntary labelling schemes from a retailer's perspective. With a few exceptions, he says, voluntary labels are 'at best much ado about nothing, at worst a misleading and potentially highly confusing market intervention'. He also raises an equity consideration that reflects Mr Adigbli's concerns: why should a small producer of wooden handicraft items in India bear the costs of environmental certification and labelling for marginal, if any, economic benefit, when its competitors based in China manufacturing in plastics need add no environmental or social qualifications whatsoever to their products? Dr Wheeler proposes a radically different approach. Governments should draw up a set of mandatory labelling requirements at least at EU level to reflect a kind of 'matrix' of where most benefit for environmental or sustainability investment lies. These should be reflected in corresponding public-sector procurement specifications and in practical and financial support for developing country producers to meet the mandatory requirements.

Part III Resolving key WTO issues

Overview

Part III addresses some of the most controversial issues in the trade–environment debate as they relate to WTO rules: the relationship between the multilateral trading system and multilateral environmental agreements (MEAs) whose implementation may require measures with trade effects, 'process and production methods' (PPMs) issues, and the WTO's dispute settlement system.

There has long been a debate about the potential for conflict between the rules of the multilateral trading system and trade provisions, or measures with trade effects, implemented by WTO members in order to meet their obligations under MEAs. Many commentators view resolution of those potential conflicts as the key priority on environment in the Millennium Round.

As to PPMs, in many respects it is this issue that lies at the heart of the North-South divide that has hindered progress in the trade and environment debate. It is generally considered that the GATT prohibits regulatory distinctions drawn between products on the basis of the overseas environmental impacts of their process or production methods. This is based principally on a GATT dispute panel's interpretation of the term 'like products' under Article III of the GATT in the controversial 1991 *Tuna/Dolphin* case (and similar interpretations in a number of later disputes) and an institutional distaste for trade-related unilateralism in the WTO. It is here that the environmental protection-versus-eco-protectionism aspect of the debate is at its clearest. Key issues include the transboundary competitiveness impacts of different environmental PPM regulations (where there is little concrete evidence but much speculation); unilateral trade measures based on 'non-product-related' PPMs (i.e. PPMs that do not have an impact on the environmental impacts or performance of the product itself); PPM-related trade measures in MEAs; and the use of PPM-based requirements in procurement or labelling.

On the WTO dispute settlement system, a perceived lack of sensitivity to environmental policy considerations is now possibly giving way, with the Appellate Body's report in the *Shrimp/Turtle* case, to a softer critique on the part of environmentalists, with developing countries voicing increasing concerns that protectionist measures may be let in by the back door in the name of environmental protection. The fact that the Appellate Body considered a non-governmental submission, annexed to the US arguments, is also adding fuel to longstanding discussions over the proper role of non-governmental representation in the dispute settlement process.

Part III opens with two 'overview' papers on some of these key issues. *Damien Geradin* sketches out the main issues associated with the interface between trade, investment and environmental regulation. For these purposes, he puts forward an analytical framework for the purposes of considering the issues within the WTO. He draws a principal distinction between unilateral environmental measures and those adopted pursuant to the provisions of various MEAs. For unilateral measures, he draws a further distinction between direct restrictions on trade, product standards and process standards. Dr Geradin also examines the 'pollution haven' hypothesis, i.e. that industries or companies located in countries with high standards of environmental regulation may relocate to low-standard countries in order to preserve their competitive position. The economic evidence, he concludes, is unconvincing, with the policy implication that it makes little sense to adopt trade measures in an attempt to equalize production costs across jurisdictions.

What of the possible solutions to the issues? Dr Geradin notes that trade disputes about product standards are particularly difficult to resolve, predicting that the focus of legal analysis in future WTO disputes may shift to the role of scientific evidence under the WTO's Agreement on the Application of Sanitary and Phytosanitary Measures (SPS Agreement). The *Beef Hormones* case, over EC restrictions on marketing of beef products from cattle treated with growth hormones, is a case in point, not to mention the real possibility of a trade dispute over genetically modified organisms. The most difficult issues, says Dr Geradin, relate to environmental process standards. Process-related trade restrictions are GATT-illegal, and here, he says, the best approach may be to encourage a greater degree of regulatory convergence across nations. The tension between WTO rules and MEAs containing trade provisions is, he says, probably the least difficult area of potential dispute to resolve in the WTO.

Magda Shahin's paper presents an overview of trade and environment discussions in the WTO from a developing-country perspective. She questions whether the debate is yet sufficiently mature to allow negotiations with a view to setting new rules and regulations in the WTO. Her view on MEAs casts doubt on the idea that this is one of the least difficult areas for the WTO: even if it is perfectly possible to devise technical solutions to the issues, the political issues none the less remain highly complex. She emphasizes the importance of 'positive measures' (such as technical and financial assistance), as distinct from trade measures, in MEAs, and suggests that changes to the rules would offer an unbalanced approach without a parallel commitment to first use and enforce such positive measures.

Turning to the *Shrimp/Turtle* dispute, Dr Shahin notes with approval the panel report's condemnation of unilaterally imposed trade-related environment measures that carry a risk of 'jeopardizing the multilateral trading system'. This, she says, reflects a political consensus among WTO members, with the sole exception of the United States, that unilateral measures should be abandoned. A WTO system based on consensus and cooperation cannot be allowed to 'adapt to … all kinds of interests' by allowing trade policy solutions to be applied unilaterally in line with what individual WTO members see to be environmental concerns. Dr Shahin is concerned that the subsequent Appellate Body report in the *Shrimp/Turtle* case may have opened up the risk of damaging the multilateral trading system through a too-liberal interpretation of Article XX(g) of the GATT.

Dr Shahin, like Dr Geradin, discounts the 'pollution haven' hypothesis, though she emphasizes that stringent environmental regulations can have a negative impact on developing-country exports. Echoing Nick Robins's paper, she points out that the resources and expertise required to adapt to new regulations in export markets are frequently not available to developing-country producers. The related issues of technology transfer and intellectual property rights are likely to feature high on the future trade and environment agenda, an agenda that must preserve a balanced approach, so that the development aspect is not overlooked.

Multilateral environmental agreements (MEAs)

The three papers in the section of this book on multilateral environmental agreements highlight some of the complexities of that debate.

Duncan Brack sketches the key controversies and potential conflicts with WTO rules. Even if a WTO challenge to a trade measure under an MEA is politically unlikely, the legal uncertainty can none the less result in a 'political chill' over the negotiation of new MEAs; and the perception that the WTO threatens environmental sustainability does not assist the growth of the multilateral trading system. In practice, Brack concludes, the existing hierarchy of international law favours the multilateral trading system over MEAs. In short, the existing situation calls for changes in the rules of the multilateral trading system. Brack's paper highlights a number of criteria for consideration in any lasting resolution of the potential conflict, assessing the pros and cons of various options for amendment to the rules. His preferred route is to seek to negotiate a new 'WTO Agreement on MEAs with Trade Provisions' during the Millennium Round – an option that could prove politically more feasible than the alternative of amendments to existing rules.

Michel Potier of the OECD makes a challenging suggestion: that discussion on amendments to Article XX has not been as fruitful as it could be, and that perhaps the focus needs to shift away from the idea that amendments to WTO rules are needed, and towards seeking to make functional cooperative arrangements between the WTO and individual MEAs.

Reinhard Quick takes a different view, addressing the issues from an industry perspective. The view of European industry, as represented by UNICE, is that the relationship should be resolved at the High Level Meeting. UNICE's preferred route is to amend Article XX(b) of the GATT, coupling it with an Understanding on the relationship between trade measures taken pursuant to MEAs and WTO rules which would include a number of criteria that MEAs would have to meet, including a test of 'necessity' of the trade measures. Controversy surrounding the Basel Convention's proposed ban on exports of dangerous waste destined for recycling to non-OECD countries illustrates the difference between his approach and that in Duncan Brack's paper – namely, the extent to which it should be permissible for the WTO to review trade measures under MEAs. 'Environmental negotiators cannot expect the international trading system to be silent on a specific trade issue if they are not able to solve the environmental issue at stake in a coherent and sustainable manner', he maintains.

Process and production methods (PPMs)

The next series of papers focuses on the controversy surrounding PPMs. Long one of the most contentious of all the issues in the trade–environment debate, there are now signs that, for some actors at least, the notion of addressing PPM issues in the Millennium Round by disaggregating them into their constituent elements is becoming politically feasible. Not all – particularly not all developing countries – would agree.

René Vossenaar considers both the key issues and some of the traditional policy responses to the use of PPMs in the context of international trade. His focus is the impact of process and production-based environmental regulation on developing countries. It is often suggested (as in Dr Geradin's paper) that harmonization of PPMs could be a vehicle for responding to competitiveness concerns. But this can go against the grain of the idea that responses to intrinsically domestic environmental problems should be tailored to the needs of individual countries. Mr Vossenaar suggests that incentives and supporting measures, such as efforts to build environmental infrastructure in developing countries, may be useful in facilitating greater convergence of standards. In other cases, minimum standards could be helpful in reducing trade frictions.

In the final section of his paper, Mr Vossenaar takes up the 'win–win' theme in the context of PPMs issues. He examines a number of options for increasing market access and generating environmental and developmental gains simultaneously. Suggestions include developing mechanisms for facilitating the transfer of environmentally sound technologies; identifying areas where removing trade restrictions and distortions can have a positive environmental effect; focusing on the potential role of transnational corporations in disseminating best environmental management practice to firms in developing countries; and facilitating certification under the ISO 14000 series of standards.

Konrad von Moltke concentrates on the issue of interpretation of the term 'like products' in the GATT, challenging the established dogma on a key conceptual ground, i.e. the basic principles of WTO rules on intellectual property rights. The WTO TRIPS Agreement distinguishes between products in trade on the basis of whether or not the rights of the holders of intellectual property have been respected; in short, it distinguishes between products on the basis of whether certain rules associated with their production processes have been respected. The appropriate starting point for debate about PPMs should therefore be to ask whether they are needed, and, if they are needed, what rules should apply. Mr von Moltke proposes a new 'PPMs Agreement', to be developed by those whose primary concern is the environment, before inserting it into the rule-based structure of the trading system.

Charles Arden-Clarke assesses the implications of the *Shrimp/Turtle* Appellate Body report through a 'PPMs' lens. Although the *Shrimp/Turtle* case did not focus on interpretation of the term 'like products', it can none the less be understood as a case about how the WTO treats trade discrimination on the basis of process and production methods. Notwithstanding its result (i.e. that the US restrictions on imports of shrimps from countries that did not require the use of turtle excluder devices were not compatible with WTO rules), Mr Arden-Clarke sees *Shrimp/Turtle* as 'irrefutable proof' that the multilateral trading system is beginning to come to terms with the issues surrounding PPMs. The fact that the Appellate Body found that the US measure could in principle qualify for the exception under Article XX(g) suggests that in principle discrimination on the basis of PPMs is compatible with WTO rules. This is precisely the point at which Magda Shahin's paper raises concerns about the implications of the Appellate Body ruling. For Mr Arden-Clarke though, renegotiation of WTO rules is still likely to be necessary. Addressing PPMs within the Millennium Round calls for an integrated approach in which PPMs and, more broadly, environmental issues, are 'mainstreamed' throughout the Round.

Conflict resolution in the World Trade Organization

Finally, in Part III two papers consider issues around one of the key institutional aspects of the debate: the future of WTO dispute settlement on environment-related issues, and the associated issues of transparency and non-governmental involvement in dispute settlement.

In their paper, *Thomas Cottier* and *Krista Nadakavukaren Schefer* give an overview of environment-related WTO dispute settlement and basic legal principles in four categories: import prohibitions; regulations on process and production methods; environmental subsidies; and disputes, such as the well-known *Beef Hormones* case, raising issues of risk assessment and perceptions and values associated with risk. Their conclusion is an optimistic one: that the trend towards a more environment-friendly WTO, evidenced by trends in dispute settlement, has not yet reached its apex.

James Cameron considers the implications of the *Shrimp/Turtle* dispute for the future of WTO dispute settlement. He sees the Appellate Body's ruling as a positive sign of the WTO dispute settlement system's receptiveness to non-governmental submissions – so far, ones that are attached physically to a government submission. But his paper goes on to consider the future of conflict resolution in the WTO. Mr Cameron calls for a more formal system for allowing non-governmental submissions to be put forward, and for the creation of a position of 'Counsel to the Panel'; a lawyer who would put forward non-binding opinions to guide WTO dispute panellists and help to promote consistency in interpretation of the rules.

Part IV Environmental regulation and international investment

The role of foreign direct investment (FDI)

Part IV focuses on the relationship between investment and environment, beginning with two papers that offer practical case studies of the relationship between foreign direct investment and environmental regulation and protection.

Veena Jha's paper is a case study of experience in India, which tends to show that generalizations about the relationship between transnational corporations and environmental protection are difficult to verify empirically, and that there is a need for more research, particularly in those sectors that are considered a high priority for foreign direct investment by the Indian government. Dr Jha stresses the importance of realizing the goal of ensuring that increased foreign direct investment and better environmental performance are mutually reinforcing.

The experience of the Bhopal disaster offers the most prominent example of environmental concerns being voiced about the operations of transnational corporations in India. But there are other examples too, for example in cases where companies have sought to use outdated machinery or have applied less than 'best practice' standards to dealing with the waste that they generate. There is also a large number of examples of transnational corporations making positive contributions to the environment, including through a 'ratcheting-up' effect. Dr Jha highlights the Indian car industry, where foreign investment has led to pressures to increase the fuel efficiency of vehicles in domestic production.

Veena Jha stresses that there are political differences among Indian states on the environmental problems associated with foreign direct investment. Against this background, she underlines that a multilateral investment regime that allows developing countries little flexibility in balancing competing environmental, economic and social concerns may find little support in India. Case-by-case obligations or codes of good business practice may better meet India's concerns.

In a second paper, *David Owen* highlights the public-versus-private-sector investment dimension of the investment–environment debate, with a focus on the water sector. He stresses the valuable role that the private sector can play in addressing the rapidly increasing need for potable water and sanitation in towns and cities in developing countries as urbanization progresses apace. The link between environmental regulation and investment in the water sector is a strong one; Dr Owen notes that, in Europe in particular, it is environmental legislation that has been a central driver of private-sector funding and operation. But if private-sector investment is to bring the maximum benefits, he cautions that there is a need for independent regulation and regulators to safeguard environment, public health and consumer interests.

Lessons from the Multilateral Agreement on Investment (MAI)

The investment aspect of the trade–investment–environment debate is likely to raise its profile, as the prospect of investment issues being discussed in the Millennium Round draws nearer. The four papers in this section of the book consider the lessons that can be learned from the failed OECD Multilateral Agreement on Investment (MAI). There is considerable reluctance to repeat the experience of the MAI negotiations: few these days are prepared to express unequivocal support for the MAI process, and the papers reflect this strongly. In a globalized economy, however, there is a strong case to be made for the WTO to provide the institutional home for any future multilateral liberalization of investment. But 'exclusivity', and lack of sensitivity to environment and labour considerations, are accusations that dog the WTO just as they dogged the MAI. Some even doubt whether there is a need for multilaterally directed liberalization, particularly given the fears that it would serve the interests of Northern multinational corporations, or that any efforts to redirect the notion of liberalization to the desirable goal of sustainable development would likely be thwarted.

Jan Huner tells the story of environment issues in the MAI, tracing the impact of NGO pressure in capitals on the negotiations themselves and the emergence of the so-called 'three-anchor' approach to environment in the MAI: (1) a reference to relevant multilateral agreements and the principles of the Rio Declaration in the preamble; (2) a provision stating that standards should not be lowered in order to attract investment (a provision closely related to the 'pollution haven' hypothesis); and (3) a provision annexing the OECD Guidelines for Multinational Enterprises to the text of the MAI. Mr Huner's account of the reluctance within the Negotiating Group to meet with NGOs is memorable. None the less, ultimately, it was the French decision that the MAI posed a 'threat to artistic and literary freedom and cultural diversity in France' that led to the 'French torpedo' causing the capsizing of the 'leaky MAI boat', rather than the opposition on environment and labour grounds.

Kristian Ehinger, who was involved in the MAI negotiations through the Business and Industry Advisory Committee to the OECD (BIAC), sets out a business perspective on the issues. He stresses that the original aims of the MAI were to develop a framework based on the principles of non-discrimination, national treatment and liberalization of foreign investment. For business, says Dr Ehinger, the main objective was to raise investor confidence. He acknowledges that a failure to include NGOs and parliamentarians in the negotiations resulted in some misunderstandings, but in substance he does not view the MAI as a failure. The OECD Secretariat's work remained in line with the main objectives of the Agreement and the 'three-anchor' approach was an appropriate and effective means of addressing key environmental aspects of the agreement. As to whether WTO negotiations would be better, Dr Ehinger stresses that the siting of the MAI in the OECD was the result of compromise in a debate about whether it was better to have broader geographical coverage or higher standards. At all times, the incorporation of an MAI in the WTO remained the ultimate goal.

Pradeep Mehta of the Consumer Unity and Trust Society in India assesses the relationship between foreign direct investment and the environment, and the lessons of the MAI negotiations, from a developing-country NGO perspective. He begins by examining whether the 'no lowering standards in the area of environment and labour' anchor of the MAI's three-anchor approach was appropriate and adequate. Do lower standards in developing countries pull in more polluting investment, or, on the contrary, is it high standards in developed countries that 'push' investors to developing countries? In fact, Mr Mehta believes that, where the relationship between foreign direct investment and environment is a negative one, at least some blame needs to be placed at the door of multinational corporations themselves, not governments. He gives a number of examples of situations where multinational corporations have double standards in their operations, applying different environmental management standards in developing countries from those that they would have applied at home. The solution, he says, should lie with the notion that businesses must respect the widely recognized principle of environmental protection, including the principle of maintaining the same standards in their operations worldwide.

A central theme of Mr Mehta's arguments is the fundamental inequity at the heart of the MAI. While its primary target was the resources and consumer markets of the developing countries, those countries were never a part of the negotiations, which took place within the closed club of the OECD. Second, there was no consideration in the negotiations of the need to ensure a proper balance of the rights of, and the obligations upon, the investors. Mehta's conclusion is that it is questionable whether a multilateral investment framework and new international rules are needed at all, given the pace at which foreign direct investment is currently increasing in the absence of such rules.

Nick Mabey of WWF characterizes the opposition to the MAI as a clash of world views: the economic and the sustainable. He sees the MAI as a threat to efforts to address the world's environmental problems through action at the national or sub-national levels. For him, and for many others among those opposing the MAI, it would have increased the power of incoming investors, reducing the ability of host countries to negotiate the best deal. For the future, Mr Mabey believes that the objective of investment agreements needs to be sustainable development. There should be more emphasis on positive initiatives such as the promotion of ethical business through preferential access to guaranteed loans and trade promotion. In short, if the investment agenda is to be passed to the WTO, it needs to be fundamentally rethought.

It remains to be seen whether negotiators of any genuinely multilateral investment regime are able to move beyond the established concepts offered by the hundreds of bilateral investment agreements already in place, or to draw a line under the unhappy experience of the MAI and start afresh. The opening stages of the Millennium Round will be critical in setting the agenda.

Finally, **Part V** contains *Halina Ward*'s summary of the discussion sections of the Chatham House conference that formed the basis of this book.

The agenda one year on

The High Level Meeting

In October 1998, when the papers in this collection were written, there was considerable discussion of the idea of a High Level Ministerial Meeting, on either trade and environment, or trade and sustainable development (depending on the proponent). The WTO and GATT Secretariats had held previous symposia on the relationship between trade and environment in 1994 and 1998, partly in response to allegations of secrecy levelled at their organizations, but this was the first time that such a degree of high-level political impetus had been given to the idea, including from President Clinton and Sir Leon Brittan.

From all sides, support for a High Level Meeting was born largely of frustration at a lack of progress in resolving the complex relationship between trade liberalization and environmental protection, particularly in the WTO Committee on Trade and Environment, the forum that was originally seen as the best location for a resolution of the issues. But what should the High Level Meeting be? A significant step towards preparing the ground for the Millennium Round, or simply an opportunity to bring together different viewpoints? The varying perspectives on the potential role of the High Level Meeting can be clearly seen in many of the papers in this book.

With the benefit of hindsight, there are probably few who would claim that the High Level *Symposia* on trade and environment and trade and development (as they eventually became), held at the WTO's headquarters in Geneva on 15–18 March 1999, represented a real milestone in the trade–sustainable development debate. Trade and environment and trade and development were split between separate symposia. This effectively frustrated NGO calls for a meeting to consider 'trade and sustainable development', particularly since only a relatively small number of people attended both meetings. More importantly, there was no ministerial participation, meaning that the events simply took the form of speeches followed by position statements from the floor, with no effort to negotiate any agreed conclusion. Thus, in practice, the High Level Symposia were little different from previous symposia and meetings organized on conformity assessment, international trade and competition policy, trade facilitation, information technology and least developed countries.

However, one idea put forward by Sir Leon Brittan at the High Level Symposium on trade and environment is rapidly gathering pace: the notion that liberalization of trade should be accompanied by an environmental or 'sustainability' assessment of its potential impacts, or even a backward-looking assessment of its impacts to date. Several WTO members and NGOs are working in this direction; but the real policy implications of such assessments, or how they might concretely feed into the Millennium Round negotiations, remain unclear for the present.

Environment in the Millennium Round: the real challenges of 'win–win'

At the time of writing, there is still a great deal of uncertainty about how environmental issues will be addressed in the Millennium Round. Some WTO members have already put forward environmental priorities for the Round, with the European Union, for example, focusing on MEAs, eco-labelling and the precautionary principle, and promoting a sustainability review of the Round. A discussion is also beginning on what place to give to the principle or goal of sustainable development in the Ministerial Declaration that will set the scene and scope of the negotiations. What does seem certain is that, one way or another, environmental issues will figure in the Round. But what is far from clear is whether they will be allocated their own negotiating mandate, or simply be dealt with on an agreement-by-agreement or sector-by-sector basis.

A number of issues have come to dominate the Northern agenda that were not previously so politically charged, not least among them the controversy surrounding the relationship between the regulation of genetically modified organisms and trade, and the February 1999 collapse of negotiations towards a Biosafety Protocol to the Convention on Biological Diversity. The area of environmental services liberalization under the built-in negotiating agenda of the General Agreement on Trade in Services (GATS) is receiving increasing attention on account of its potential to promote the win–win theme at home in WTO member countries with strong environmental service industries. The roll-back of agriculture subsidies under the built-in agenda of the Agriculture Agreement is also coming in for environmental scrutiny, as is the reduction and possible elimination of subsidies in other areas, such as fisheries – both areas with win–win potential. Whether the controversial topic of investment liberalization will be included in the Round is still, however, uncertain.

Among developing countries, there is considerable concern at the idea of incorporating *any* environmental agenda items into the Round, notwithstanding the increased attention being devoted to the idea of win–win options. This leads to some critical questions. What does win–win mean when it is no longer a call to action but a guiding principle for tough negotiations? The detail of how win–win options might relate to a trade negotiation framework in which cross-sectoral trade-offs are a key to progress remains to be explored; though the idea of a genuinely win–win option being traded off against anything is intuitively difficult to grasp. Can a consensus on trade and environment in the Millennium Round ever amount only to an 'absence of sustained opposition' (to borrow a phrase from the international standards community)?

Even more difficult, in many areas it is clear that what is sought by developing countries is positive measures outside the Millennium Round, for example to facilitate compliance with multilateral environmental agreements, or to assist in the development of domestic environmental certification capacities (just two of the suggestions put forward in the papers that follow). Responding to such calls in the context of a *trade-related* negotiation, and making the necessary linkages to bodies and initiatives outside the Millennium Round so that the results have an impact on negotiating positions, presents a huge challenge. Whether the developed-country negotiators of the Millennium Round will be able to rise to that challenge and put financial and technical assistance on the table remains to be seen.

If the creation of a World Trade Organization was the biggest surprise and innovation from the limited Punta Del Este Declaration that formed the basic negotiating mandate for the Uruguay Round, then it is genuine institutional and policy integration of this kind and scale that should be the focus for aspirations for innovation in the forthcoming Millennium Round. Only then will it be possible to claim that the WTO has become properly integrated into a system of global governance fit for the new millennium.

Part I
A strategic overview of the debate and the key issues for the future

Renato Ruggiero

Fifty years of the multilateral trading system

This year marked the 50th anniversary of the multilateral trading system – a system that, together with the United Nations and the Bretton Woods institutions, emerged out of the tragedies of the Great Depression and the Second World War. Certainly our world today is in many ways still unacceptable. Poverty and hunger remain with us. The promise of development has yet to be redeemed for much of the emerging world. Civil war and ethnic strife mar the global peace. And in contrast to the dark history of the first half of this century, the second half has shone immeasurably brighter – in no small part because of the vision and contribution of the postwar international system.

Now, on the threshold of a new century and a new era, we ask what the next 50 years will bring. Will it be a time of conflict or cooperation? Stagnation or progress? Another dark age, or one filled with light? Today I want to comment on the realities of this new globalized age – and what these realities mean for the evolution of the international system in the time ahead.

The current financial crisis marks an important turning point in the process of globalization – but not in the way that its critics now predict. As difficult and destabilizing as the past 16 months have been, the crisis has reinforced, not weakened, the reality of globalization. It has underlined in a stark and powerful way just how interconnected we have become financially, socially, politically, as well as economically. It has further blurred the distinction between domestic and foreign issues, fatally undermining the notion that a country's internal policies or practices are the concern of no one else. And it has created new pressures for more – not less – international cooperation, across a much broader policy front.

This is because globalization is about much more than trade and capital flows. Technology is linking us together to an unprecedented degree – through communications, information and ideas, as well as services and investment, shrinking distances and time. And this process, in turn, is creating an awareness of interdependence on a planetary scale. Television, fax machines, mobile phones and the Internet are erasing barriers not only between economies, but between people, allowing us to see and understand how interconnected we are. There is a globalization of our consciousness, as well as of our economies. And this dimension of globalization, more than any other, will prove impossible to slow down or reverse.

The financial crisis has dominated our discussions over the past year, with its moments of pessimism and moments of renewed hope. It is clear that this is first and foremost a financial crisis, and the solutions must be found from within the financial and monetary systems. But it is now equally clear that continued financial and exchange rate instability can – and will – have a negative effect on world trade, investment and development. Declining commodity prices, weakening imports in the affected countries, excessive export competition in the advanced markets and the threat of further devaluations – all of these forces are introducing new uncertainties, new risks and new protectionist pressures into the global economy.

The reality is that the questions raised by the financial crisis go to the heart of the major challenge of our time: the challenge of global governance in this complex and interdependent era. Can we maintain a stable and increasingly borderless global economy, with rising trade, employment and growth, without a stable global financial and monetary system? Will the integration of our economies require a more coordinated approach to fiscal, monetary, development and environmental policies, as well as trade policy? Does the logic of globalization force us to re-examine the global architecture?

A new international consensus will have to develop for improving the management of the global economy if we are to continue to liberalize markets, and if globalization is to fulfil its promise.

First, we need to open up the international system to wider participation at the highest level of the decision-making process. This implies that we must move from a predominantly unilateral leadership to a more collective leadership – and one with a more balanced share of responsibility. This does not mean that US leadership is any less important. What it means is that Europe, Japan, the transition regimes and the developing countries that make up a growing share of the world economy must be prepared to play their part. The recent G-22 meetings are good initial steps in this direction.

And this in turn means that the nature of international leadership must change. During the Cold War, leadership was about solidarity, discipline, the possibility of force in the common defence of our values. By contrast, leadership in an interdependent world is the art of cooperation and consensus. It is about recognizing that our national interests are increasingly global interests, and that our national security increasingly hinges on the security of others. I do not suggest that the voice of internationalism is an easy one in the present climate – only that it is essential in our globally interdependent world.

Second, we need to broaden the scope of the issues that are part of the international agenda and at the highest level of the system. We can no longer afford to view issues through a sectoral lens. We need to look at the challenges we face from a broader perspective, and as pieces of a larger, interconnected puzzle. Globalization has given rise to a lengthening list of issues that now cross borders, from environmental standards and development concerns to the distribution of resources, labour standards, health issues, human rights, education, technological empowerment – even foreign security. More and more, we are dependent on each other's financial stability, economic development, environmental security and political reform. More and more, there is pressure to widen the scope of international coordination, and to define institutions that can bridge the gap between an economic and technological system that is increasingly global, and a political system that is still predominantly national.

The environmental dimension

In this widening of the international agenda, the environment will occupy a very important part. Environmental challenges such as acid rain, deforestation, global warming or the protection of endangered species clearly demand approaches that are global rather than national in scope.

The recent *Shrimp/Turtle* appeal in the WTO is the clearest sign yet that the trading system is fully supportive of policies to protect endangered species or the environment – but that it is up to the environmental community itself to provide this policy framework, or to implement the policies without discrimination. It strongly reinforces the growing need to negotiate global environmental rules and standards – and to reach a global consensus about environmental issues. And it underlines the need to strengthen existing bridges between trade and environmental policies, a task that would be made immeasurably easier if we could also create a house for the environment to help focus and coordinate our efforts.

This *Shrimp/Turtle* appeal is extremely important because it clarifies one essential issue in the debate between the trade community and the environmental community: that there are no political, economic or legal obstacles to the harmonious development of both environmental objectives and free trade objectives. And here it is important to put on the record the conclusions of the Appellate Body in this case:

> We wish to underscore what we have not decided in this case. We have not decided that the protection and preservation of the environment is of no significance to Members of the WFO. Clearly it is. We have not decided that the sovereign nations that are Members of the WTO cannot adopt effective measures to protect endangered species, such as sea turtles. Clearly, they can and should. And we have not decided that sovereign states should not act together bilaterally, plurilaterally or multilaterally, either within the WTO or other international fora, to protect endangered species or to otherwise protect the environment. Clearly, they should and do.[1]

This appeal makes it even more impossible to say that trade policy does not consider environmental issues. It is clear not only that the trade system takes environmental concerns into account, but – if they are implemented without discrimination – that these concerns prevail over free trade objectives.

This is of fundamental importance, because if we want to succeed in defining our objectives – both the trade community and the environ-

[1] *United States – Import Prohibition of Certain Shrimp and Shrimp Products*, para. 185, WT/DS58/AB/R (12 October 1998).

mental community – we have to define the real challenges we face, and not create false obstacles. To pretend that environmental concerns stand in the way of free trade is to create a false obstacle. To pretend that free trade stands in the way of environmental concerns is also to create a false obstacle. And if we focus our attention on these false obstacles instead of the real problems that we face, we are only losing time and resources without coming any closer to reaching our shared goals.

One message must come out loud and clear. The WTO is a strong institutional friend and supporter of the environment. And we must proceed, the trade and environmental communities hand in hand, to improve and strengthen this alliance. This is also the message that must be sent from the High Level Dialogue proposed by both President Clinton and Sir Leon Brittan, and strongly endorsed from the outset by me. We are making substantial progress in the preparations of this dialogue and we are not far from launching this initiative – probably together with another High Level Dialogue on Trade and Development at the beginning of next spring. There is still a lot we must do together to improve and clarify the relationship between trade and environment. But this task will be much easier if we move forward as friends, not as opponents.

To characterize the WTO (as we have read recently) as an organization that 'refuses to reveal its deliberations to the public, or be held responsible for the social, political and environmental costs of its decisions'[2] is a false representation. No one can claim this. Certainly, there is more that we can, and must, do to improve transparency and our alliance with environmental, social and development policies. But those who follow the activities of the WTO know that we are strongly committed to that course, and that we are already moving towards these objectives within the rules that have been adopted by consensus by all our members and ratified by each of our parliaments.

---

[2] *Newsweek*, 12 October, 1998, p. 24C.

The social dimension

A second important issue is the social dimension of globalization. At the WTO's first Ministerial Conference in Singapore, we emerged from a difficult debate with a clear and strong consensus on the issues of labour standards – a consensus, first, that members were committed to the observance of core labour standards; second, that the ILO was the relevant body to address these issues; third, that standards are best promoted by growth and development, fostered by trade liberalization; and fourth, that labour standards should in no way be used for protectionist purposes or to put into question the comparative advantage of countries. It is this consensus that has opened the door for the International Labour Organization and its Declaration[3] to make real progress on the issue of the social clause. Perhaps not everyone is fully satisfied with this progress. But the reality is that we would have made no progress at all if we had still been fighting over the issue of the ILO's or the WTO's competence.

Least developed country needs

The third step was the WTO initiative last year to provide assistance, in collaboration with UNCTAD, UNDP, the World Bank and others, to address the needs of least developed countries. The proposed High Level Dialogue on Trade and Development has to give priority to this urgent problem. One objective is to give least developed countries better access for their exports in advanced markets, and here I have strongly advocated that we provide bound duty-free access – a call that has now also been taken up by many world leaders, and that must be answered during the next multilateral negotiations in 1999. In addition, we must continue to work towards a more integrated approach to capacity-building in these countries. And we must build upon our efforts to link the least developed countries via the Internet to all the resources and expertise of the WTO – a powerful symbol of the new kind of dialogue that is needed in our global electronic village.

[3] *Editors' note:* In June 1998, the International Labour Conference adopted the 'ILO Declaration on fundamental principles and rights at work.'

Towards a vision for a world of deeper integration

We need to define a vision for the post-Cold War era. For four decades, the strategic imperatives of the Cold War created a degree of cohesion and singlemindedness of purpose that helped sustain the international system. But we have lost the 'cement' of the Cold War. And no one has yet articulated a clear vision of what the post-Cold War order should be. Instead of one common enemy, we face thousands of complex problems. We need to define a new global vision to match the realities of a new global age – a technology-driven age which is shrinking time and space.

To sum up, if we consider the present financial turmoil, it seems that an answer cannot be found unless we keep our markets open. At the same time, it will be increasingly difficult to resist protectionist pressure unless stability is restored to the financial and exchange rates systems. If we look beyond the financial crisis, we can see that there is a new global reality emerging – and even a new global economy – which is much more complex than trade or capital flows. What we need is an architecture that will take into account, at the highest political level, a number of players that goes beyond a few industrialized countries, and includes developing countries and economies in transition.

And, just as we have to increase the number of players in the highest international decision-making process, so too must we increase the number of issues that have to be taken into account in this globalized world, to develop a more balanced and global vision to accommodate our more complex and technology-driven global system.

If the challenge of the past 50 years was to manage a divided world, the challenge of the future will be to manage a world of deeper integration. It is a challenge that will in many ways be much more difficult and more complex. We find ourselves in a new world today, and in a new economy, whose characteristics are not fully understood even by its most prominent actors. And yet the choices we face are enduring ones – between moving into the next century on the basis of shared global rules or on the basis of power, between stability or uncertainty, consensus or conflict. How we manage these challenges in the months and years ahead will depend on the choices we make today, not on globalization.

Globalization has enormous potential to generate growth, to spread the benefits of technology, and to weave a more stable planet. But it also challenges the status quo. It demands that we adapt. This is not the moment to retreat from the future and to turn back to the past – a past that has shown us with such stark clarity how building barriers to one another can only make our economies poorer and our world less secure.

Brian Wilson

Introduction

We are faced by global problems and we need to find global solutions. We will only achieve this by greater cooperation and dialogue between the people from all interested groups. We have all begun to understand better the links between our interests in trade, investment, environment, development and wider issues.

The UK government is strongly committed to the creation of open markets around the world, supported by effective multilateral rules. Free trade benefits developing countries by providing access to overseas markets. It brings better quality, more choice and lower prices to consumers. It stimulates the efficiency and innovation of business. And, by giving them access to competitively priced components and services, it allows businesses to profit and grow. Throughout the last 50 years, growth in world trade has constantly outstripped the growth of GDP. It has been estimated that the Uruguay Round of negotiations alone when fully implemented will add US$500 billion each year to world income. We are all more prosperous as a result.

But clearly, there remains much more to be done. There are genuine benefits, for economic growth, improved living standards and new job creation across the world, to be gained from further liberalization. Obviously these are difficult times for the world economy. The temptation is to take the easy populist approach – to try to close domestic markets. But protectionist measures will get none of us anywhere in the medium term and must be resisted.

There are other threats to the liberalization agenda, and one of the most important of these is the belief that free trade must be bad for the environment. So in the longer term our objectives are to pursue open markets in a way that recognizes that there are genuine concerns about sustaining the environment and therefore that we should pursue our objectives in a way that is compatible with these concerns.

There are two strands of questions outstanding in the trade–investment–environment debate: what are the issues we are currently facing, and how can we take these issues forward?

The issues

We need to look at the development of both trade policy and environmental protection rules. We are currently working with our EU partners to build support for a comprehensive approach to a new round of trade negotiations. We are also actively pursuing the development of key existing and future international conventions tackling global environmental problems such as climate change and ozone layer depletion.

Protecting the environment and maintaining an open, and equitable non-discriminatory multilateral trading system are both essential to the achievement of our objective of sustainable development. There are many effective internationally recognized measures which aim to protect our environment. There is more to be done, although significant progress has been made in the last 20 years or so with a number of multilateral environmental agreements (MEAs). Liberalizing trade helps to ensure that resources are used efficiently, it helps generate the wealth necessary for development and environmental improvement, and it encourages the spread of clean technology.

It is clear that these two systems – trade and environment – must accommodate each other in order to be fully effective. It has been argued that the WTO Agreements could frustrate the aims of some environmental protection measures. Some have pointed to the report of the WTO dispute settlement panel in the *Shrimp/Turtle* case as evidence of this. But the Appellate Body has now reversed some of the panel's judgments.

Although the Appellate Body ruled against the US measure in that case because of the application of the measure, it acknowledged that the measure was legitimate in principle – a very significant decision. The report certainly promoted the need to interpret WTO rules so that they do not undermine environmental protection measures: 'We have *not* decided that the protection and preservation of the environment is of no significance to the Members of the WTO. Clearly, it is.'[1] The report of the Appellate Body could be interpreted as evidence of the complementarity between the two systems. We must all reassess the position.

The roles of the world trade system and the framework for environmental protection should be complementary. To consider the need for action, I intend to highlight briefly three of the subjects we are currently considering: the interface between MEAs and the WTO rules; the relevance of process and production methods; and the issue of labelling.

The MEA–WTO interface

On this first subject, we are all aware of the growing number of MEAs and international conventions aimed at protecting the environment. The majority of these have little or no trade implications. However, some conventions have the specific purpose of imposing controls on the free movement of goods, for example of hazardous substances or species requiring protection, and some MEAs include trade restrictions as part of an integrated policy package agreed by the parties to achieve broader objectives on the production and consumption of substances harmful to the environment. Under the right conditions, and in the absence of better alternatives, trade measures in MEAs can be useful instruments.

There has been much discussion in recent years in the WTO and in other international fora about the relationship between MEAs and the multilateral trading system. No consensus has yet emerged among WTO members on whether or not the status quo is acceptable. I believe that there is a need to clarify the interface between MEAs and the GATT. But I do not think it is yet obvious how this relationship should best be clarified.

To some, amending the text of GATT may seem an attractive option. But it is not a readily available short-term option. Amending GATT legal texts is a difficult task because WTO members are not likely to

---

[1] *United States – Import Prohibition of Certain Shrimp and Shrimp Products*, para. 185, WT/DS58/AB/R (12 October 1998).

relinquish well-established legal rights and obligations without advantage. And because many among the developing countries fear that any amendments would be aimed squarely at them, they are the least able to respond, and are unlikely to support that approach.

We should also be clear of the context. We must be sure of the consequences of any changes. It is not possible to hold this debate in isolation, as case law is continuing to clarify the meaning of the WTO Agreements.

There may be other approaches. If a group of countries agree to apply trade restraints to each other, perhaps relinquishing their rights under WTO Agreements, then why should anyone object? However, if the proposal is to apply trade restraints to unwilling trade partners, then the issue becomes more complex. My view is that there is no way of setting aside the WTO rights of member countries against their will. That is why no country, developing or otherwise, need fear wider discussion. Nothing will – or can – change without consensus.

Process and production methods (PPMs)

Closely linked to the case of applying trade measures to unwilling partners is the debate surrounding process and production methods (PPMs). Environmental policies are increasingly concerned with avoiding environmental degradation at all stages in the life cycle of products.

Controlling the processes of production is an increasingly important element in strategies for environmental protection. The logic of the life cycle approach in environmental policy is sound. We must ensure that the international community does all it can – once more, by agreement – to develop measures to ensure adequate environmental standards in production methods.

But I would be deeply concerned at any attempt to reinterpret WTO rules to permit trade restraints to coerce trading partners to adopt the domestic policies of others. And I think it is worth stressing that discriminatory or arbitrary application of legitimate measures is unlikely to lead us towards the development of effective global policies. We have to be aware that measures may need to be tailored to local conditions to meet a common objective. For example, globally we may be concerned about water usage in production, but the means of achieving our common objective may require different actions around the world.

In discussing PPMs, it has been argued that the solution could be the amendment of GATT rules to allow discrimination between like products. At the moment, such a solution looks rather theoretical. The prospects of consensus in the WTO are low on this kind of proposition. We should work to build consensus in this subject, and not only in the WTO. The WTO alone cannot be used to reach a consensus on how to deliver all environmental policy objectives. It is not a body for making regulations on the environment. We should certainly be pushing for improved standards, but we should consider which approach will lead us most effectively to that objective.

Labelling

On labelling, we know that consumer demands in this area are increasing. We are, for example, committed to ensuring better labelling of genetically modified foods. Consumers are looking for information on the environmental effects of a product's production and disposal. This desire has led to greater use of suitable labelling by producers and retailers. Voluntary initiatives of this kind in the marketplace should be welcomed, especially if they open markets for sustainably produced goods from developing countries.

Labelling schemes should be simple, non-discriminatory, transparent and capable of independent verification. The process of verification for such schemes should be achievable and affordable by smaller companies and by those in the developing world. At the level of broad principle, schemes that meet these criteria should be a useful complement to a liberalizing trade policy.

Consumers should be able to purchase goods on a properly informed basis. This is another area where the development of international standards can help establish the right degree of transparency both for government schemes and independent single-issue certification schemes.

There are clearly many more issues that we should address when formulating policy, but there is simply no time to cover each one here.

The way forward

Let me be clear. The UK government is very serious about its obligation to protect the global environment. But part of this obligation will be delivered by ensuring the effectiveness of the world trade system. We need a strong world trade system which delivers real opportunities for economic growth, not least to those developing countries that desperately need more access to our markets in order to grow out of poverty.

The Appellate Body in the *Shrimp/Turtle* case reiterated that our agreements under the WTO already recognize that the multilateral trading system must accommodate the framework of laws needed to protect our environment. I accept that it is not altogether clear where the line between the two systems is drawn. That is an area where we have to look very closely at the Appellate Body report and seek clarification on it.

In the context of applying the general exceptions in GATT Article XX, the Appellate Body said that the location of the line 'is not fixed and unchanging; the line moves as the kind and the shape of the measures at stake vary and as the facts making up specific cases differ'.[2] This willingness to address the issues on a case-by-case basis should be viewed positively, especially as the Appellate Body also recognized that elements of the WTO agreements must be read in light of contemporary concerns. We should consider carefully the balance between our need for certainty and the value of flexibility.

Investment

So far, I have been talking mainly about the interaction between trade liberalization and environmental protection. An equally important issue for the future will be the relationship between environmental issues and the liberalization of international investment.

The investment issue has been given a higher public profile by the negotiation of the Multilateral Agreement on Investment, or MAI. It now looks most unlikely that we will conclude the MAI in the near

[2] *United States – Import Prohibition of Certain Shrimp and Shrimp Products*, para. 159, WT/DS58/AB/R (12 October 1998).

future. But the issues that came up in the MAI context are still relevant.

I am optimistic that these issues can be addressed in a way that everyone can find satisfactory. In principle, there should be no conflict between the fair treatment of investors and the protection of the environment. Our aim is to make sure that these two goals are not allowed to undermine each other in practice. The UK government – at least since May 1997 – took a leading role in forcing this issue up the agenda in the MAI negotiations and will continue to give it a high priority.

The priorities

So how should we be channelling our energies now? I think we should concentrate on two areas.

First, we must recognize the value of international consensus on environmental protection. And we must continue to work to expand the scope and the reach of the consensus. The United Kingdom will continue to play its full part in the development of key existing and future international conventions tackling global environmental problems such as climate change and ozone layer depletion. And we will work to build consensus and develop mutual recognition of standards, and, where desirable, to harmonize standards while ensuring that trade rules are not used to impose unfair standards on developing countries.

Second, we must ensure that there is a better understanding between the global trade and environment communities. It may be that a solution to some of our concerns will be found in a clarification of the interface between the systems rather than in the alteration of established principles. This will become apparent only with improved dialogue.

We need a continuing dialogue within government, between government, business and civil society organizations, and on an intergovernmental level. For this dialogue to be fully effective, we will also have to push for greater transparency in international organizations, and in particular in the WTO, so that it can shed its image of a secret body and deflect unwarranted criticisms about its deliberations.

Cooperation within and between governments will underpin the compatibility of both sets of policies and their coherent development.

I think that the trade and environment frameworks are less in conflict than some might claim. That does not mean that I dismiss the possibility of any conflicts. Governments themselves have a duty to balance the objectives of both protecting the environment and upholding the multilateral trading system, whether they are negotiating in a trade forum or an environment forum. It is therefore for parties to both existing and new agreements to ensure individually and collectively that they do not sign up to conflicting requirements.

A High Level Meeting and towards a new round

We need a strategy for taking all of these ideas forward. Central to our strategy should be a dialogue between all parties. Earlier this year, Sir Leon Brittan called for a High Level Meeting on trade and environment to add impetus to the debate. We are working to build support for this idea within the WTO. I would like such a meeting to explore the interface between trade and environment policies: to consider what the potential conflicts between the two might be and to examine possible solutions. The meeting might also look forward to the new trade round, and provide the opportunity to exchange views on what might be achieved there.

Conclusion

Trade, investment and the environment are all increasingly global issues. The international community has made great inroads into dealing with these concerns at a global level. What we do not have is a framework for how each of these systems overlap with or complement the others. This is the area that we must explore and resolve. Solutions to global problems will be found only through that consensus.

As a nation, we should not shy away from a leadership role and we should be seeking opportunities for progress. But progress will come only from an improved dialogue between all interested parties. We cannot hide from the fact that environmental concerns can be used as a smoke-screen for protectionist measures – with very immediate impacts on people's welfare in other parts of the world. So I want to see solutions that will lead us down the path of sustainable development. We need to get the balance right, both on policy and on timing.

Gary P. Sampson

It can be stated with some objectivity that the General Agreement on Tariffs and Trade (GATT) and now the World Trade Organization (WTO) have been successful over the past half-century at doing what they have been clearly mandated to do. The WTO has two primary objectives: first, to progressively remove those trade restrictions and distortions that protect uncompetitive producers and deny consumers the possibility of purchasing goods and services at the most competitive international prices; second, to maintain the open, liberal and non-discriminatory rules-based multilateral trading system as a means to ensure predictability and stability in world trade. The reduction of barriers to trade in the postwar period has been dramatic, and the concepts, principles and rules on the basis of which legally binding rights and obligations are negotiated apply to thousands of billions of dollars' worth of goods and services trade between 132 countries at all levels of development. What this means in practical terms is that there will be strong resistance to change an organization that is considered by many to be working well with respect to what it is supposed to do.

Notwithstanding this success, the WTO is strongly criticized by many groups of environmentalists. While the WTO does not have as its primary objective the protection of the environment, the importance of this policy goal is clearly acknowledged in its Preamble and in various Agreements. The WTO places no constraints on governments pursuing within their borders whatever legitimate policy options they wish with respect to the environment. Nevertheless, the view widely held by many representatives of civil society is that WTO rules constrain their democratically elected governments from acting as they should to protect the environment. This dissatisfaction relates to, among other things, a lack of flexibility at the national level to use trade discrimination as a means of extending domestic environmental standards beyond national borders, or to discriminate against imports that are seen to undermine environmental standards that are established to reflect domestic societal preferences.

A point that is sometimes overlooked in directing these criticisms at the WTO is that the meaning ascribed to the World Trade Organization depends very much on the context in which it is used. The WTO can be taken to mean at least four things. First, it is a set of Agreements which create legally binding rights and obligations for all 132 members. Unlike many other multilateral agreements, these rights and obligations are enforced through a disputes settlement mechanism that provides for both compensation and retaliation in cases of non-compliance. WTO procedures do not, however, foreclose the options of governments agreeing to forgo their rights by joining other Agreements that provide for measures that would otherwise violate WTO rules.[1] Second, the WTO is a forum for reviewing the trade policies of its members and discussing other recent developments in the multilateral trading system. Third, the WTO is a relatively small secretariat with no enforcement powers or role in the interpretation of the legal rights and obligations of members.

Finally, and most importantly for present purposes, it is sometimes forgotten that the WTO consists of 132 governments that have agreed to act in a certain manner – in particular, not to discriminate against each other in international trade unless they have agreed to do so in some other context, such as a multilateral environment agreement, or in the event of exceptional circumstances. In this context, the WTO is a collectivity of governments acting on behalf of their own constituencies in accordance with multilaterally agreed principles that have been adopted by consensus.

There is a realization in a number of quarters that there is a need to build support for the process of trade liberalization in the WTO, and in fact for the WTO itself. Thus, a call has come from a variety of groups to convene a meeting to address the concerns relating to trade and the environment.[2] This, in turn, has led to a consensus among WTO members to hold the High Level Meeting in March of 1999.

[1] Examples include CITES, the Montreal Protocol and the Basel Convention.

[2] The proposal to hold a High Level Meeting is reflected in the Quad Ministerial Communiqué of 29–30 April 1998, the Report of the European Parliament adopted on 30 April 1998, various initiatives of the European Commission (e.g. the speech of Sir Leon Brittan to the Bellerive Foundation on 23 March 1998), and, most recently, the call by

In large measure, the challenge facing the member governments of the WTO is to find a way of dealing with the criticisms of civil society without severely damaging the credibility and usefulness of the WTO as a body responsible for the rules of the non-discriminatory trading system and the progressive liberalization of trade in both goods and services. Conducting international trade according to rules rather than commercial or political power is accepted by all WTO members to be one of its most important characteristics.

It could be reasoned that there is a now a window of opportunity to address the concerns of the trade community and representatives of civil society. First, the negotiations leading to the formulation of the agenda for the WTO Ministerial Meeting in December 1999 will provide the opportunity for serious consideration of the issues to be addressed in whatever form the multilateral negotiations take in the year 2000. Second, much groundwork has been done in the WTO to introduce change if this is thought necessary; comprehensive proposals on most of the major issues have been discussed at length. Third, a great deal of work is already under way in the regular bodies of the WTO, including the General Council, addressing ways to improve the transparency of the WTO and to accelerate the derestriction of an increasing range of documents. Fourth, there is a political awareness that something needs to be done, expressed most recently in the call for the High Level Meeting itself. For this opportunity to be realized, there must be an appropriate level of ambition on the part of all interested parties. While it is important to be ambitious, it is equally important to be realistic with regard to what can be done in the WTO within particular time frames.

Various stages determined by forthcoming events need to be taken into account in ascertaining what issues are to be addressed and when. The first is the preparatory stage for the High Level Meeting. Second, there is the High Level Meeting itself and what could be the outcome

[2] (cont)
President Clinton for a joint Ministerial Conference of Trade and Environment Ministers. President Clinton asked that 'a high-level meeting be convened, to bring together trade and environmental ministers, to provide strong direction and new energy to the WTO's environmental efforts in the years to come, as has been suggested by the European Commission'.

of this meeting. Third, there is the preparatory stage for the WTO Ministerial Meeting taking place at the end of 1999 in the United States, and the negotiations surrounding the formulation of the agenda for this meeting. Fourth, there is the Ministerial Meeting itself and perhaps the launching of a new round of negotiations.

Given the manner in which the WTO proceeds, it would seem reasonable to divide the issues to be addressed, and the possible outcomes, into categories, depending on the degree of government involvement or negotiation in each case. Given the consensus-based nature of the WTO, the need for members to take decisions requires collective decision-taking, probably intensive negotiation, and certainly not a rapid outcome. On this basis, it is possible to envisage three sets of objectives and outcomes. First, there are those that can be achieved if there is enough informal support for the Director-General or the Secretariat to undertake initiatives without formal discussion and decision-taking on the part of the members. In such cases, consultation is important but negotiation is not. Second, there are initiatives that require the collective approval of members, but not necessarily changes in rules, rights or obligations. Each WTO member has joined the organization because the existing balance of rights and obligations is seen to be satisfactory. Upsetting this balance may require negotiation in areas quite outside those under discussion. There are, however, numerous examples where members can operate expeditiously within the existing framework of rules to achieve objectives that are considered important. Finally, there are those objectives that can be achieved only through a change in rules. The procedures for changing rules in the WTO are complex. In practical terms, rule changes can be achieved only in comprehensive rounds of trade negotiations where cross-sectoral trade-offs are possible.

The coming twelve months could be important for the trade and environment debate in the World Trade Organization. To take advantage of the window of opportunity that exists at the present time, however, will require careful consideration of the content of the proposals presented and the timing and nature of forthcoming important meetings.

Reconciling trade and investment liberalization and environmental sustainability

In the developed world, concern about the environment is here to stay. We have broadly reached an acceptable standard of living and we are now looking for more than just the material benefits and comfort that the industrial revolution, technological advancement and trade have created. We can now afford to be more critical about the environment and the impact that our production processes, products and lifestyles have on the environment. There is also a general recognition that we cannot continue to extract natural resources, produce, consume, create waste and pollute our surroundings in the way we have done in the past; this is simply not sustainable.

The link between a high standard of living and improved environmental standards is clearly evident. The link between the progressive liberalization of trade, investment and wealth creation has also been clearly proven by the GATT and WTO over the past 50 years. It can therefore be deduced that more liberalized trade and investment creates wealth that leads to higher environmental standards and improved sustainability. Conversely, without wealth creation environmental standards would not be improved and environmental sustainability would have a far lower priority.

Trade and investment liberalization and environmental sustainability are thereby mutually supportive. It is only the rate at which we progress and the degree of improvement of environmental performance and sustainability that needs to be reconciled.

It is also essential for developing countries to create wealth and thereby to adopt very much higher environmental standards.

What challenges will the next few years pose?

In the next few years one of the main problems will be avoiding global economic decline. Without wealth creation in developing countries, environmental standards will remain unsatisfactory and sustainability will be sacrificed for short-term wealth creation. A reversion to protectionism will also prevent global solutions to global environmental problems.

Environmental issues are currently addressed by a farrago of international organizations. There is no coherent or prioritized approach, and activity is driven to some extent by fashion and political motivation. Failure to address environmental issues coherently and effectively leads to greater expectations being placed on the WTO to solve the problem. We are like startled rabbits in the light of the WTO.

A more coherent and prioritized approach to environment issues through a single powerful, dynamic and respected international agency is absolutely crucial. If this is not possible, then there should at least be an organization to coordinate the individual organizations' or agencies' activities. This would focus resources on internationally agreed priorities, and reduce duplication and the inefficient use of limited resource to address environmental concerns.

Another major challenge for the future is to modify the culture of individuals towards the environment. Individuals in their own lifestyles cause more pollution and create more waste than companies which, through a combination of regulation and voluntary action, are in my opinion extremely good citizens in the main, committed to good environmental management.

Failure to create the right culture and individual approach to the environment will encourage an onerous regulatory approach which ultimately will become self-defeating as companies become buried in regulatory burdens and authorities are no longer able to monitor compliance with all the regulations. In the case of regulations covering trade, there is a whole range of border controls all of which are extremely important in their own right and most of which are growing in their own requirements.

We already have the Montreal Protocol, the Basel Convention and the Convention on the Prior Informed Consent procedure, each of which is enforced through a different process. While the controls are manageable at present, if more different types of trade control are introduced and the current ones become more widely applicable, they will become extremely difficult, if not impossible, to manage. Effective enforcement must be considered carefully in all future conventions and agreements related to trade controls.

Environment in the Millennium Round?

If the Millennium Round goes ahead at the end of 1999, one of the major tasks will be to defend and strengthen the agreements achieved in the Uruguay Round.

Second, agriculture and textile trade need to be further liberalized to enable developing countries to benefit from increased trade with developed countries in these products.

Third, it is my view that the Millennium Round should also be used as an opportunity to get a consensus on the need for the establishment of a World Organization for the Environment.

Finally, I hope that the future will not be a reflection of the past in the way that this issue is handled. There has been a distinct 'us-and-them' approach. We need trade policy specialists, environmentalists, industrialists and authorities working together to achieve a workable and necessary environmental improvement.

Tom Burke

The dangers of trade and the environment

Trade and the environment is an area with enormous dangers. My most intimate acquaintance with the kind of dangers that this set of issues can produce occurred when I was deeply involved in the leghold traps dispute that took place during 1996-7.[1] During the course of that dispute, I watched Sir Leon Brittan – who believes in democracy, is very much in favour of trade liberalization and is a strong pro-European – get himself bent completely out of shape as he sought to reconcile the conflicts between trade and environment. He became someone acting in an extraordinarily undemocratic fashion in order to thwart the democratic will of all 15 environment ministers of Europe who wished to protect animals by prohibiting the use of leghold traps. In doing so, he deeply undermined both the case for trade liberalization and the case for strengthening Europe. None of these were things he intended to do: they were things that the deep logic of the trade–environment conflict produced.

One of the other dangers in this field is that we focus enormously on wonderfully intricate policy with deeply difficult technical corners to get locked into, and we ignore the politics. The politics is at least as important as the policy in this issue – indeed, perhaps more important. We need to understand that there are political risks as well as policy risks and that they are sometimes in conflict with each other. There is a clear policy risk (and it is easily understandable) that environmental

[1] *Editors' note*: The EC 'Leghold Traps Regulation' (Council Regulation 3254/91 of 4 November 1991) was concluded in 1991. It provided for imports of pelts of specified species to be banned with effect from 1 January 1996 *unless* the Commission had determined that the country from which they originated had taken adequate steps to prohibit the use of the leghold trap, or that the trapping methods used for those species in that country met internationally agreed humane trapping standards (which were the subject of ongoing negotiations between the EU, Canada, Russia and the USA). In late 1995, Leon Brittan decided to delay the introduction of the ban following complaints from the USA and Canada that its introduction would be a breach of WTO rules.

measures might be used to act as a cover for trade protection. An example of this can be found in the way in which the US CAFE standards were constructed.[2]

There is an equally clear political risk that the strict application of the policy will collapse public and political support for it, and it is that risk that is bubbling away in such matters as the *Tuna/Dolphin* and *Shrimp/Turtle* issues. However, if we think these issues were troublesome, wait until we get into GMOs in the next 12 months. And particularly wait until we get to GMOs in the light of the recent emergence of a Red–Green alliance in Germany as one of the dominant political actors on the world stage. It is important, therefore, to balance the notion of policy risk with the notion of political risk.

Setting the debate in the context of globalization

The debate needs also to be set in the context of globalization. Globalization of opportunity will, and must, be accompanied by globalization of responsibility, just as nationalization of opportunity was accompanied by nationalization of responsibility.

It is easy to forget that national markets are a relatively recent creation in economic history. They may have begun in the 1750s, but national markets did not really start to be a dominant feature until the 1850s. It was not until we had created national markets that we began to create national standards: standards on child labour, standards on environment, standards on public health. The process in which we are now engaged is a replication on a global scale of the process that went on in the nineteenth century of responsibility following opportunity.

How do we create the means of responsibility to accompany the means of opportunity? One thing is certain: to offer the notion that there can be globalization of opportunity without globalization of responsibility is to offer a very false prospect indeed.

---

[2] *Editors' note*: The US 'corporate average fuel efficiency (CAFE) payment was the subject of a GATT dispute between the United States and the European Community. The European Community argued that the payment had the effect of discriminating against the EC car industry. The GATT dispute settlement panel upheld the complaint (*United States – Restrictions on Imports of Tuna*, DS29/R, June 1994).

The two rule systems for global responsibility in the second half of the twentieth century, the trade rule system and the environment rule system, are among the most significant political accomplishments of this period. And the development of both is an essential part of making the transition to sustainable development. Without both sets of rules, both commanding public confidence and both working efficiently, there is no prospect of making a transition to sustainable development. Therefore, the need to avoid collision between the two rule systems is the paramount policy and the political goal of this debate. It is therefore alarming to look at the extent to which there are structural factors that are promoting that collision. In other words, it is not a question of people's aspirations, the strengths or weaknesses of individuals (or indeed of individual institutions), but, much more, the depth to which some of the structural factors are embedded.

There is the prospect of the World Trade Organization adding 30 new members and having rigorously to insist, as it tries to absorb these 30 new members (including China, which is the biggest and most important of all), on maintaining its standards in the perfectly natural fear that they may be dissolved in the extension of the club. There is a very strong sense, particularly now, that economic turbulence will act as an excuse for relaxing some of the disciplines of the trade system. There is fear of an increased backsliding on these hard established rules, the sort of fear that led a former assistant trade secretary in the United States, writing in the *International Herald Tribune*, to talk about the 'protectionist juggernaut' that he saw developing.

At the same time as that structural dynamic is working, insisting on a more rigorous application of trade policy, environmental degradation is occurring at a very strong and accelerating pace. People look around and they see the deterioration in environmental quality, whether at local, regional or global level, increasing ever more quickly. At the same time, there are powerful policy messages coming from a number of quarters that, in order to deal with these issues in an economically efficient way, the policy response must be pushed further and further up the production chain, so that we are designing out solutions rather than fixing them at the end. That whole agenda – eco-efficiency, life cycle assessment, eco-labelling, environmental management systems and much else – is driven structurally. And incidentally, it is driven in part by the OECD, the same body that promotes trade liberalization policies as essential ways to address environmental problems efficiently.

The role of companies

As the whole momentum of adapting consumption and production cycles gathers pace, and as we move out increasingly further into the idea of the consumer's responsibility in all this – so that it is no longer just companies and governments having to resolve these questions – it seems to me that the structural momentum to ensure that consumers are given clear signals about the environmental impacts of their purchases, not just what is made but also how it was made, can only grow, enhancing that potential for conflict between the environment rules and the trade rules. It is here that companies find themselves trying to work out where they should position themselves inside this enormous potential for turbulence.

We tend to talk about multinational companies as if they were all the same. There are in fact different kinds of multinational companies. Not all of them have the same interest in the trade–environment debate and not all of them have the same behaviour or impact on either trade or the environment. The companies that are engaged in the flows of capital around the world, and the people who market capital – money – around the world, have very different sorts of behaviour, time scale, view and perspective from the companies that are purchasing goods and commodities, whether they are Nike in the famous case,[3] or other companies in a similar role who are sourcing goods for trade from different parts of the world. And both types have a different interest from those companies that are putting direct investment into the extractive industries or into large capital equipment, chemical plants, and vehicle manufacturing plants. Not all multinational companies behave in the same way, and it is important to keep that distinction in mind.

[3] *Editors' note*: Nike is one of a number of sportswear manufacturers whose labour practices – particularly in developing countries – have been targeted by NGOs. In 1997, Nike hired an external expert to report on the company's global sportswear operations. The resulting report was questioned by NGOs, triggering debate about the role of monitoring and verification.

Sinking several billion dollars into a hole in the ground that cannot be moved and being able to push a button and get half a billion dollars' worth of capital out of the country in literally a split second create very different views of how you want the world to be. The former gives a much greater interest in stability, be it global or local stability, and a much greater interest in a rounded perspective of what constitutes development. Such companies operate inside a single information space where, increasingly, the standards to which they have to operate on the environment are global standards – and are also the standards that operate in their home country.

For Shell, Rio Tinto, BP or any of the major companies, there is very little choice but to operate to the same standards abroad as those at home, because if they do not somebody will point out the difference and they will find themselves in deep reputational trouble. Therefore, to a very considerable extent, this makes that sort of company very different from the procurers and the capital merchants. It makes them a very powerful mechanism for the transfer of standards, because it is extremely important for them to ensure that the standards to which they operate abroad are in some very real way compatible with the standards to which they operate at home, not just for competitive reasons but also so that they can make sure that their assurance chain works and that their suppliers and contractors are operating in ways that they can live with.

It is that sort of company in particular that has an overwhelming interest in ensuring that there is not some inadvertent collision between the two rule systems, environment and trade. Therefore, to put the point more positively, we need to work hard to achieve some sort of successful merging of the rule systems, and we need to do that sooner rather than later. Therefore it is important to have a grasp of what the differences are, both in the theory and the culture. And the differences are far more important than the similarities.

The cultures of trade and environment

The trade culture is a culture of deal-making. It calls itself *law*, and since the creation of the WTO it has more of the appearance of law, but in practice it has consistently been a process whereby people arrive at deals with all the incoherence and inconsistency that deal-making involves. That has been the accepted culture for trade rule-making. Environmental rule-making has had the appearance of law, but the appearance is often all it has had. It has not been law in the sense of being binding in outcomes, but it has had the appearance of law, with all the requirements for consistency that law has. This meets its most difficult and interesting challenge when you look at the Basel Convention, where all of the conflicts and difficulties come about because it is extremely difficult to come up with a legally consistent notion of what constitutes waste.[4]

The trade culture, for reasons that are all to do with the necessity of deal-making, is a deeply secretive culture. What matters is the outcome, not the process by which the outcome was arrived at, because the process is inevitably going to be somewhat incoherent and inconsistent. The environment rule-making culture is entirely one of transparency, with everything open. Anybody who sat through something like the Kyoto Protocol negotiations will know just how transparent the system is. The basis of trade rules is that you do not make discriminations between people. The basis of global environment rules is precisely that you do make discriminations between people; you differentiate responsibilities because you recognize that there are different circumstances.

The trade rules, both in practice and in intent, have been exclusive in their processes. They have excluded people who did not have a direct and immediate interest in the discussions. The environment rules, partly because of the pressures that have led to them, have been enormously inclusive and participative in both intent and in culture.

The trade rules have real bite; there really are some sanctions that you can impose and they act powerfully to enforce the disciplines. There are no sanctions in the environment rules. The environment rules

[4] *Editors' note*: A key problem faced by the Basel Convention is that the definition of 'hazardous waste'– the object of its regulation – is contested. The Basel Convention includes as wastes hazardous materials that are intended for recycling, whereas the recycling industry often regards those same materials as 'products' or 'secondary raw materials' and argues that they should not be subject to 'waste' regulation. See Jonathan Krueger, *International Trade and the Basel Convention* (RIIA/Earthscan, 1999), pp. 99 *et seq*.

are obeyed globally only to the extent to which countries agree to obey them, and there is nothing anyone can do if someone does not want to obey them. This is why, when most countries fail to achieve their framework climate convention target – and most of the industrialized countries will do that some time around the year 2000 – nobody will say or do anything, because there won't be anything that can be said or done.

The trade rules are frequently opposed by the public – all sorts of different publics with all sorts of different interests – but, by and large, the environment rules are supported by the public.

These are important differences in culture. They are particularly important differences as we look at the prospects for merging the two sets of rules. This is not just a question of merging two sets of language on two pieces of paper: it is about merging two different cultures, different institutions, trying to bring together two different political contexts. It is a very complex and elaborate task and one of which the full scale needs to be understood if there is to be any prospect of success.

Merging the cultures

Let me conclude by making two points on what I believe are essential components for success in that task. I do not agree that it can be done only by case law and that a change in the theory is too difficult to accomplish. In practice, that will not be adequate. It will be necessary to look for some way of achieving a much better shared analytical base for policy-making in both areas. That cannot be done by the WTO and its Committee on Trade and the Environment. It needs to be based on the OECD model of getting the relevant policy-makers together in a sustained and focused way. This is not, however, to suggest a job here for the OECD itself – particularly given the poor job it has made on the Multilateral Agreement on Investment.

This said, there is a real need to revisit the key theoretical concepts in both aspects of the debate – 'like products', 'trade restrictive', 'precautionary principle' – and we need to reconcile some of these conflicts at a theoretical or analytical level, and to create a forum in which to do that. If a high-level panel meets and achieves some success, one of the key elements in that success will be the creation of a political impetus for some of this policy resolution to take place outside of the negotiations.

The key aspect of the OECD model is that people accept that they are not negotiating: they are simply analysing and sharing their analysis. That has often provided a very sound basis of future policy development through negotiation. I do not see how a resolution of the conflicts, real and potential, between trade and environment rules can be accomplished without some sort of forum like that to take on that task. However, the WTO will not be halted in its tracks while this task is being carried out, and therefore, in some very real sense, many of these issues will continue to be resolved through case law.

If we do not create the sort of forum we are talking about, and if we leave it to case law alone, we will simply be overwhelmed by events, and not in a way that any of us would like very much. As Winston Churchill once remarked, 'if something be not done, it will do itself and in a manner pleasing to no one'.

If we are going to do things by case law, the one area where we could make significant progress relatively rapidly is in enhancing public confidence in the disputes process. The WTO disputes process currently commands no public confidence, and the only reason why it is not a source of greater outrage than it now is in some communities is simply because most people do not have any idea of what it is doing. The confines of the existing debate will not be adequate.

First, we need to create a transparent disputes process in which all of the steps are open and visible, quickly and rapidly, so that people can see not just the outcome but also the process and how the process is working. Second, we need to create access to that disputes system by right, not by permission. It should not be considered progress when you are allowed to submit *amicus* briefs. It should by right be the case that those people who have an interest in the outcome of a trade dispute should be able to submit whatever they think in the way of input to the process of a dispute. Third, the selection of dispute and appellate panels needs to be very much more open and clear, and people need to know who is taking these decisions on their behalf, how they came to be selected, what their qualifications for selection were and what their background, antecedence and interests are. We are not dealing with judges inside a framework in which the authority of judges is unquestioned. In some sense, you certainly do not want the WTO determining environmental policy for you; but if it is going to do so by default, you had better make sure that it has on its Appellate Body expert assessors who know what they are doing.

These seem to me to be three elements that are essential for creating more public confidence. There are probably many more that we need to get right in the disputes process in order to create some space for a more sustained and off-line examination of how to resolve the analytical conflicts, so that we are able to achieve a successful merging of the trade and environment rules.

John Gummer[1]

Matching national and international actions

I wonder how it is that we have managed to get ourselves into a position in which we do internationally what we would not dream of doing nationally. It has usually been the other way around. Usually we have demanded from international agreements standards and values which not all the participants could honourably sign up to at home. We ask for democracy in the United Nations, although at times less than half the members are democratic at home; the nations that have signed up to the anti-slavery concordat are not all, in the strict sense of the matter, carrying that out at home. But for some curious reason, we have allowed the World Trade Organization to operate in circumstances in which we would not accept any such protection of free trade to operate at home.

In the UK for example, where we have a long tradition of free trade internally, we have only seen it as possible to have that kind of commercial freedom because we have had first of all the rule of law; second, a series of protections for the vulnerable; and, third, a series of protections for the credulous. In other words, we protect people who cannot protect themselves, and we are protecting people who are stupid enough not to try to protect themselves. That is the basis upon which we operate trade within our society.

Of course, the argument is not that we should not do this: the only argument is how far we should go. Nobody in the UK, not even the most extreme of free market thinkers, seriously suggests that all of these protections should be swept away. The difference between political parties here is either about the way in which you protect or about the degree to which you protect – but not about the principle in the first place.

It is a very curious structure that we have invented internationally; one which *prima facie* demands an apology – an apology that is not so

[1] *Editors' note:* This is an edited version of Mr Gummer's paper presented at the conference.

far forthcoming. It is also a matter of significance that in many ways this is the only international arrangement that appears to have sufficient teeth to make it work. If you look at almost everything else we are talking about, not just at the margins but fairly centrally, we do not quite get there globally.

Let me take one of those arrangements which is seen to be an enormous success – the Montreal Protocol. Let us just look at two things there which perhaps detract from its success. First of all, we have never been able to get anybody seriously to face up to, and certainly not seriously to sign up to, the kind of reductions in methyl bromide that are necessary. I myself spent hours of fruitless negotiations late into the night debating with the Africans, particularly the Kenyans, the question of changing over from methyl bromide, whereas they were *increasing* their use of methyl bromide. I even offered to pay for it – and that is very hard for a British minister. And it is still the case that the use of methyl bromide, a potent destroyer of the ozone layer, is increasing in the world rather than decreasing.

As a second example, we tried to get the Americans to sign up to an understanding that deals with substitutes for CFCs. They have done a deal with their industry. They know that the manufacturing process of CFC substitutes itself contributes to the ozone layer's depletion, but they have decided to stick to the deal they did. We can't get that to change. So there is the most successful of the international arrangements that we have, and I am not at all sure that there are not some very large holes even in that.

But watch what happens to any advanced nation, and to most less advanced nations, if you threaten them with the WTO. That is taken seriously, as seriously as almost any kind of internal threat, because it is a legal system which appears to be recognized as something that is absolutely effective. Where the law is concerned, what matters most is whether you think it will be enforced. If you think it will be enforced, you are pretty likely to obey it.

So we ought to be thinking seriously in dealing with the issues of trade and the environment about the fact that here we have an international operation which does not have the restrictions that we have in similar operations in our own nations, and which also seems to have a degree of credibility that is unparalleled in other international agreements.

If you then take the word 'environment' and say to yourself, 'Faced with the sort of issues that we now have environmentally, will we be able to solve them without having international agreements of a similarly solid kind?', the answer is 'no'.

Cooperating in the common interest

Whatever you may think about what will happen at the climate change talks in Buenos Aires later this year (1998), all of us who are going there will be saying that the issue we are facing – the change in our climate – is still subject to all kinds of arguments. But any sensible politician will have to accept that it is something that cannot be ignored and that must be dealt with – unless you intend to make a special exception and say 'it is so nasty I prefer not to think about it', which is the US Republican Party's policy.

The truth is that this is an issue which is going to affect policies throughout the world, because politicians throughout the world – outside the United States – have now accepted that if they apply their normal judgment this is not something they can avoid. They also know that if they want to do anything about it – and an increasingly large number of them do – they have to get out of a position in which their population can say, as the British population could so easily say, 'We account for only 3 per cent of the world's emissions; whatever we do in the next ten years will be counteracted by what China does, and therefore why don't we say we won't do anything until China does something.'

The problem is that this is a very powerful argument; and it becomes more powerful the smaller the nation is and the more advanced it is, because if that 3 per cent can be pulled down to 2 per cent and 1½ per cent and the cost of changing anything is significant, then two arguments begin to evolve: one, that it does not make enough difference to matter; and the other, that the cost of doing it in Sweden is so much more than the cost of doing it in Bangladesh that we really have to wait until we can do it in Bangladesh because you get so much more for your money. Of course you do if you spend it; but what they really mean is that you would get so much more for your money, and you will get even more if you don't spend the money! That is the difficulty with that argument, so it is one that we have to watch very carefully, because it is a very powerful argument.

One has to say very clearly that here is an area where governments, politicians, are clearly going to act, where most of us think they ought to act, but where they know perfectly well that they cannot act in the long run unless there is some kind of global agreement. Although we can get people to do it now – and I can usually shame an audience into accepting that it is our fault so we have to do our bit first – there comes the moment at which that argument ceases to have quite the impetus. It started in America, and we will have to get over that in some way; and somewhere in the early years of the next century we will find it quite impossible to continue unless there is a clear connection between what we are doing and what the developing countries, as they grow, are doing.

Of course, if there is to be such a connection it has to be one that involves justice. There is no point in discussing this issue with developing countries unless you are prepared to accept that, if there is a global problem that involves reducing emissions globally, then that reduction cannot be on the basis of historical use: it has to be on some kind of basis that has some connection with justice.

Historical use of course has to come into it. You cannot ask people to change from having four per cent of the world's population and 25 per cent of the world's emissions to having four per cent of the world's emissions overnight. Not only would it not be possible for them politically, but it would be extremely bad for the world economy. However, at some point along this trajectory there is a hugely important element of justice, which has to be seen not just by the poorer countries but also by the richer countries. It is only by understanding what interdependence really means that they can begin to evolve a system that properly represents a global solution to a global problem.

Tackling 'economic imperialism'

A word about interdependence. The trouble with all of us is that we are fundamentally imperialist; everybody is imperialist unless you are right at the bottom of the heap where there is nobody to be imperialist about! It reminds me about the story of the Baptist minister who once made a speech, building to huge crescendo as he said 'Catholics have persecuted people. The Church of England has persecuted people. Lutherans have persecuted people. The Calvinists have persecuted people. Only we Baptists have never persecuted anyone, and that is because we have never had the chance!' To some degree, that ought to be thought of in terms of imperialism.

People are imperialist about other people, and they are imperialist in whatever is the fashionable area. This used to be overrunning people and taking over, and then it was something rather less elegant than that, and now it is a different kind of imperialism. It is about helping other people because you know best, and that is the sort of imperialism which is very well illustrated in a speech I often hear when I am in the United States, which goes like this.

The United States is the engine of world trade. Without the United States, world trade would be very, very much less powerful and would contribute very much less to the well-being of the world, and we are in it in order to contribute to the well-being of the world. (Sometimes that is not put in but it is thought of.) Therefore you cannot complain if we do all this emitting because it is the price not just of our riches but of such riches as Bangladesh has.

You will see the mistake in this economic argument, but very often the most powerful economic arguments are fundamentally faulty. After all, Marx conned the world for a hundred-and-a-bit years on a totally false economic argument, without any practical expression – totally wrong, known to be wrong every time it was expressed, but he got away with it because it was always not quite right there: 'This isn't really Marxism; Marxism is really different' – and we go back to the real theory of it. That is not just on the left: it is on the right and everywhere else. There is always a reason why your theory does not fit the facts. It is not the theory's fault: it is the fact's fault, always!

This is the difficulty for those who put the argument forward that somehow or other you must not stop the engine of world trade, and that therefore there is a kind of inherent fairness about it because everybody benefits. Of course it will not stand up; but it is very deeply ingrained. If we want to talk about fairness, we have to do so in circumstances where people understand that it does not matter what they think about it: it is the practical price you pay for what you need. In other words, we should stop talking about fairness in the sense of it being a moral responsibility – although I happen to hold that this is so – indeed, to stop talking about it even as a religious responsibility (although I happen to hold that too). What we have to say is that it is just a practical necessity. It doesn't matter what your argument is about it: either you find a way that is seen to be fair enough for others to join in, or others won't join in.

This is no longer a matter of theology or ideology, it is now a matter of practical necessity. So if you want to solve this environmental problem and, I suspect increasingly, others – for example the environmental problems related to the oceans – then it can only be done if you create a context of fairness. I define 'fairness' simply by the matter of saying that it is a context which those who sign up to it think is fair, or better still fair enough. That is, after all, the basis of most international agreements. It is not that you actually agree with it, but that it is the best you can get and it is reasonable enough for you to sell. That is the sort of situation in which we have to work.

Now let us bring that back to the context of the WTO. In the WTO we have a tough, effective, almost universally accepted system. It is one that people take seriously, and yet one that has none of the restrictions, none of the value judgments, that we have in our own countries. We are faced with environmental problems which, if we are to solve, will demand answers that will not be strictly amenable to the sort of measurements the WTO has used up to now. These two things run absolutely counter to each other. It is not just a matter of making sure that the WTO is more environmentally friendly and thinks a bit more about this, that and the other, and does not actually fall out with the Convention on International Trade in Endangered Species; it is something much more fundamental than that.

Accommodating different values

It is here that I want to bring in the last point. For one moment, think not about the environment or the WTO but about the question of genetically modified organisms – GMOs. One of the problems of discussing GMOs is that many of those who want to exult in them are fascinated by the primacy of science. They are science-based to a degree that blinds them to the fact that most people are culture-based. One of the difficulties between the United States and the rest of the world is that the United States is much more science-based and science-friendly than the rest of the world and, curiously enough, is much less culture-based and much less culture-friendly in that sense than the rest of the world.

These two attitudes very often come into very deep contrast. If you listen to people talking about 'why the French think this' or 'the Germans think that' or 'the British think this' or 'Europeans think like this', very often behind the question, if they are Americans, is a sort of feeling that they ought *not* to think differently, that rational people should not come to different conclusions, because scientifically rational people can come to only one conclusion, whereas we all know that the world is not like that.

The reason we know it is that we have to move in that world – and anybody who has negotiated around the table with the European Union moves in it all the time. Indeed, you have to learn that what you think is science-based is not so at all: it is also very deeply culture-based, so that your reaction to many things is different because you are different, and you are different because you are not as simple as is made out if you take the very simplistic rational approach.

Apply that for a moment to the issue of the environment and trade. Because it is more complicated for most people, you cannot have the simplistic answer that forms the basis of the WTO. You have to find something that is able to take into account people's wider interests. That is, after all, what we do with our own countries. Why is it that we protect the vulnerable? Why is it that we protect the credulous? Why is it that we have the rule of law? It is overwhelmingly because we do not think that trade is absolutely the only good, that free trade is the only thing that matters. Even if you can be an enthusiast for free trade and the free market, as I am, I do not believe it is the most important thing in life.

I very rarely make a party-political comment, and this is not a party-political comment but just a quote from Quintin Hogg which I use because it is a parallel. In defining Conservatives, he said that 'Conservatives never think that politics is the most important thing in life. Intelligent Conservatives think that religion is more important; rather less intelligent Conservatives think that hunting is more important', and he said 'Some Conservatives think that both are more important'.

It is a good parallel with what we are talking about. What Hogg is saying is that people who are committed to a certain political party, who think it is an important thing, who work for it, spend a lot of their time on it, still do not think it is the most important thing in life. That seems to me to be the way we ought to look at trade. I think that trade is very important. Free trade is vital. It is the only thing that will change the future for people. The only way in which we will get the sort of raising of standards of living in areas that so desperately need it is via the trading mechanism. But I do not think it is the most important thing in life. I certainly don't think it is the only thing in life.

In a sense, what we are battling with here is a curious absolutism in world decision-making, which is entirely absent in national decision-making. I come at the end to where I started. If we are going to discuss trade, investment and the environment, we need to do so bearing in mind our own experience of how we have dealt with trade, investment and the environment in our own countries. We have dealt with them in a non-absolutist sense. We have said you have to make them work and mesh together; that you cannot ignore any one of them; that you must have environmental protection; that if you are going to have investment there must be protection for the investor, but there must also be protection for those whom his investment affects.

When you deal with trade, you accept that you want a business-friendly society. We now have no disagreement with that at all. Everybody thinks it is good to have a business-friendly society, but everybody also thinks that a business-friendly society does not mean that you have a free-for-all, a system that is uninterested in the ability of all members of that society to pay for the basics of life.

Bringing home the issues

My personal key to this very fraught discussion is to bring people back all the time to what they would accept at home, and then ask how is it that what they propose abroad should be different? How can they propose that something they would not for one moment accept in their own nations should be the pattern of world affairs?

Second, I would ask them how they expect us to deal with the great issues which can only be dealt with globally unless we recognize that what has to be done has to be seen to be fair enough? And fairness does demand a much broader vision than the mere concentration upon trading issues.

Third, because I do not think they ought to be allowed to get away with it, I would have to say to them that nobody is prepared now to have a commercial programme, a commercial system, a nation with parameters within which business operates, unless it recognizes environmental concerns for trading reasons; because nationally we recognize that, if we are totally unable to take the environment into account, we will not have those business opportunities in the future because we are so rapidly reducing the range of resources and the ability that we have to utilize them. We are saying all the time that the productivity of resources must grow. We are saying it not just because it is right, but because it is necessary. And if we say that at home, we have to say that abroad.

Lastly, I want to say something even more challenging to them than that. It is simply this: what decent person wants to live in a world in which the only good is free trade? In Samuel Butler's wonderful book *Erewhon*, everything is transformed, and he has people going on a Sunday to the bank with their purses in their hands as against going to the church with their prayerbooks in their hands. He is making a joke, of course, about the ostentatious performance of religious duties, but it is the sort of world that we are increasingly pretending is the one we want. Of course it is a liturgical form of it, but the truth is that we are suggesting by our aggrandizement of the WTO over and above everything else that we really believe that, at the most solemn moments when we remember what we most care about, we should be carrying our purse.

Previous generations have admitted that many people do think like that, and many people – if not most people – act like that. Politicians increasingly say that is why people vote, that in any case it is like that. But if we give in to this argument internationally, we will be the first generation that actually says publicly, liturgically, in a sense morally, that this is the sort of world we want. I think that particularly those of us who care about the environment should say to the world, ‘It is not the kind of family we want; it is not the kind of local community we want; it is not the kind of region we want; it is not the kind of nation we want, and therefore it will not be the kind of world we want.’

Part II
Towards win–win solutions?

Poverty and sustainability

David Batt

Introduction

It is perhaps worth starting with the underlying question: What is the relevance of trade, investment and environment policy linkages for developing countries? Trade and investment lead to growth, which in turn creates the resources for poorer countries to tackle the problems they face including those of an environmental nature. The linkages between trade, investment, environment and development can, however, be more complex. Certain patterns of growth and development can themselves cause environmental degradation, particularly in the case of countries whose environmental policies are weak or unenforced. Also, there is no guarantee that resources provided by trade will be used on environmental improvements, though the evidence suggests that, as a country's income rises beyond a certain level, the negative effects of growth tend to lessen.

Moreover, developing countries themselves are concerned that environmental policies may restrict their market access, or could be used as a protectionist tool. More progress clearly needs to be made at the multilateral level to reconcile different interests.

Addressing the concerns of developing countries on these issues is therefore an important part of the resolution of conflict at the international level on trade, investment and environment. And the UK is committed to ensuring that developing countries are fully integrated into the multilateral trading system. The timing is critical. We need to be prepared to negotiate about the concerns of developing countries in the Millennium Round, where the environment will be one of the important issues on the agenda. Unlocking the debate on trade and environment will help make progress on a range of other trade issues.

This paper outlines broadly the range of activities that the UK Department for International Development (DFID) has initiated to take this work forward, particularly those activities that stem from the recent White Paper on International Development.[1]

DFID and White Paper commitments

DFID's primary objective in this area is to ensure that UK and EU policy reflects our commitment to eradicate poverty and to promote sustainable development, and to take into account the concerns of developing countries.

Against this background, we in the UK have recognized the value of strong links between trade, environment and development ministries. They are vital to allow us to pursue a consistent line in international forums. DFID is working closely with colleagues in Whitehall, particularly the DTI and DETR. We need to encourage others to develop and maintain these links.

Reflecting this close coordination between different departments, the Government's White Paper on International Development identified three main strategies for integrating a development perspective into trade and environment policy-making:

- work to ensure that trade rules do not impose unfair standards on developing countries or discriminate unfairly against their goods – a point emphasized by the Prime Minister speaking at the WTO Ministerial Conference in May;
- work with producers and importers to increase trade in sustainably produced products and services from developing countries;
- work with developing countries to support their efforts to raise their domestic environment standards and to help them tackle global environmental problems.

Ensuring fair trade rules

In this first area – ensuring that trade rules do not impose unfair standards or discriminate unfairly – our work covers the following key areas:

[1] *Eliminating World Poverty: A Challenge for the 21st Century*, DFID, November 1997.

- commissioning research to identity the most serious issues faced by developing countries, so we can focus energies on addressing the right problems;
- working to help increase the capacity of developing countries themselves to identify their interests and to play a full and active part in negotiations. We are delighted to be funding a project in this area which builds on ideas put forward by the Foundation for International Environmental Law and Development, and which has been developed in close consultation with UNCTAD. The model that has emerged here, of close collaboration between a multilateral agency and a leading NGO, is I think an innovative and exciting one;
- working ourselves closely with Whitehall colleagues and EU partners to identify any real problems and determine appropriate solutions.

Increasing sustainable trade

Moving to the second strategy, that of increasing trade in sustainably produced products and services, the following initiatives are under way:

- building the capacity of producers to benefit from changing consumer demands; for example, the Kenya Flower Association has asked us for help with the independent validation of the criteria in the ethical and environmental code that the Association has adopted;
- funding research by the International Institute for Environment and Development (IIED) to identify the positive opportunities for developing-country exporters which arise from changes in consumer demand in the North; examining which preconditions need to be in place to stimulate sustainable trade;
- supporting further analysis of who benefits from sustainable trade – are the poorest people, the smallest enterprises, actually able to take advantage of these new opportunities, and if not how can we address this issue?
- supporting use of trade policy instruments to promote better environmental performance, for example the EU's GSP (Generalized

System of Preferences) scheme. On the environment side, this offers improved market access in return for satisfactory implementation of International Tropical Timber Organization (ITTO) standards. On the labour side, the criteria are the adoption of core labour standards. We have successfully pressed not only for this incentive structure, but also for financial and technical assistance to help developed countries meet these standards;
- looking at how support for voluntary initiatives on the one hand, and increased regulation on the other, can work together; we have asked the New Economics Foundation to undertake research into this.

Raising environmental standards in developing countries

The third main White Paper strategy area is that of helping developing countries raise domestic environmental standards to meet commitments under multilateral environment agreements (MEAs). In this area, we are:

- working to improve environmental performance rather than focusing solely on the amendment of regulations – enabling developing countries to implement standards is as important, if not more so, as the standard setting process itself;
- providing support to partner countries on a range of both domestic environmental issues, such as soil degradation and urban water, and global environmental issues, such as air quality, oceans and greenhouse gas emissions;
- providing support for the transfer, development and adaptation of environmentally sound technology;
- helping partner countries to develop and implement environmentally sound policy, and in particular supporting partner-country efforts to develop national strategies for sustainable development, which integrate environmental issues into socioeconomic plans and programmes at regional and sectoral levels, as well as at the national level, and in line with international targets. These targets require such strategies to be in place by 2005 so as to ensure that current

trends in the loss of environmental resources are effectively reversed at both global and national levels by 2015;
- looking into the area of environmental management systems, particularly the ISO 14000 series. Companies may require developing-country suppliers and producers to follow these systems. We are therefore considering the need for technical assistance to raise awareness of the ISO 14000 standards in developing countries and to help suppliers and producers meet these. The Pakistan Chamber of Commerce has already asked DFID for assistance in this area.

In relation to MEA commitments, DFID recognizes the importance of assisting developing countries to tackle global environmental issues. As the White Paper said, the impact of developing countries on the global environment is growing rapidly; and so too is their vulnerability to adverse changes. The UK sees the MEAs as an important means of coordinating global actions. We have a major voice in MEA negotiations and are major contributors to them. For example:

- The UK is the fifth largest contributor (over £215 million) to the Global Environment Facility, which is the major multilateral channel for assisting developing countries meet their obligations under MEAs.
- DFID spent over £23 million on biodiversity projects in 1996–7.
- On climate change DFID is funding work on climate-friendly technologies and policies through its Energy Efficiency programme.
- DFID has committed £69 million to the Montreal Protocol's Multilateral Fund which meets the cost to developing countries of phasing out ozone depleting substances.

Win–win approaches

Finally, there is a fourth area which was not drawn out explicitly in last year's development White Paper. This is the 'win–win' approach. In brief, this means identifying areas where the removal of trade restrictions and distortions has the potential to yield both direct economic benefits for developing countries and positive environmental results.

As a principle, this has been signed up to by developed and developing countries alike. It has been widely discussed within the Committee on Trade and Environment (CTE) at the WTO. A certain amount of work has been undertaken, looking most recently at how to apply this principle at a sectoral level. And looking ahead, there are clearly a number of opportunities to take this work forward as we move towards the next WTO Ministerial Conference, including next February's meeting of the CTE and the possible High Level Meeting on Trade and Environment.

It is clearly an attractive approach. Indeed, it sounds almost too good to be true. But is it? And what do we need to do to move this work forward?

First, I think we need to pin the terminology down a little. The term 'positive environmental effects' is a beguilingly simple one, but of course policy changes do not always have simple effects. It is possible to imagine changes that would produce a mixture of environmental effects, some positive and some negative, with maybe a positive, neutral or negative balance sheet overall. And the economic effects will not always be clear-cut either. There may be a mixture of 'winners' and 'losers'. We need a clear analytical framework for dealing with this issue.

Second, we need to start pinning down the sort of areas where we think there are likely to be the strongest balance of 'win–wins', and where we should therefore focus research. One broad area would clearly be where there are barriers (tariff or non-tariff) to the entry of products that are sustainably produced and can be sustainably consumed, and that have the potential to replace, if barriers are lowered, products that are either not sustainably produced or not sustainably consumed, or both. A second broad area would be where we can see that subsidies in developed countries, whether domestic or export subsidies or both, are leading to unsustainable patterns of production, unsustainable exploitation of resources or increased environmental damage at the point of consumption, and at the same time are restricting economic opportunities for developing countries.

Third, we need to start building up our list of examples in this area. Some countries in the CTE have already begun to suggest areas. For example, the United States and New Zealand have identified fisheries as a sector where subsidies have led to over-capacity in developed countries' fishing fleets and depletion in certain varieties of world fish stocks. The argument runs that the reduction or removal of these subsidies would provide both a developmental 'win' (because it would provide increased market opportunities for developing-country exporters, who would no longer need to compete on a playing field tilted against them through subsidies to the fishing fleets of developed countries) and an environmental 'win' (because it would slow down depletion of stocks).

Fourth, in order to develop this list of examples, we need to undertake more research. Two points about this. First, I do not think this research need involve going out and collecting extensive primary data. Our assessment is that a lot of the basic data needed are already available, for instance in UNCTAD and elsewhere, but that what has not yet been done is to use the data to try to answer the sort of questions I have been touching on. Second, this is the sort of work that DFID is now supporting. This is not research for the sake of research: it is research specifically linked to policy challenges. It is the sort of policy-based research that DFID wants to undertake more and more of, in partnership with others, not just on this crucial part of any forthcoming multilateral round, but on others too.

Finally, important as this research is, I do not think that the questions are capable of being answered fully by a process of analysis on its own – by my asking someone, or a group of people, no matter how expert, to go off into a room on their own with a pile of papers and a pot of hot coffee. We need the ideas, the intuition, the experience, of a larger group of people.

Building sustainable markets

Nick Robins

The challenge

It is now clear that achieving sustainable patterns of production and consumption will involve long-term structural change in the world economy. In the post-industrial economies of the OECD, improvements in environmental performance of a factor of ten could be required over the next half century. Increasing global interdependence means that this transformation will inevitably have trade implications. The issue facing the world trade system is to work out how it can contribute to this transition, and thereby generate sustainable flows of trade.

In essence, sustainable trade is deceptively simple.[1] Sustainable trade takes place when the international exchange of goods and services meets the four core criteria of sustainable development:

1. it generates economic value;
2. it reduces poverty and inequality;
3. it regenerates the environmental resource base;
4. it is carried out within an open and accountable system of governance.

Making sustainable trade the norm is a different matter and will require a long-term transformation of global markets, involving fundamental changes in the policy and institutional architecture, in corporate practices and patterns of consumption. For developing countries, the challenge of sustainable trade is to ensure that they realize positive benefits from this shift in terms of strengthened trade performance, improved

[1] The International Institute for Environment and Development (IIED) has launched a three-year project, 'Stimulating Sustainable Trade', aimed at providing practical guidance on the mechanics of encouraging trade in sustainable goods and services, from the developing world to the European Union.

environmental quality and, importantly, reductions in poverty. Critical to this will be managing these impacts so that the principles of open trade are respected and the trading relationship provides additional incentives for local action to improve social and environmental performance rather than imposing 'further burdens', in the words of President Mandela.

Achieving sustainable trade requires two complementary strategies. First, we need to squeeze the trade in unsustainable goods and services out of the world economy through international law and national regulation. Slow progress has been achieved on the international front for endangered species, hazardous wastes, ozone depleting substances and toxic chemicals. This has been supplemented by national restrictions on imports containing materials that could damage consumer health, such as bans on the use of certain dyes and controls on pesticide residues. But fierce disputes continue to rage over the legality, feasibility and equity of measures to extend this approach – notably, to allow importing countries to specify social and environmental performance requirements of production methods – through reforms to existing trade law and institutions.

Second, we need to stimulate the trade in sustainable goods and services through market incentives, extended corporate responsibility and new forms of consumer demand and citizen action. This is now perhaps the most promising area for immediate action, given the difficulty of achieving consensus for the restructuring of the international legal architecture and the growing evidence of a range of initiatives leading to significant financial, social and environmental benefits – particularly for developing countries, where opening up new trade opportunities is so central for development. But these initiatives are still new, and many barriers remain to be tackled through concerted action.

Describing the experience and prospects for this second strategy is the subject of this paper. What is particularly noticeable at the moment is the growing convergence of previously parallel initiatives to strengthen the social and environmental dimensions of trade. For example, a recent study conducted by UNIDO in the textile industry showed that 'improvements in environmental protection can be achieved faster and would be more sustainable if accompanied by improvements in the social aspects of the production process'.[2] This integrated approach to sustainable trade holds out the promise of important synergies between environmental improvement, better working conditions and enhanced competitiveness.

The global market for sustainable goods and services

In the past, sustainable goods and services have been viewed as a 'green' niche within a largely unchanged economic structure. Thus, in the early 1990s, estimates of environmental market suggested an annual turnover of over US$200 billion rising to nearly US$600 billion by 2010. However, these figures dealt mostly with pollution control and resource management technologies. Now, change in core sectors of the economy – such as agriculture, energy, manufacturing, transport and tourism – is opening up the prospect of a more substantial and mainstream demand for sustainable goods and services.

Unfortunately, it is difficult, if not impossible, to give an accurate picture of the scale of this demand. Statistics are not collected, and in most cases there is no consensus on what constitutes sustainable goods and services. For example, there are no data on the sales of eco-labelled products worldwide. Nevertheless, some rough indicators of growth can be given.

Agriculture Health and environmental concerns among consumers are driving the world market for organic produce. This now stands at about US$11 billion and is growing at about 20–30 per cent per year. Because of the imbalance between supply and demand, organic products command premium prices, and for developing countries this premium alone could be worth US$500 million a year. In the next ten years, the world market could grow to over US$100 billion. Beyond organic products, there are also increasing requirements for social and environmental conditions (such as integrated crop management) for a range of crops, from flowers to fruit and vegetables.

[2] See R. Kumar et al., *Responding to Global Standards: Case Study of the Textile Industry in India, Indonesia and Zimbabwe*, UNIDO, Vienna, 1998.

Forestry Led by the Forest Stewardship Council (FSC), demand is growing among retailers and other institutional purchasers for certified timber products. Since November 1996, the area of forest certified as under sustainable management has more than doubled to 6.3 million hectares in 20 countries, and it was expected that ten million hectares would be certified by the end of 1998; within the next five years, this could quadruple to 40 million hectares. Purchasers of paper products are also specifying recycled content and restrictions on chlorine bleaching.

Textiles After a short-lived fashion for 'green textiles' in the early 1990s, there is now a more sustained demand for clothing products that can demonstrate compliance with high health, environmental and social standards. One indicator of this is the expansion in the use of the Eco-Tex 100 certificate[3] from none in 1992 to almost 6,000 now, midway through 1999, with an annual rate of growth of 20–30 per cent per year. Some standards, such as the organic certification agency SKAL's criteria for sustainable textile production, integrate social and environmental norms from farm to factory.

Manufacturing Although the ISO 14001 environmental management system does not specify norms for sustainable production or product design, its rapid uptake is a sign of business-to-business demand for increased assurance that environmental responsibilities are being managed effectively. By the end of 1997, about 5,000 certificates had been awarded worldwide, with Japan, the UK and Germany dominating so far; growing numbers of companies in Asia, including China, India, Malaysia and Thailand, are also getting certified. Leading the way are the electronics, automobile and chemical industries. The value of goods and services from these companies is not known, however.

Tourism The tourism sector is now the world's largest industry, and social and environmental concerns are of increasing importance in deciding the choice of destination. As part of this there is a growing eco-

[3] The Eco-Tex label is an independent labelling system that tests textile products for the presence of harmful chemicals.

tourism movement; although precise statistics are difficult to come by, some estimates put the eco-tourism market at about US$200 billion per annum.

Fair trade Beyond these largely environmentally driven initiatives is a growing market for fairly traded and ethically sourced products from developing countries. Fair trade has been promoted by development organizations as a way of benefiting disadvantaged producers through the provision of stable and premium prices and assistance with market access. The value of fairly traded products is now around US$500 million, and successful brands such as Café Direct have captured about three per cent of the UK coffee market. Environmental considerations such as organic production methods are rising in importance, as exemplified by the new criteria for fair traded bananas and the International Banana Charter.

These examples merely give indications of the upward trends in the demand for sustainable goods and services. Although the long-term implications are uncertain, for developing-country producers that can adapt to these rising expectations and start moving to anticipate trends, new trade opportunities are emerging and bringing a range of benefits, such as premium prices, increased sales and new markets, as well as job creation, environmental improvement and better client relations.

Driving forces for sustainable trade

For developing-country producers, these changing market conditions are translated into a series of often powerful driving forces that affect their export prospects.

Consumer demand Although the 'green consumer' movement has waned since the late 1980s, there is evidence that in some areas active demand from consumers is driving trade flows, notably for organic produce and more recently for fair trade coffee, tea and bananas. For example, three-quarters of EU consumers say that they would buy a 'fair trade' banana if it were available in the shops, and a third would pay a premium of ten per cent. In response, alternative and mainstream retailers and processors are providing new product ranges to meet this demand. However, in most markets active consumers who seek out sustainable goods and services are unlikely to represent more than a tenth of sales.

Citizen campaigns A more potent force has been citizen campaigns to improve the social and environmental performance of trade. A prominent tool has been the organization of consumer boycotts of allegedly damaging goods and companies – tropical timber being a notable example – and pressure on European and North American corporations to integrate social and environmental criteria into their trading practices. A prime example is the Clean Clothes Campaign, which has been pressing for the adoption of social codes of conduct in the garment industry with third-party verification in order to eliminate sweat shop conditions.

Corporate supply chain management These campaigning pressures have fused with an extended sense of corporate responsibility among leading corporations for the wider impacts of their trading operations. A growing number of companies in Europe and North America are now incorporating social and environmental requirements into their purchase requirements, extending the scope of quality management to include risks to corporate reputation. Rather than just developing green, ethical or sustainable niche products, the purpose of supply chain management is to provide assurance that all goods and services meet certain standards.

While companies are clearly seeking market advantage from these initiatives, they often take place ahead of consumer demand, driven by a combination of market creation and precautionary concerns. Notable examples include Levi Strauss, Timberland and Patagonia in the USA and Otto Versand, B&Q and Coop Suisse (see Box 1). In addition to individual corporate codes of conduct, there are a growing number of sectoral or national supply chain initiatives, such as Eurocommerce's social sourcing guidelines, and the specification of evidence of an environmental management system in purchasing contracts. Leading companies such as IBM and Daimler-Benz are already asking their suppliers to seek ISO 14001 certification.

Box 1: Examples of international supply chain management

- *The Body Shop* The Body Shop, a leading cosmetics company, has over 1,500 branches in 47 countries, and has long been a pioneer of ethical business practice. At the end of the 1980s it launched its 'Trade not Aid' programme, which aimed to use trade as a mechanism to bring income, employment and social benefits to communities in need. Today, 30 organizations are involved in the renamed Community Trade Programme. The proportion of The Body Shop's overall sales generated by the Community Trade has fluctuated and in 1996–7 stood at seven per cent. Products include nut oil and bracelets from Brazil, cocoa from Ghana, jute and cotton from Bangladesh, sisal from Mexico and honey and beeswax from Zambia. The Body Shop is working to improve communication and forecasting with suppliers and to help them to diversify their product and customer base. Overall, the Community Trade programme is held to have brought significant environmental and social gains to its partners.
- *C&A* A Dutch-based family firm with more 2,000 clothing stores worldwide, C&A contracts out most of its production, sourcing 25 per cent of its merchandise from the Far East and ten per cent from other non-European countries. As part of its environmental policy issued in 1996, the company's General Delivery Instructions to suppliers contain information about products that must not be used and the maximum permitted quantities of potentially harmful substances. A small but increasing proportion of merchandise carries the Eco-Tex label, including C&A's own brand of jeans, Jinglers. Environmental issues are also part of C&A's broader Code of Conduct for the Supply of Merchandise. This covers legal requirements, employment conditions forbidding the use of child labour or forced labour, environmental aspects and freedom of association. All suppliers are required to sign a compliance form. To monitor implementation, C&A set up the Service Organization for Compliance Audit Management (SOCAM), which makes unannounced inspection visits to around 1,000 production units a year. Its first report was issued in May 1998, and as a result of its work, by the end of March 1998, C&A had suspended contracts with 80 suppliers, mostly because of evidence of child labour or intolerable working conditions; 30 were reinstated after a corrective plan was put in place.
- *Sainsbury's* One of the largest UK supermarket chains, Sainsbury's has taken a number of steps to improve the social and environmental performance of key parts of its supply chain. For its food products, the company has worked with its UK suppliers to reduce the use of pesticides through the use of Integrated Crop Management (ICM). In 1997, six years after the launch of the initiative, 88 per cent of all UK produce is grown according to ICM standards. Less progress has been achieved with overseas suppliers. Sainsbury's also supports the use of FSC certified timber, and in 1997 the company transferred £8 million worth of business to suppliers meeting FSC requirements, and exceeded its target of stocking 150 producers using FSC timber. The company has also issued guidelines to its suppliers on the sourcing from the wild of plant and animal material for products in order to meet legal requirements – for example within the Convention on International Trade in Endangered Species (CITES) – and consumer concerns. Examples include shells, moss, crocodile meat, plant bulbs and seafood.

Donor initiatives Environment and development agencies, both from the public and from NGO sectors, have also been a powerful driving force for change, investing in a variety of initiatives to smoothe the transition process for developing-country producers. Priority areas have included information and training on new market demands (e.g. the Dutch GreenBuss database), investments to boost the supply of sustainably produced goods (e.g. UK funding for certified timber in Mexico) and joint policy initiatives to build common positions (such as the Indo-German Export Promotion Project). Alongside this, the non-governmental environment and development sector has been at the cutting edge of support to community-based producers, enabling them to access international markets through fair trade and eco-trade schemes.

Creative partnerships One of the more innovative driving forces is the establishment of creative partnerships between governments, the private sector and citizens' organizations to promote more sustainable trade. In Germany, for example, the Federal Environmental Ministry is supporting a Network of Eco- and Fair Trade Initiatives to increase the profile of sustainably produced and socially sound products from developing countries. In Britain, the Department for International Development (DFID) has established the Ethical Trading Initiative (ETI), bringing together companies, non-governmental organizations and trade unions to work together to improve the quality of life of workers involved in international supply chains of companies importing into the UK. Although the ETI does not deal with the environmental dimension as yet, DFID has committed itself to supporting an increased trade in sustainably produced products and services from developing countries.

Innovative producers Last, but not least, sustainable trade is also being driven by innovative producers in developing countries who see opportunities for community and commercial development from tapping these emerging export markets – some of whom are profiled in the next section.

Sustainable trade: case studies

In spite of often unfavourable conditions, a number of producers in developing countries are starting to take advantage of these driving forces. In its 1997 report, *Unlocking Trade Opportunities*, the International Institute for Environment and Development (IIED) profiled ten producers who had turned new demands to their advantage.[4] The following examples highlight the main types of producers that have so far been able to respond positively to the challenge.

(a) Large-scale private sector: Century Textiles, India

Century Textiles is a major player in India's textile industry: it operates the country's biggest mill and is the largest exporter of cotton textiles, with export earnings growing a hundred-fold since 1975, reaching US$81 million in 1996–7. Century is accredited to the ISO 9002 quality series and has won awards for its energy conservation and clean production efforts. From the beginning of the 1990s, the company became increasingly aware of new environmental standards in its export markets. In 1994, the German government introduced measures to prohibit the import of textiles containing potentially harmful azo dyes. Half of India's textile industry exports to Germany, and so the regulation had direct implications.

For Century, the need to phase out azo dyes was indicated by Otto Aversano, one of the company's major German clients. Six months of investigation led to the phasing out of azo dyes and the award of an independent Eco-Tex certificate. Although the new dyes are more expensive than their substitutes, Eco-Tex certification has resulted both in premium prices, which were still being maintained in 1998, and new market opportunities in the USA and UK. Century is now aiming for ISO 14001 certification.

Century's entrenched commitment to quality, responsiveness to customer requirements and rising environmental awareness lies behind its successful switch to azo-free dyes. Even for a corporation the size of Century, close relations with its client in Germany were crucial for

[4] Nick Robins and Sarah Roberts, *Unlocking Trade Opportunities*, IIED, London, 1997.

making the transition. Yet, the small-scale sector that makes up the bulk of India's textile industry often lacks the skills, information and resources to make the transition cost-effectively.

(b) Fair trade cooperative: Coocafe, Costa Rica

Coocafe is a consortium of eight coffee producers with 3,500 members, set up in 1988 in response to a financial crisis in the sector. It produces about 3 per cent of Costa Rica's coffee output, most of which is exported. As part of its overall strategy of marketing, economic and social support for its members, Coocafe has formed close links with 'fair trade' organizations in Europe, such as Twin Trading in the UK.

To get listed on the International Fair Trade Coffee Register, Coocafe had to meet a number of criteria, such as being independent and democratically controlled by its members and committed to improving the quality of the coffee, and supporting social development and promoting sustainable production techniques that minimize the use of chemical inputs. In return, those buying from Coocafe pay a price premium (more for organic production), establish secure contractual arrangements and are subject to external review. Initially, Coocafe received start-up funding and technical assistance from the Friedrich Ebert Stiftung in Germany.

Coocafe's fair trade sales almost doubled between 1991 and 1996, gaining a fair trade premium of over US$250,000 in 1996, which was spent on education and women's development projects. In the UK, Coocafe beans are marketed under the Café Direct brand – blended with coffee from 13 other producer organizations in seven countries – which now has a 3 per cent market share for ground coffee, despite being 10 per cent more expensive than conventional competitors. Apart from the financial benefits, the fair trade relationships have also provided the stability to enable Coocafe to begin the transition to organic production. Coocafe has begun converting to organic production with the aim that their entire production will be organic by 2002. The decision was taken as part of a long-term economic and marketing strategy and was based on financial as well as environmental considerations since, organic certification will give them an extra premium.

(c) Donor supported cooperative: Lango Cooperatives Union, Uganda

The Lango Cooperatives Union in Uganda is made up of 5,500 cotton growers, and was selected by the Swedish International Development Agency (SIDA) in 1995 as a pilot for its new 'EPOPA' programme, which aims to promote exports of organic produce from Africa to help fill the increasing gap between supply and demand in Europe.

SIDA has provided US$45,000 to Lango, which has been used for research, farmer support, inspection, certification and marketing. In 1996 the cooperative exported 400 tonnes of organic cotton, about 2 per cent of Uganda's cotton harvest; one of the companies that has bought cotton from Uganda is Patagonia, whose cotton clothing range is now entirely organic. Lango producers receive on average a 20 per cent better farmgate price. The contractual relations are also more secure as the Dutch-based African Fair Trade Association helps to provide crop finance, often a major barrier for small producers. The Swedish organic certification agency KRAV is also training local inspectors to bring down the cost of third-party inspection.

Support from SIDA has helped to ease the difficulties in becoming certified, a process that can be both laborious and costly, currently adding nearly 2 per cent to the price of the cotton in Europe. Lango has implemented an internal quality control system, and by going for group rather than individual certification has helped to reduce the burden on individual farmers.

The organic sector has high potential for developing countries, as there are few technical constraints since farmers already practice low-impact agriculture. The main stumbling blocks are getting certified and identifying export opportunities, and international partnerships can be critical for overcoming these.

(d) Fair trade partnership: Solomon Western Islands Fair Trade (SWIFT)

SWIFT has helped small producers in the Solomon Islands to gain a reasonable livelihood from the sale of sustainably produced timber to high-value European markets. SWIFT is supported by the Dutch church aid development agency ICCO, which has helped provide access to European markets: over 90 per cent of the timber produced is exported, the majority to The Netherlands. This has enabled communities to resist pressure to sell their logging rights to foreign companies, most of whom are only interested in one-off logging. SWIFT provides forestry support and distribution and marketing services to 300 producer groups covering 50,000 hectares of forest. In 1997, 1,200 cubic metres of five different species of timber was exported, of which 500 cubic metres was FSC-certified, to a range of companies, including some of the major DIY retailers in The Netherlands, where it fetched price premiums of as much as 20 per cent. Revenues from the trade are distributed within the community according to agreements drawn up by the groups, which vary according to the make-up and priorities of the particular community.

But developing the market for SWIFT timber has been a considerable struggle. The first major barrier was that few of the common species in the Solomon Island forests were well known in Europe and SWIFT had to put considerable time and money into understanding Dutch buyers' specifications, testing the species, gaining the Dutch quality certificate KOMO and raising awareness of the properties and availability of the lesser-known species.

The five-year history of SWIFT demonstrates clearly the costs and benefits of certification. FSC certification has brought 20 per cent premiums and has been crucial in developing markets. But the organization has found the certification process to be costly and bureaucratic and a particular burden for small-scale producers with low literacy in a country where tenure arrangements may not be formally documented. Initially, SWIFT had some of its producers individually certified by the European agency Société Générale de Surveillance (SGS), but it found this far too expensive.

The development of a 'Green Umbrella' group certification has made the process easier, and SWIFT is now in the process of designing a simplified Kopu Huda ('hold onto your trees') scheme, which it hopes will satisfy the sustainable forest management principles and its overseas customers. SWIFT has also investigated the prospect of Fairtrade certification as a means of maintaining at least its premium. But in the long term, questions have been raised about the sustainability of long-distance timber trade and the possibility of opening up regional markets for their output.

(e) Environmentally driven enterprise: Tagua Initiative, Ecuador

The Tagua Initiative was set up in 1990 by Conservation International (CI), a US-based environment group, and CIDESA, an Ecuadorean NGO working on environmental training and development. The aim was to find ways of conserving the rich biological diversity of the Cotacachi Cayapas Reserve through socioeconomic development of the local population, which suffers from extreme poverty. The solution was found in reviving the use of the tagua nut for making buttons, a traditional material recently overtaken by plastic substitutes.

The Initiative is run as a business, with the local producers paying for the services they receive from the NGOs. Conservation International and CIDESA have helped local people to process the nuts and then link them to local and international markets. Although tagua is more expensive as a raw material, lower processing costs and economies of scale have meant that they are now only slightly more expensive than plastic.

About US$5 million worth of buttons have now been sold, sustaining over 2,800 jobs. CI has captured a 5 per cent premium from the button sales which is invested in community development and conservation. Tagua buttons are now used by 60 major manufacturers, including GAP, Banana Republic and DKNY. In many cases companies are unaware of the social and environmental benefits of the buttons, and choose them purely on style and quality grounds. The project demonstrates that social and economic development is a critical foundation for conservation, and that providing quality goods is essential to achieve long-term market success.

Lessons and challenges for the future

These case studies present snapshots of producers that have been able to ride the wave of changing market conditions. They are by no means perfect or represent an ideal of sustainable trade; in most cases, only a limited number of the life cycle social and environmental aspects of production, trade and consumption have been dealt with. All represent work in progress and give a sense of the possible.

Reviewing the cases, it is clear that two factors have been critical for success.

1. *Partnership* Effective partnerships along the supply chain are vital to speed the flow of information, skills and resources necessary to make the change. Even in the case of Century Textiles, the largest mill in India, a close working relationship with its clients in Germany was central for its rapid transition to higher standards. In the fair trade cases, forging new marketing channels for small and often disadvantaged producers was an essential part of the overall strategy.

2. *Quality* Product quality is a basic precondition for success. No longer can sustainable products hope to succeed on the basis of ethical criteria alone. Indeed, social and environmental requirements have to be seen as part of an overall drive to improve productivity. This need not mean excessive prices for consumers, and as supply expands economies of scale could help to bring sustainable products from developing countries within reach. Independent verification of social and environmental claims is also critical to maintain consumer trust and provide recognition for producers.

But showing that a small and growing number of producers are gaining new opportunities from sustainable trade does not mean that these are open to all. There are many real barriers that have to be overcome to ensure that rising social and environmental expectations do not become 'further burdens' for developing countries. Not just at the political level, but also within markets themselves, there is often a lack of trust about both the motivations and the impacts of rising social and environmental demands. This lack of trust is rooted in real problems over decision-making, institutional capacity, distributional issues, governance, the prospects for smaller producers, and continuing policy distortions and trade barriers.

Decision-making Developing country producers often lack access and influence in the decision-making processes that determine new requirements, such as criteria for environmental management systems, certification and eco-labelling. One route out of this is through mutual recognition, an option currently being explored between Indonesia and the FSC for forest certification. This problem is compounded by the array of public, semi-public, corporate and private bodies now setting standards in this area, resulting in a blizzard of norms, particularly in Europe.

Institutional capacity Beyond these problems related to decision-making, developing country producers can be disadvantaged by an absence of the institutional capacity to respond. A key problem is the lack of local standards and certification bodies that are recognized and respected by corporations in the North. This can lead to what organic producers in Latin America refer to as 'bio-colonialism' – the imposition of international consultants and certifiers, bringing higher costs, often without in-depth understanding of local conditions.

Costs and benefits Where special fair trade conditions have been established, or where demand outstrips supply, producers can gain a price premium. But this can be temporary phenomenon and can dissolve, as has already been the case for certified timber products. As a result, social and environmental criteria simply become a basic requirement for doing business, with producers facing the full costs of investment and certification without offsetting price or market share advantages.

Governance The issue of who benefits is central to the broader issue of governance along the supply chain.[5] Inequalities in market power between retailers, traders and producers means that the standards can be imposed on suppliers and the burden of change shifted onto the weakest member in the chain.

Scale All these problems weigh most heavily on small and medium-sized firms, which often lack the skills, information or resources to

[5] See Konrad von Moltke et al., *Global Product Chains*, UNEP, Geneva, 1998, for a detailed analysis of market power in commodity chains.

grapple with new market requirements. Collective solutions, such as group certification, the formation of producer cooperatives and taking a cluster approach to problem solving, can help to overcome the issue of scale.

Policy distortions and trade barriers Beyond these market failures, the potential for sustainable trade is often considerably constrained by continuing policy distortions in importing countries. These range from protectionist barriers (especially for agricultural and textile imports), to often unnecessarily bureaucratic regulations which effectively discriminate against foreign producers. In addition, many government programmes in both North and South continue to subsidize unsustainable production practices, and social and environmental regulations that do exist are often not effectively enforced. As a result, while opportunities are emerging for sustainable trade, widening access to these opportunities cannot be left to micro-solutions in the marketplace. Strategic interventions will often be required to tackle these obstacles through a package of policy reform, public investments and new partnerships.

Over the next three years, IIED will be working to provide practical guidance on how to overcome some of these barriers. There are a number of key priority areas:

1. Better understanding is required of the actual experiences, hopes and fears of producers and traders in the South trying to improve the social and environmental of the goods they export to Europe and North America – as a prelude to a targeted reform of the barriers that exist in today's policy frameworks and market practices.
2. More work is required to develop effective models for partnerships along the supply chain, models that produce more open and accountable systems of governance.
3. Options need to be explored for more regional trade to tackle issues surrounding international freight.
4. Joint design and mutual recognition of standards and norms need to be encouraged.

5. There is a need for practical tools to be designed to enable producers – particularly smaller firms – to generate productivity improvements from social and environmental standards.
6. Investment in the necessary institutional and productive capacities is required to help make the transition to higher standards.
7. A strategic policy dialogue and support programmes between importing and exporting countries must be established to enable producers to understand and anticipate trends and to provide additional incentives to local action groups to improve performance.

'Green consumerism' and trade: a Ghanaian forestry perspective

Moses Adigbli[1]

Introduction

I am employed by Ghana's Timber Export Development Board and I am based in London. The Timber Export Development Board has the task of promoting Ghana's tropical wood and wood products in international markets. It is a government organization responsible to the Ministry of Lands and Forestry, and is financed by levies on industry. This paper outlines the trade and environment problems of the tropical timber sector, focusing on the issues as they affect Ghana.

For some years there has been a selective environmental focus on loss of tropical forest arising from the impacts of human activity. In some countries there has been aggressive campaigning against the use of tropical wood with an impact on market access and market success. I aim to address these specific issues and to try to draw some conclusions with wider relevance to the debate on the relationship between trade, environment and investment.

Ghana's forests

Geographically, Ghana extends to the north into drier savannah and semi-desert which accounts for two-thirds of the land area, but the south includes the wetter regions. The tropical forest covers about 7 per cent of the land area, and a large proportion of it is in the form of legally constituted forest reserves.

Ghana is not a rich country. Its 14 million inhabitants include a large number of low-income earners and land-reliant families. The country's export trade depends on a handful of products, gold, cocoa and timber being the principal components. All three of these have environmental

[1] This contribution is made in a personal capacity.

impacts on the forest. Ghanaians also look to the forest for other goods and services, using huge amounts of wood for fuel and charcoal, and relying on the forest to supply meat and other non-timber products.

There was a time, as in Britain three hundred years ago, when the productivity and existence of the forest could be taken for granted. This is no longer the case. Britain has used up most of its own forests and now relies on imports to supply more than 80 per cent of its wood and wood fibre needs. Ghana is not yet in that position, but we are aware that there are finite limits to our forests. The ever increasing demands on it have to be regulated and supplemented if we are to have a permanent forest resource capable of enabling a sustainable flow of products to meet the needs of our own people and have a surplus for export. There is now a widespread realization that urgent and strong measures are needed to ensure the continuation of material, environmental, cultural and communal benefits.

Our forest lands are owned by communities, and although significant areas have legally and democratically been put under the care of the government as forest reserves, outside these areas the forest is still subject to the old ways. Rights of access and utilization are embedded in the traditional and sometimes complex rights exercised through chiefs and elders and recognized by government. Environmental groups are often fiercely supportive of the rights of local communities, and such rights are strongly in evidence in Ghana. But one cannot presume that this automatically protects the forest. The rights for timber extraction are matters of exclusive concessions or contracts involving the private sector, government and community. These three sectors of society all have to be involved in, and support, the ways in which forests are used if there is to be successful commitment to sustainability. Each group has rights and each group has responsibilities.

Environmental concerns in Ghana

Ghana is classified as a 'developing nation'. People in developing nations all round the world have anxieties about their environment. They do not wish to live in unhealthy air, with impure water, or to exist in poverty, in poor housing, with poor protection against disease and famine. Such environmental considerations have in my opinion a high priority. Concern may become less egocentric when people in such countries become a little more affluent, a little more secure and have more regular income. Then they may be more able to worry about wildlife, conservation, ecosystems, biodiversity and global warming.

The residual natural forests of Britain may be seen in terms of public access and leisure pursuits, such as picnics, rambling, and enjoying the visual impact of conifers and broad-leaved trees. Ghanaian forests are working forests. They are sources of meat, wood for fuel, shade for cocoa production, land for farming. The environmental priorities are different, but environmental campaigners, in their fund-raising enthusiasm, appear not to acknowledge the real conditions of under-resourced developing countries, or to want to use any of their money to actually help such countries improve standards.

Instead, their campaigning often misinforms buyers and customers and sets out deliberately to create discrimination against the use of tropical wood. For me, this is a trade barrier, a vindictive and totally negative approach to a real problem: that of putting better forest management in place. Trade is a positive element. Forest royalties from logging finance better forestry; export duties help in the evolution of sustainable economic and social development. It is time that environmental groups relied less on threats of boycotts and more on assisting the process of change. Governments of importing countries should, in the spirit of trade liberalization, find ways to actively discourage discrimination, particularly in areas of guidance for national government departments and subnational governments. If there can be any bridges between the more extreme environmentalists and tropical forested countries, then they will have to be constructed on more helpful attitudes on the part of our critics.

Encouraging sustainable use

Ghana's Timber Export Development Board exists in a world of supply and demand, where price, quality, delivery, competition, exchange rates, finance and corporate reputation are all important. The Board also works to see that concepts of corporate reputation embrace good environmental practice. Corporate responsibility in relation to society is in reality infinitely variable. Around the world, in every sphere of activity, there are 'crooks' and 'good guys'. Illegal activities are, sadly, common in all walks of life. There are those who operate just on the right side of the law, those who flout it, and those who do more than is mandatory in order to be seen to be good citizens. Our environmental worries are not about the good guys but about the others. It is in our own national interest to formulate laws and regulations to ensure good behaviour. For this to be successful, it is not really enough just to apply a heavy punitive hand. People have to see that the laws make sense, and are necessary and in the longer term beneficial to them. In environmental affairs, it may take time for local communities to understand and support environmental measures, especially when it means moving away from practices that have been used for generations.

In Ghana the government has worked hard to create the right laws, policies, regulations and effective institutions to ensure the perpetuation of forests and their proper economic, environmental and social use. For example, it has laid down and implemented clear practical requirements for timber companies working in the forest reserves. The task is more complex in community-owned lands outside the reserves, where land is allocated by elders to members of the tribal group and specific traditional responsibilities and tribute requirements rest on individuals. Changes in traditional ways take longer.

The key point is that every effort is being made to meet the environmental expectations of the international community, but progress is of necessity slow. It is therefore unfair that environmental groups work to inhibit our international wood trade.

Adding value to Ghana's forest products

Our Forestry Department has calculated that industry should not take more than 1 million cubic metres of logs from the natural mixed-species forest each year. This is the level the forest can sustain year after year. It allows bigger trees of particular species to be harvested on the basis of minimum fellable diameters. It allows a cycle of time for the younger smaller trees to grow to harvestable size. We also have a conservation rating for commercial species which is firmly in place.

Because we have this limit to forest harvests, we cannot increase income by stepping up the gross volume taken from the forest. We have to find other ways. These avenues of opportunity direct us towards processing wood to a higher degree before export, thus providing a higher value per unit of volume. We are encouraging industry to develop linkages and activities within Ghana that will lead to higher production of wooden components, furniture parts and finished wood goods. With the very welcome help of the World Bank, the International Tropical Timber Organization, the European Commission, the UK Department for International Development, the Danish International Development Administration (DANIDA) and others, we are strengthening our capabilities in this sector. We are endeavouring to open up new markets. All of this means that we are attaching even more importance to the perpetuation of forests – forests that will support more jobs, more careers, more families, as well as contributing to government revenues and building, through capital formation and profit, the foundations for industrial evolution and the raising of living standards.

The export of value added products relies on market access, and on the ability to compete on an equal footing. The trade liberalization successes of the WTO help us compete in world markets, particularly in markets where consumers have greater discretionary spending power.

The International Tropical Timber Organization (ITTO), an intergovernmental body inspired by UNCTAD/GATT, is at present undertaking a market access study. As a direct result of very strong anxieties expressed by its producer member countries, this study will focus more on barriers to trade arising from environmentalism than on matters of competition and protection. Some politicians in the tropical world even harbour suspicions that environmentalism is a smokescreen designed to give more opportunity to non-tropical and domestic wood producers in the developed world.

This is true of course, if only by accident; because, if a buyer is persuaded that there is something bad about tropical wood, then he will have to find alternative materials. There is also a perceptible shift in tropical wood exports to less sensitive markets.

Environmental exactitude is harming the process of world trade liberalization for processed wood. This poisoning of opportunity exists, to take Britain as an example, through pressures exerted by environmental campaigners in the media, threats of demonstrations and pressures applied to local government, retail groups, specifiers and importers. It is a process embodying intolerance, almost a fundamentalism, and demands pass-or-fail judgments against standards set by the environmental community itself. Unlike the underlying, and perhaps unspoken, philosophy of the system of British Standards, which concentrates on what industry itself thinks it can achieve in practical terms, environmentalists extend their demands beyond forest management into ethnic problems, wage levels and workers' rights. Yet their demands carefully avoid and fail to recognize the often extreme political and economic constraints that may exist in some countries. The whole approach is grossly simplified, with blanket accusations levelled at the entire tropical world encapsulated by the assertion that logging destroys tropical forests.

Discouragement of investment

This deliberate souring of the purchasing climate seems to be ignored by governments of importing countries discussing world trade in international forums. On the one hand, international agencies and sources of bilateral aid are actually encouraging better forest management, but on the other they are doing nothing to keep markets open. Governments of importing countries are seldom inclined even to give guidance to their own departments or to subnational governments on the unacceptability of discrimination.

The situation may be affecting the development of Ghana's forest products industry in other ways. International institutions continue to provide valued help, but an injection of capital and skills from investment sources in Britain are markedly absent. Historically there have been political reasons for this, but today one suspects that investors are frightened that their reputations would immediately come under fire from the environmental extremists. One suspects that this discouragement applies particularly to investors who have a keen sense of responsibility towards the environment.

My colleagues and I are well aware that there are many different kinds of environmentally concerned groups and that many do understand the problems and try to help, but the extreme groups do us damage and we resent it. Discouragement of potential investors deprives us of capital, management and production skills and market linkages. This is a negative aspect of the relationship between environmentalism and investment.

Likelihood of environmental premium

Claims that financial rewards flow from higher environmental standards are expressions of wishful thinking, except perhaps for tiny niche markets. In practice, any environmental surcharge at the retail level is difficult to pass back through the distribution chain to finance forest improvement or to those who might be identified as having incurred extra costs on environmental grounds. Some years ago the British timber importing trade tried to interest governments in an import levy on timber that would go into a fund for forest management. There were obvious problems and the endeavour failed, but at least it was an attempt to be positive and helpful.

It is recognized that improved forest management has to be paid for. In an ideal world, the timber industry and users of wood coming from natural forests would pay the total notional value of the tree, encompassing not just the extraction process but also the cost borne by Mother Nature in nurturing a tree to commercial maturity. Raising forest rents and royalties to such levels cannot be done at the expense of commercial competition, or beyond the ability of industry to pay. In industry no company can act in ways that render it uncompetitive through higher costs, nor can it overstep the limits of affordability. Industry should not be expected to carry the costs of national parks and totally protected areas, or for open-ended environmental research or social work for indigenous forest groups who are outside the market economy. It is better that the forested country itself impose forest charges and that it does so as close to the forest as possible in order to ensure that money raised is actually used for forest improvements. If the developed world wants a high level of environmental protection in the developing world, then it should be prepared to pay for it. Countries like mine do have a desire to see improvements in the way the human race reacts with the world's lands, seas and air, but we are less able to indulge them because we don't have the money.

The role of wood products certification

Even though reliable statistics on how much demand there actually is for certified timber products are difficult to come by, there is nevertheless an awareness in Ghana that the introduction of forest certification will further strengthen the positive forestry management currently in existence. Ghana has made some progress towards evolving a certification scheme; it is not sponsored by the Forest Stewardship Council (FSC)[2] but is based on international principles and criteria supported by the numerous international agencies and intergovernmental forums. Draft standards were to be debated before the end of 1998. Pilot tests on the forests are to be carried out by the middle of 1999, and it is hoped that forest certification will commence towards the end of that year.

The international debate

There is no shortage of environmental theorizing, and no shortage of international fora where the search for global principles and global solutions is discussed. Much of the world's concerns about the environment were identified at the Earth Summit meetings of the UN Conference on Environment and Development (UNCED) in Rio de Janeiro in 1992. For those of us in the forestry sector, a whole set of forest principles and Agenda 21 together covered the subject extremely well – so much so that the subsequent work of the UN Commission on Sustainable Development (UNCSD), through the International Panel on Forests and more recently the Intergovernmental Forum on Forests, had comparatively little to add except in the important areas of avoiding duplication of effort by international agencies, consideration of imple-

---

[2] The FSC is an international non-governmental body that is involved in the certification of forests and the labelling of forest products according to principles, standards and criteria laid down by its governing council.

mentation of desirable aims and activities, and whether there should be a Forest Convention. The focus had always to shift, sooner or later, from broad principles to encouraging and assisting individual nations to achieve global desires for the Earth's environment.

Under existing conventions, the tropical forested nations are already having to digest commitments on endangered species, biodiversity and climate. At this time it is difficult to see how a Forest Convention could be shaped, other than as a lowest common denominator to allow what is achievable in practice with current resources. Were such a convention to exist, it might be taken as a point of reference in international trade negotiations.

At present there is an extraordinary wave of environmental awareness from myriad sources and affecting all levels of society. It would be very surprising if there are any governments or industries that remain ignorant of the need to improve environmental standards and practices. Closer examination of developing countries that appear not to be acting positively may uncover specific reasons – civil unrest, political indifference, more pressing social problems or a lack of resources. Within these wider determinants, industry itself needs an enabling investment climate which would include, among many things, a clear picture of the environmental rules and the industry's ability in commercial terms to absorb them and contribute to sustainable, environmentally healthy development. The environmental measures of a country may be above or below those of other countries with which it trades. There is a great deal of difference between what can be achieved on the ground within a particular set of circumstances and the continual search for global truths, which often invoke emotional or academic logic which effortlessly slides away from practicalities.

World trade policies and agreements cannot ignore the environmental dimension. The policies of intergovernmental bodies usually rule out specific criticism of individual member countries. It may rebound. Neither can there be suggestions of sanctions. There can be encouragement towards international standards, and mutual recognition of national processes. There can be recognition of the individual responsibilities of international organizations in health, labour, industrial development, agriculture and forestry.

There can also be factual reporting on progress towards environmental goals. In the tropical forestry sector, this is how the ITTO keeps up to date with the progress of its member countries towards its Objective Year 2000.[3] For example, some tropical countries, including Ghana, Indonesia and Malaysia, are well advanced towards authenticated national certification of good forest practice.

This paper has focused on the tropical forest problems in relation to world trade. Anything that places specific environmental duties and costs on internationally traded tropical wood products must surely require equitable expectations of other products of metal, plastic or mineral base. This raises other problems. Criticism of the timber trade is devoted to the issue of forest loss, yet the pluses and minuses of the environmental equation embrace all stages of the life of a product, including energy uptake in processing, air pollution from such processing and biodegradability on disposal.

In conclusion, I believe that an international trade organization cannot avoid having stated policies on environmental matters, and that it has to recognize national, regional and international environmental initiatives in ways that are essentially helpful and positive, discourage discrimination, and do not disadvantage the developing world.

[3] The International Tropical Timber Organization (ITTO) has set the year 2000 as the date by which timber from all tropical forests will be judged as being sustainably harvested. This means that by that date each member country's forest operations are expected to meet the requirements of principles, criteria and management standards that were approved in 1995.

'Green consumerism' and labelling: a retailer's perspective

David Wheeler[1]

Introduction

These comments are based on The Body Shop's experience of retail trading in 47 countries around the world and extensive experience of both voluntary and certified approaches to the provision of consumer information. There are few elements of the green consumer agenda with which The Body Shop has not been involved on an international scale over the years, whether environmental, social (including fair trade) or animal welfare-related.

The Body Shop believes that the scope for voluntary environmental labelling to promote significant environmental benefits is limited. We have experience of numerous international and national schemes operating in the consumer field. There is not a single scheme in any country on the planet that we could say has made a significant impact in the cosmetics and toiletries marketplace from the perspective of consumer behaviour. The more general conclusion that we would draw is that, with a few honourable exceptions, voluntary labels are at best much ado about nothing, at worst a misleading and potentially highly confusing market intervention.

There have been some successes, for example in organic labelling, where there is a very active producer movement and a direct link to consumer human health and well-being; another is the Forest Stewardship Council (FSC), where the issue is quite specific and significant effort has been devoted to consensus-building across producer, NGO and retail sectors. However, recent experience with the EU eco-labelling

[1] *Editors' note*: This is an edited version of David Wheeler's evidence to the House of Commons Environment Select Committee Inquity into the Environmental Impact of Consumer Products. See *Reducing the Environmental Impact of Consumer Products*, House of Commons Environment Select Committee 11 Report, HC 149, Vol. II, July 1999.

scheme[2] leads to the conclusion that voluntary *generic* labelling is highly likely to create the illusion of activity by manufacturers and retailers while in reality simply adding to the plethora of competing claims of variable validity.

Along with a number of other commentators, The Body Shop is now highly sceptical that the current very technical practice of Life Cycle Analysis (LCA) has much to contribute to resolving the fundamental issues raised by the social and economic dimensions of sustainable development with respect to environmental labelling. We have included a streamlined version of LCA in our own product stewardship programmes for several years. However, it must be recorded that, in the context of the EU eco-label, the various expert groups and the competent bodies signally failed to develop an LCA methodology that would adequately reflect societal values in the process of developing label criteria. The exclusion of ethical issues (for example animal welfare from cosmetics or household product labels) or social issues (for example human rights), from any product category exposed the fundamental inadequacy of a generic voluntary labelling scheme as ambitious as the EU eco-label. We believe that this contributed significantly to the scepticism of opinion-formers and a consequent failure to enrol consumers.

Product stewardship and LCA are now becoming the province of ISO processes designed to achieve common denominator systems of management. However, ISO processes typically do not set normative standards: they simply require management systems and processes to be in place. Undoubtedly ISO has a role – indeed, The Body Shop uses ISO standards for some of its own ethical management procedures. However, they are fundamentally process-driven, not necessarily amenable to implementation by SMEs or accessible to producers in the less industrialized world. We do not see much long-term prospect for ISO systems to underpin consumer labels or claims except as part of an integrated approach to environmental management subject to indepen-

[2] Council Regulation (EEC) No. 880/92 of 23 March 1992 on a Community eco-label award scheme, OJ L 099 11.04.92, p. 1.

dent verification, for example within the context of the EU EMAS Regulation.[3]

Finally, in public policy terms, it is difficult to justify why companies that produce environmentally or socially less damaging goods and services should be required to internalize costs for appropriate management and certification systems (or, indeed, why consumers should pay more for voluntarily labelled goods) when companies that do not take such care escape their obligations and indeed are able to charge their customers less without the requirement for any labelling at all. This is a direct contradiction of the principle that consumers and companies should be given incentives to do the right thing and economically penalized for excessive or environmentally inefficient consumption – a principle, like the polluter-pays principle, that will become increasingly important in public policy, e.g. eco-taxation. Why should a small producer of wooden handicraft items in India bear the costs of environmental certification and labelling (e.g. via the FSC scheme) for marginal, if any, economic benefit, when its competitors based in China manufacturing in plastics need add no environmental or social qualifications whatsoever to their products?

A way forward

If we were starting from first principles, The Body Shop would advocate completely downgrading the public policy importance of voluntary, generic labelling initiatives. They will always exist, and certainly will need to be made more transparent and honest through codes of practice or regulatory intervention. But with the planet facing such urgent social and environmental challenges, such initiatives should not be allowed to distract us from more serious opportunities for progress. Hence the Body Shop believes that the British government, in concert with its global trading partners, should:

[3] Council Regulation (EEC) No. 1836/93 of 29 June 1993, allowing voluntary participation by companies in the industrial sector in a Community eco-management and audit scheme, OJ L 168 10.07.93, p. 1.

1. agree the global priorities for action on sustainability, e.g. global warming, human rights, forestry, etc.;
2. carry out a rapid audit of all consumer products and identify where the *significant* sustainability impacts lie, for example:
   - washing machines – water;
   - refrigerators – electricity;
   - textiles – labour standards;
3. draw up a matrix of where most benefit for ecological/sustainability investment lie, for example:
   - all washing machines could (and should) be 50 per cent more water-efficient;
   - all refrigerators could (and should) be 50 per cent more energy-efficient;
   - all textiles should be produced consistent with ILO criteria;
4. draw up a set of mandatory labelling requirements, at least at EU level, to match the matrix, for example:
   - all washing machines must be marked with a five star system on water efficiency;
   - all refrigerators must be marked with a five star system on energy efficiency;
   - all textiles must be marked with a certificate of compliance on labour standards;
5. back up the above with public-sector purchasing policy and specifications, for example:
   - 'The government will specify only three star and above washing machines up to the year 2001 and only five star thereafter';
   - 'The government will specify only refrigerators that are three-star-rated and above up to the year 2001 and only five-star-rated ones thereafter';
   - 'The government will specify only textiles with a certificate of compliance on labour standards by the year 2001';
6. provide practical and financial support for developing-country producers to meet mandatory labelling requirements and/or exempt small producers altogether.

Conclusion

The approach advocated here is unashamedly pragmatic, but I believe it would generate significant market signals and would help cut through the current confusion in the market-place. It would accelerate environmental and social change and would be consistent with wider objectives on sustainability and poverty alleviation in developing countries.

This sort of approach does not remove the opportunity for consumer action; it merely shifts the main motive force in the market-place to standards for government procurement. And, being pragmatic and 'single issue' based, it would not attempt to resolve every social/environmental and ethical issue within a relatively weak, consumer market-based framework, or indeed via voluntary and generic labels which create little real motivation either for producers or consumers.

Good initiatives like FSC and organic certification would fit well within such a scheme. There is absolutely no reason why government purchasing standards should not prioritize sustainable forestry and healthy food. Moreover, the approach could be readily applied to social and ethical criteria as well. Why should not certified 'child-labour-free' be the main social criterion for government textile purchasing?

Part III
Resolving key WTO issues

Overview

A lawyer's view

Damien Geradin

Introduction

The objective of this paper is to provide a short overview of the various issues created by the interface between trade, investment and environmental regulation. Most of the paper will concentrate on the links between trade and environmental protection, though investment aspects will also be dealt with when relevant. Because of its introductory character, this paper will inevitably contain a number of simplifications. More sophisticated analysis may, however, be found in my recent publications.[1]

As a starting point, it is essential to observe that the various interlinkages between trade, investment and environmental protection can be properly identified only by making a number of basic distinctions. Indeed, the impact of environmental regulations on trade and investment – and, conversely, the impact of trade and investment on environmental regulations – may vary depending on the type of environmental measure concerned.

A first distinction should be drawn between environmental measures depending on whether they have been adopted unilaterally or pursuant to multilateral environmental agreements (hereafter, MEAs). Each category is considered in turn.

---

1 See, in particular, D. Geradin, 'Trade and Environmental Protection in the Context of World Trade Rules', *European Foreign Affairs Review*, Vol. 2, Spring 1997, p. 33; D. Esty and D. Geradin, 'Market Access, Competitiveness and Harmonization: Environmental Protection in Regional Trade Agreements', *Harvard Environmental Law Review*, Vol. 21, 1997, p. 265.

Unilateral measures

A further distinction should be made here between three categories of environmental measures: direct restrictions on trade; product standards; and process standards.[2]

Direct restrictions on trade

Direct restrictions on trade generally take the form of import or export bans. Countries can, for example, restrict the imports of hazardous substances or waste in their territory. They may also restrict the exports of scarce ecological resources, such as endangered species of fauna and flora.

Such restrictions are contrary to Article XI of the GATT which prevents quantitative restrictions on trade. The question then becomes whether such measures can be justified under Articles XX(b) or XX(g). Those Articles permit members to adopt measures that would normally be incompatible with GATT if they are 'necessary to protect human, animal or plant life or health' (Article XX(b)) or if they 'relate to the conservation of exhaustible natural resources if ... made effective in conjunction with restrictions on domestic production or consumption' (Article XX(g)).[3] Such measures can, however, be legitimized under these exceptions only if 'they are not applied in a manner which would constitute a means of arbitrary or unjustifiable discrimination where the same conditions prevail, oir a disguised restriction on international trade'.

So far, the Article XX exceptions have been interpreted relatively strictly in the context of GATT disputes. In the two *Tuna/Dolphin* cases, dispute settlement panels held that US import bans on certain categories of tuna products – tuna fished in a dolphin-harmful manner – did not fall within the scope of the Article XX exception because they at-

---

[2] For a discussion of these different categories of environmental measures see D. Geradin, *Trade and Environment: A Comparative Analysis of EC and US Law*, Cambridge University Press, 1997.

[3] Generally on these exceptions see S. Charnovitz, 'Explaining the Environmental Exceptions in GATT Article XX', *Journal of World Trade*, Vol. 25, 1991, p. 37.

tempted to coerce foreign countries to modify their domestic regulations.[4] This type of 'extrajurisdictional' measure would therefore be *per se* illegal.

In its recent *Shrimp/Turtle* decision,[5] the Appellate Body seems to reject this analysis, focusing on 'categories' of measures, and on the 'specific circumstances' of each case.[6] Nevertheless, it considered that Section 609 of US Public Law 101-162 pursuant to which the US government had adopted a controversial import ban on shrimps from certain countries could not be justified under Article XX because this provision had been applied in a manner constituting 'arbitrary and unjustifiable discrimination between countries where the same conditions prevail'. Among the flaws identified by the Appellate Body in the application of Section 609 were the fact that the US government required all exporting Members to apply the *same* policy as the one adopted by the United States; that it did not ensure that its policies were appropriate for the specific local and regional conditions prevailing in other countries; and that it did not seriously attempt to reach a multilateral solution to the turtle problem through negotiation.

Though this decision was perceived by environmental NGOs as an additional illustration of the lack of consideration given by the WTO dispute settlement machinery to ecological questions, it was welcomed by some legal commentators as a balanced decision setting forth 'clear guidelines as to how the US might both comply with GATT requirements and still implement legislation designed to protect a shared, but endangered world resource, the migrating sea turtles'.[7]

[4] See *US: Restrictions on the Imports of Tuna*, 16 August 1991, reprinted in *International Legal Materials* ('Tuna/Dolphin I'), Vol. 30, 1991; and *US: Restrictions on the Imports of Tuna*, 20 May 1994, reprinted in *International Legal Materials*, Vol. 33, 1994.

[5] See *US: Import Prohibition of Certain Shrimp and Shrimp Products*, WT/DS58/AB/R (12 October 1998).

[6] See G. Shaffer, 'The U.S. Shrimp Turtle Appellate Body Report: Setting Guidelines toward Moderating the Trade-Environment Conflict', *Bridges Between Trade and Sustainable Development*, Vol. 2, No. 7, October 1998, p. 9.

[7] Ibid.

Product standards

Product standards regulate the (environmental) characteristics of products. They include, for instance, packaging rules, sanitary requirements, vehicle exhaust emission standards, etc. Although such rules do not impose direct restrictions on international trade, they may nevertheless have a trade restrictive effect on such trade in two categories of circumstances.

First, product standards may be used as an instrument of protectionism when they discriminate on their face or in their effects against imported products. This is, for instance, the case when a standard expressly imposes heavier requirements on imported products (formal discrimination) or imposes similar obligations on domestic and imported products, but in practice it has the effect of protecting the domestic products to which it applies or other categories of domestic products (material discrimination). As illustrated in the *Reformulated Gasoline* dispute,[8] such discriminatory standards are incompatible with the national treatment principle contained in Article III. Unless they can be justified under one of the exceptions contained in Article XX, they will therefore be contrary to GATT.

Second, even when they do not discriminate on their face or in their effects against imports, product standards may nevertheless have the effect of making such imports more difficult. This may, for example, be the case when countries require the use of certain types of labelling or packaging. Such regulations impose an extra burden on manufacturers located in other countries since they will have to meet both the standards of their own country and those of the country of sale, or perhaps of several countries of sale. Despite the potentially restrictive effects on trade of such standards, they are not contrary to Article III of GATT, whose national treatment principle only prevents discrimination.

[8] See *US: Standards for Reformulated and Conventional Gasoline*, WT/DS2, (29 January 1996), where a dispute settlement panel found that a US EPA regulation treating imported gasoline less favourably than domestic gasoline was not compatible with GATT Article III. This panel decision was subsequently confirmed by the WTO Appellate Body, WT/DS/AB/R, (29 April 1996).

There might, however, be some opportunity to challenge such standards under the Technical Barriers to Trade (TBT) and the Sanitary and Phytosanitary Measures (SPS) Agreements. For instance, the TBT Agreement requires its members to 'ensure that technical regulations are not prepared, adopted or applied with a view or with effect of creating unecessary obstacles to international trade'. It might be inferred from this provision that non-discriminatory regulations that would be valid under GATT Article III's national treatment principle might be challenged under the TBT Agreement as unnecessary obstacles to trade.

Similarly, the SPS Agreement requires members to ensure that 'any sanitary or phytosanitary measure is applied only to the extent necessary to protect human, animal or plant life or health, is based on scientific principles and is not maintained without scientific evidence'. This agreement also requires that in the assessment of risks members take into account, *inter alia*, 'available scientific evidence'. As illustrated by the *Beef Hormone* Appellate Body decision,[9] this language may provide an effective instrument for countries seeking to challenge equally applicable, but none the less trade-restrictive, sanitary regulations.

Process standards

Unlike product standards, process standards regulate not the characteristics of products, but the production methods by which they are made. As such, process standards do not restrict trade and there is nothing in the GATT that prevents its members from regulating domestic producers that engage in polluting activities.

Difficulties may, however, arise when WTO Members attempt to use trade measures in order to control the production processes used by foreign producers. In order to achieve such control, Members can, for instance, deny market access to products that have been produced pursuant to inadequate process standards, or impose a duty on such products (hereafter, 'process-related trade restrictions').

[9] *EC Measures Concerning Meat and Meat Products (Hormones)*, WT/DS26/AB/R, WT/DS48/AB/R.

Before assessing the compatibility of such process-related trade restrictions with the GATT, the question must be asked in what circumstances members may be tempted to resort to such restrictions. There are two main sets of reasons.

The first is ecological. The enforcement of lax environmental process standards by some countries may put pressure on the local, regional or even global environment.[10] For instance, the burning of environmentally unsound high sulphur coal in China may have adverse effects on the local population, produce transboundary air pollution and contribute to the global warming process. This is why some nations may decide to use trade restrictions as a weapon to force low-standard nations to improve their environmental practices.

The second set of reasons is economic. Variations in the stringency of process standards may affect the conditions of competition.[11] Other things being equal, companies operating in jurisdictions with lax process standards will face lower compliance costs and hence will be able to bring their goods to market at lower costs than those operating in high-standard jurisdictions. It is also often argued that variations in the stringency of process standards may induce those located in high-standard jurisdictions to relocate to low-standard jurisdictions in order to preserve their competitive position. This industrial migration to 'pollution havens' would result in lost jobs and in reduced and downward pressure on wages in high-standard nations. As a result of these perceptions, high-standard nations' governments are often under pressure from industry or labour groups to adopt trade measures to correct such distortions.[12]

The research that Dan Esty and I carried out last year casts some serious doubts on the validity of the second set of reasons.[13] Most eco-

---

[10] See J. Trachtmann, 'Internationalization, Regulatory Competition, Externalization and Jurisdiction', *Harvard Journal of International Law*, Vol. 34, 1993, p. 47, 57.

[11] See R. Carbaugh and D. Wassink, Environmental Standards and International Competitiveness, *World Competition*,Vol. 16, p. 81.

[12] See, e.g. 'Gephart Bill to Allow Sanctions for Not Enforcing Environmental Laws', *International Trade Reporter*, Vol. 11, 30 March 1994, p. 500 (reporting Congressman Gephart's intention to propose legislation treating any failure to adopt proper environmental standards as an unfair trade practice actionable under Section 301 of the Trade Act 1974).

[13] D. Esty and D. Geradin, 'Environmental Protection and International Competitiveness: A Conceptual Framework', *Journal of World Trade*, Vol. 32, 1998, p. 5.

nomic studies we read tend to suggest that there is no specific link between the level of environmental regulation adopted by a country and its economic performance in terms of the competitiveness of its industries on domestic and international markets, or its levels of investment. Differences in environmental standards do not necessarily penalize high-standard nations. Hence it seems to make little sense to adopt trade measures such as bans or eco-duties in an attempt to equalize production costs across jurisdictions.

A more difficult question is whether WTO Members should be allowed to adopt trade measures to force low-standard nations to increase their process standards in order to achieve specific environmental objectives. From a legal standpoint, process-related trade restrictions violate GATT Articles I and III, and, for reasons discussed above, it is unlikely that they are justifiable under Article XX. Moreover, from a policy standpoint, there is general hostility among most WTO Members for this type of restriction.

This hostility is motivated by two main objections. First, there is the concern that one or several nations could use their superior commercial power to impose their environmental standards on other nations without their consent or participation in the development of such standards (the 'eco-imperialism' objection). Second, to use John Jackson's words, there is the concern that, 'if a nation is allowed to use the process characteristics as the basis for trade restrictive measures, then the result would be to open large loopholes in the GATT'.[14] The use of environmental process characteristics as a basis for discrimination between products could trigger similar claims in other areas of social policies, such as human and labour rights (the 'slippery slope' objection).

Thus, it appears that, from both law and policy standpoints, a multilateral approach though which high-standard nations attempt to encourage low-standard nations to improve their environmental practices by using incentive regimes will generally be more acceptable than any form of unilateral restriction.

[14] J. Jackson, 'World Trade Rules and Environmental Policies: Congruence or Conflict?', *Washington and Lee Law Review*, Vol. 49, 1992, pp. 1127, 1243.

Multilateral measures

As we have seen, countries frequently resort to unilateral trade restrictions to advance environmental objectives. However, countries may also adopt trade restrictions in order to implement trade provisions that are contained in MEAs. Examples of MEAs containing trade provisions are the Washington Convention on International Trade in Endangered Species of Wild Flora and Fauna (CITES), the Montreal Protocol on Substances that Deplete the Ozone Layer, and the Basel Convention on the Control of Transboundary Movement of Hazardous Wastes and their Disposal.

In agreements such as CITES and the Basel Convention, the rationale for trade restrictions between parties is clear. Trade must be reduced or eliminated because it represents the vehicle through which the environmental damage occurs. Trade restrictions applying to non-parties may be based on similar reasons. As illustrated by the Montreal Protocol, such restrictions may also be designed to ensure that, by staying out of the agreement, non-parties are unable to take a free ride, i.e. to benefit from the environmental efforts brought about by the agreement without bearing any of the costs it entails. On the contrary, these trade provisions will generally place non-parties in a disadvantageous position, thereby giving them an incentive to join.

Domestic measures adopted to implement these trade provisions may, however, conflict with GATT in a number of ways. First, measures discriminating between parties and non-parties may violate Article I's most favoured nation (MFN) obligation; an example is the adoption of an import or export ban on CFCs and CFC-containing products and technologies against a WTO Member that is not a party to the Montreal Protocol. Second, measures subjecting imported products to more stringent obligations than like domestic products may violate the national treatment provision contained in Article III; an example is the adoption by a party to the Basel Convention of a total ban on foreign waste. Finally, import or export prohibitions, such as those contained in CITES, may amount to quantitative restrictions contrary to Article XI. In addition, the exceptions contained in GATT Articles XX(b) or (g) may not be available to justify such restrictions. As in the case of unilateral measures, a number of restrictions adopted pursuant to multilateral environmental agreements may therefore be found to be inconsistent with the GATT.

It seems, however, that there are good reasons for distinguishing between unilateral trade measures and trade measures adopted pursuant to multilateral environmental agreements. First, multilaterally adopted standards present less risk of being motivated by protectionist concerns than unilaterally adopted ones. More generally, as acknowledged by the *Shrimp/Turtle* Appellate Body report, negotiation of MEAs is to be preferred over unilateral actions as a way of addressing environmental problems. However, because of the collective nature of the goods protected and the constant economic struggle between countries, it may be difficult to negotiate such agreements successfully without having recourse to some form of trade restriction. Would it not therefore be somewhat inconsistent for GATT to, on the one hand, call for increased multinational cooperation but, on the other hand, deprive the international community of one essential instrument for generating the consensus necessary for collective action?

So far, there has not been any case of a GATT member challenging trade restrictions adopted by another member to implement the trade provisions contained in a MEA. However, to the extent that this type of challenge is possible, the situation should be clarified. In this regard, several approaches have been suggested for how MEAs might be reconciled with the GATT. One option would be the adoption of a waiver allowing the functioning of trade restrictions in a limited number of agreements. Another option would be the development of a new Article XX exception modelled on the exception that already applies to international commodity agreements. Finally, building on the example provided by the North American Free Trade Agreement (NAFTA), it might be envisaged incorporating directly into the GATT a list of MEAs whose obligations would prevail over GATT obligations in the event of inconsistency.

Conclusions

The above discussion illustrates that the interface between trade, investment and environmental regulation raises a set of complex issues that have created a considerable degree of tension among WTO members. Things are, however, evolving, and it seems that some of these issues could find a happy solution.

Among the issues raised above, it seems that the tension between MEAs containing trade provisions and the WTO is probably the least difficult to solve. First, there is a high degree of consensus that MEAs are the best approach to dealing with environmental issues. Moreover, as discussed above, this tension could be suppressed through relatively modest amendments to the existing rules.

The use of unilateral trade restrictions to coerce foreign countries to modify their domestic regulations has been rejected by GATT dispute settlement panels. However, as observed above, in its *Shrimp/Turtle* decision, the WTO Appellate Body rejected the view that trade restrictions adopted by WTO members to protect resources outside their jurisdiction are *per se* contradictory to the GATT. In this regard, this decision seems to suggest the conditions under which such restrictions could be compatible with the GATT.

Trade disputes involving product standards may be particularly difficult to solve, especially when they involve tricky sanitary issues. As illustrated by the *Beef Hormone* case, the role of scientific evidence in trade cases will be one of the most important issues in the years to come. From a general standpoint, the best way to prevent trade disputes over product standards from arising is to encourage a greater degree of regulatory convergence across nations, for instance through harmonization or mutual recognition. In this regard, ensuring more regulatory convergence between the European Union and the United States is one of the essential objectives of the so-called transatlantic agenda.

The most difficult issues relate to environmental process standards. Process-related trade restrictions are GATT-illegal and, in any event, appear as a second-best option from a policy standpoint. Here again, the best approach is to encourage a greater degree of regulatory convergence across nations. Convergence is, however, less easy to achieve in the case of process standards than in the case of product standards because of the existence of differences in geographic circumstances and levels of development. In a recent article that I co-authored with Dan

Esty, we nevertheless explore various possible options to encourage some degree of process standards harmonization.[15]

In this paper, I have not said much about institutional issues, but this does not mean that these are not important. The existence of a proper institutional framework is essential to the good functioning of any organization, and the WTO is no exception. From the point of view of environmental protection, the creation of a Committee on Trade and Environment (CTE) is a good first step, though so far this body has not produced a great deal of results. The setting up of an Appellate Body is also welcome. Although it is too early to say what its impact on the trade and environment debate will be, I believe that stronger and more independent courts make more balanced judgments. An example is the European Court of Justice, which, despite the key importance of the creation of a single market in the European Union, has not hesitated in some cases to give precedence to environmental values over trade considerations.[16]

One aspect that is often ignored in the international economic sphere is the role of NGOs.[17] The recent collapse of the proposed Multilateral Agreement on Investment (MAI) illustrates, however, that NGOs represent an increasingly powerful voice. One of the reasons why this agreement collapsed – apart from the fact that it contained some objectionable provisions – is that it was negotiated behind closed doors. In the future, it will be increasingly important to take the views of NGOs into account.

---

[15] See Esty and Geradin, supra n. 1.

[16] See D. Geradin, 'Free Trade and Environmental Protection in an Integrated Market: A Survey of the Case-Law of the United States Supreme Court and the European Court of Justice', *Journal of Transnational Law and Policy*, Vol. 2, 1993, p. 141.

[17] See generally, D. Esty, 'Non-Governmental Organizations at the World Trade Organization: Cooperation, Competition, or Exclusion', *Journal of International Economic Law*, Vol. 1, No 1, 1998, p. 123.

A view from the South

Magda Shahin

Introduction

Addressing the relationship between trade and environment has become an integral part of any strategy for promoting exports of developing and developed countries in order to enable them to compete in the world market. To that end, countries are striving to understand better this relationship with a view to pursuing their interests and advancing their economies in a sustainable manner. It is noteworthy to recall here how Rubens Ricupero, the Secretary General of UNCTAD, perceives this complex and cumbersome relationship as a relationship between two poles in a dialectical thesis, where the resulting synthesis should conciliate the two ends. In contrast to many who would like to conceive of the trade and the environment aspects as two sides of the same coin, Ricupero stresses that linking trade to environment does not come as something natural. It necessitates tremendous and enormous sacrifices to reconcile these two ends. One should seek to integrate environment into decision-making processes from the very beginning rather than attempting to rectify a wrong-doing at the end by having recourse to sanctions and trade embargoes. Technology, financing, market access, knowledge and expertise are essential for the preservation and protection of the environment.

So far, such considerations have been given little attention in the ongoing debate in the WTO. Some would argue that the WTO is neither a development forum nor a financing institution; others believe that the debate has not yet been exhausted, and that some of these considerations could find their way into future negotiations. If we today would like to assess the prospects for the future of the trade–investment–environment debate, we cannot shy away from addressing this complex relationship in its entirety. In fact, it is now beyond any doubt that one of the prime reasons behind the collapse of the negotiations on the MAI in the OECD was the failure to integrate environment considerations into the negotiations from the outset. Any future negotiations on trade/investment/the environment will have to answer first the basic question: are we ready to make recommendations on whether any modifications of the provisions of the multilateral trading system are required? Has the debate been exhausted? Are we prepared to set rules and regulations?

Basic elements

Having said this, let me stress that the relationship between trade liberalization and environmental benefits is not a direct one. It is an indirect relationship which passes through different production and consumption patterns, levels of development, standards of living and the extent of poverty in the society.

Let me also reiterate that the debate in the WTO to date has been set within certain parameters and following a clear consensual mandate which clarifies the extent to which such a debate is viable and legitimate. In this context, I would like to base my assessment of how work may continue on the trade–environment debate on three basic realities.

First, with regard to the Preamble of the 'Marrakesh Agreement Establishing the World Trade Organization',[1] no one denies the importance assigned to the protection and preservation of the environment in the Preamble. But it is equally true that the Preamble emphasized that this be done 'in a manner consistent with the countries' needs and concerns at different levels of economic development'. What is of significance here is that the importance given to environment is not set in absolute terms, but linked to the needs and concerns of the countries and their levels of development. I could even argue further that priority is attributed to development, as the protection and preservation of the environment can be undertaken only to the extent *consistent with* the level of development.

Second, the Marrakesh Ministerial Decision on Trade and Environment was clear in setting the terms of reference for WTO work on trade

[1] The text of the Agreements can be found in WTO Secretariat, *The Results of the Uruguay Round of Multilateral Trade Negotiations: Legal Texts*, Geneva, 1995.

and environment. It stipulates, in its fourth preambular paragraph, that attempts to coordinate the policies in the field of trade and environment should be carried out without exceeding the competence of the multilateral trading system. It then goes on to explain that the 'competence of the multilateral trading system' is limited to trade policies and those trade-related aspects of environmental policies that may result in significant trade effects for its members. Of utmost significance here is the framework the negotiators have agreed upon within which the environment could be dealt with in the WTO. They were adamant in making clear that it should not exceed *the competence* of the multilateral trading system, whose policies are confined to trade and/or trade-related aspects of environmental policies.

Third, for the purpose of discharging any possible fears of a new 'green' conditionality attached to market access opportunities, thus nullifying the benefits accruing from trade liberalization within the context of the Uruguay Round, the Singapore Ministerial Report (1996) on Trade and Environment[2] stressed the following points:

- The WTO is not an environmental protection agency and the WTO itself does not provide an answer to environmental problems.
- Environmental problems require environmental solutions, not trade solutions.
- There should be no blank cheque for the use of trade measures for environmental purposes.
- Trade liberalization is not the primary cause of environmental degradation, nor are trade instruments the first-best policy for addressing environmental problems.
- GATT/WTO Agreements already provide significant scope for national environmental protection policies, provided that they are non-discriminatory.
- Secure market access opportunities are essential to help developing countries work towards sustainable development.
- Increased national coordination as well as multilateral cooperation is necessary to adequately address trade-related environmental concerns.

[2] *Report of the Committee on Trade and Environment*, WT/CTE/W/40, 7 November 1996.

The state of play

In order to assess the possible trends and directions of the future debate on trade, investment and environment, we need first to take a quick look at where we stand today. I will refrain from going into each of the ten items that form the work agenda of the Committee on Trade and Environment. But I will certainly base much of my assessment on the Singapore Ministerial Report, which I believe was comprehensive, educational and extremely useful in clarifying many misunderstandings and which will help set a sound basis for any further negotiations.

The results that were reflected in the Singapore report satisfied many, but not all. This is because the results were confined to the various positions and views of countries and stopped short of coming up with any agreed conclusion. This lack of clear-cut solutions is attributable not to the weakness of the negotiators, but rather to the complexities of the issues at hand. It is hard to believe that these are solvable in the near future. However, this does not and should not preclude us from discussing further and in greater depth the issues at hand, although I believe that the trade–investment–environment debate has not yet matured to the stage where negotiations with a view to setting rules and regulations in this complex relationship can be established. Views on this subject were wide apart, which only indicates the difficulties of defining the relationship between multilateral environmental agreements (MEAs) and the WTO.

The issue of the relationship between the WTO and MEAs has raised numerous controversies, ranging from the hierarchy and compatibility between the two entities to the proper scope of a comprehensive framework *within* MEAs to deal with negative environmental externalities that necessitate the more frequent use of positive measures. In the framework of MEA negotiations, positive measures such as improved market access, capacity-building, additional finance and access to and transfer of technology were considered effective instruments to assist developing countries to meet multilaterally agreed environmental targets. This was in drastic contrast to the much-disputed effectiveness of trade measures applied as sanctions in the purview of the WTO. And lastly, the issue of the scope for trade measures pursuant to MEAs under WTO provisions, and their unilateral application to environmental problems that lie outside a country's national jurisdiction, raised wide disagreements and was sternly contested.

Trade measures are one of the options in the package of instruments that can be used to achieve MEA objectives. Singling out trade measures 'pursuant to MEAs' for some kind of WTO 'accommodation' would mean determining whether those trade measures are necessary or effective. This would require holistic consideration of all other measures, including positive measures, taken within the framework of an MEA, a task that is clearly outside the WTO's scope. Positive measures are more efficient and effective. Therefore, changes in WTO rules to accommodate MEA trade measures that are inconsistent with WTO rules offer an unbalanced and isolated approach as long as there is no parallel commitment to first use and enforce positive measures.

In fact, this item remains one of the problem areas. The European Commission continues to press for the introduction of new rules or an 'Understanding' that would prioritize the environment or make it an exception, through what they would like to perceive as an 'environmental window', which would basically mean legitimizing inconsistent trade measures in the WTO.

The debate has clearly shown that there is no quarrel with depicting the WTO as an environment-friendly organization. As a matter of fact, the GATT allows for any action to be taken at the national level to protect the environment, provided that it is in compliance with its basic rules and regulations. Article XX of the GATT,[3] the Agreement on Technical Barriers to Trade (TBT Agreement),[4] and the Agreement on the Application of Sanitary and Phytosanitary measures (SPS Agree-

[3] Article XX, entitled 'General Exeptions', gives ample opportunity to use measures to protect (a) public morals and (b) human, animal or plant life or health, etc., provided that, as the *chapeau* of the article stipulates, they are not applied in a manner that would constitute a means of *arbitrary or unjustifiable discrimination between countries where the same conditions prevail, or a disguised restriction on international trade...*

[4] The TBT Agreement deals basically with technical regulations and international standards, including packaging, marking and labelling requirements, and procedures for assessment of conformity, and makes sure that they do not constitute a means of arbitrary or unjustifiable discrimination between countries where the same conditions prevail, or a disguised restriction on international trade.

ment)[5] are all cases in point, giving each WTO member the right to set the level of protection that it deems appropriate for the environment, provided that it does not act against the basic principles of the WTO as stipulated in Articles I and III of the GATT.[6] If, however, a state imposes stricter regulations on imported products than on those domestically produced for environmental purposes, it is in violation of GATT Article III. Once a substantive GATT requirement has been violated, analysis shifts to Article XX, which incorporates a number of General Exceptions, though this Article remains a cause of the greatest uncertainty and continues to be a subject of controversial interpretation.

The *Shrimp/Turtle* dispute

The latest developments regarding this specific issue were double-edged. I will look briefly at the main panel and Appellate Body findings and conclusions from this dispute as they are key and decisive for the future debate on the relationship between the WTO and MEAs.

The Panel report

To many, the famous *Shrimp/Turtle* case between the United States on one side and Malaysia, Indonesia, India, Pakistan and Thailand on the other has exterminated all the remaining doubts about the interpretation of Article XX as authorizing unilateral measures for the sake of protecting and preserving environment. To others, the results of the panel findings have only intensified their belief in the need for a drastic change in the prevailing WTO rules, under the pretext that they do not serve the environment well.

---

[5] The SPS Agreement, which forms an integral part of the Agreement on Agriculture, reaffirms in its preamble that no Member should be prevented from adopting or enforcing measures necessary to protect human, animal or plant life or health, subject to the requirement that these measures are not applied in a manner that would constitute a means of arbitrary or unjustifiable discrimination between members where the same conditions prevail, or a disguised restriction on international trade.

[6] GATT Article I: Most Favoured Nation Treatment; GATT Article III: National Treatment.

It is worth noting that the *Shrimp/Turtle* case is the first conflict that has arisen between the WTO and a MEA, in this case the Convention on International Trade in Endangered Species (CITES). The report is precedent-setting after the two *Tuna/Dolphin* reports, which were not adopted because the United States blocked adoption. The *Shrimp/Turtle* ruling is the first adopted WTO ruling concerning a trade embargo based solely on domestic environmental legislation. The United States is the only country that interprets Article XX so broadly as to allow for extra-territorial measures to protect the environment beyond its territories.

For the United States the case focused on the right of WTO members to take measures under Article XX of GATT 1994 to conserve and protect natural resources, as reaffirmed and reinforced by the preamble to the WTO Agreement. For the complainant, it was a case about the imposition of unilateral trade measures designed to coerce other members to adopt environmental policies that mirrored those in the United States. The United States based its entire defence on Article XX, which allows countries to take measures contrary to GATT obligations when such measures are necessary to protect human, animal or plant life or health. In this case the United States argued that the trade measure was necessary because sea turtles were threatened with extinction and the use of turtle excluder devices on shrimp nets was the only way to protect them effectively from drowning in shrimp nets. Overall, the panel stressed the WTO's preference for multilaterally negotiated solutions.[7]

Furthermore, the panel focused its analysis on the headnote or *chapeau* of Article XX, which requires legitimate trade restrictions to be applied 'in a manner which would not constitute a means of arbitrary or unjustifiable discrimination between countries where the same conditions prevail or a disguised restriction on international trade'. The panel found that interpreting the *chapeau* in a way that would allow importing countries to restrict market access according to exporters' adoption of 'certain policies, including conservation policies' would mean that 'GATT 1994 and the WTO Agreement could no longer serve

[7] *United States – Import Prohibition of Certain Shrimp and Shrimp Products*, Report of the Panel, WT/DS58/R, 15 May 1998, pp. 278–300.

as a multilateral framework for trade among Members'. Such an interpretation, the panel felt, could lead to 'conflicting policy requirements' since exporting countries would need to conform with different domestic policies in importing countries, thus threatening the 'security and predictability of trade relations' under WTO Agreements. It therefore drew the conclusion that 'certain unilateral measures, insofar as they could jeopardise the multilateral trading system, could not be covered by Article XX'.

Based on the above arguments, the panel ruled that the US measure did not fall within the scope of the measures permitted under the *chapeau* of Article XX.[8] The panel also observed that WTO Members could adopt GATT-inconsistent measures (falling under the 'General Exceptions' clause of GATT Article XX) for the protection of the environment or the conservation of exhaustible natural resources. It is not clearly spelled out in the Agreement that the resources being protected could fall outside the jurisdiction of the party adopting the environmental controls. The United States argued that there is nothing in the text of Article XX that indicates that it applies only to policies to protect animal or plant resources or conserve natural resources within the territory of the country invoking the provision. Thus, the United States insisted that Article XX allows a country to take any measure for the purpose of protecting environmental resources even if those environmental resources lie outside its jurisdiction.

The issue of process and production methods (PPMs) was also one of the top matters addressed by the panel. The panel said that, on the basis of information provided by scientific experts, it considered turtle excluder devices (TEDs) to be 'one of the recommended means of protection within an integrated conservation strategy'. The panel does not seem to have been convinced that TEDs are the only, or even a key, component of marine turtle protection.

Against this background, one can hardly find any reason to revise Article XX, when the panel ruling was so straightforward and without any room for doubt. On the other hand, at the time of negotiating the Singapore report, all countries except the United States wanted an *ex-*

---

[8] Ibid.

plicit commitment by WTO members to avoid using trade measures unilaterally for the purpose of protecting environmental resources outside the jurisdiction of one's own country. The Singapore Report came out with only a vague reference. Many would say that this is reason enough to go for negotiations in which an environmental window would be traded against an explicit denial of the use of unilateral measure. Fair enough. But the US Congress clearly rejected the idea that any such recommendations should be explicitly included in the Singapore Report, as they would have touched on US sovereignty. Are we to consider that the future US position will alter in this respect? To those like the United States who still hold out some hope for the permissibility of unilateral measures, let me simply underline that the entire Uruguay Round was started, negotiated and concluded on the basis of a premiss that unilateral measures were to be abandoned.

The Appellate Body report

The Appellate Body report in the *Shrimp/Turtle* case did not reverse the panel report in its main findings and conclusions,[9] but it has none the less left the door open to reinterpret Article XX(g) in a way that goes beyond its conventional interpretation. Many would tend to see risks emanating from the fact that the Appellate Body interpreted Article XX(g) so as to suggest that it was *a priori* GATT-consistent to protect the sea turtle as an endangered species. The Appellate Body has thus bypassed GATT tests of necessity and effectiveness for the measure itself.

In fact, many would perceive that the openings within the system that the Appellate Body provided with its reports in the two cases of *Reformulated Gasoline* and *Shrimp/Turtle* carry inherent risks of damaging the multilateral trading system – the system we have so long fought for, developing and developed countries alike, and which in a relatively short time has gained in seriousness and credibility.

[9] *United States – Import Prohibition of Certain Shrimp and Shrimp Products*, AB-1998-4, WT/DS58/AB/R, 12 October 1998.

The risks of going beyond trade

The WTO is a trade organization. No one can refute that. If WTO members have recourse to the WTO to settle their disputes, it is to settle problems of 'trade' concerns – not finance, not technology, not exchange rates and not the environment *per se*. That does not mean, as some would have it, that trade concerns 'in the world' must prevail over all other concerns, but trade concerns prevail in the GATT trading system and are the only concerns that GATT rules address or are entitled to look at. That we today want to look at the GATT rules in a broader manner, addressing trade concerns from different perspectives, with the excuse that the WTO does not function in a vacuum, is a risk and a danger to the system. That today we want to have a larger environmental perspective, tomorrow a social perspective, the day after tomorrow a good governance perspective – without knowing where it all will end – carries the seeds of damage to the whole trading system. We cannot allow this system to adapt to or safeguard all kinds of different interests. That would then rightly become, as the *Shrimp/Turtle* Panel put it, 'a real threat to the multilateral trading system', in the sense that, in order to defend different interests, WTO members would then feel free to pursue their own trade policy solutions unilaterally in line with what they perceive today to be environmental concerns. This would certainly amount to an abuse of the GATT Article XX exceptions, and thus would be a threat to the preservation of a multilateral trade system based on consensus and multilateral cooperation.

However, I should emphasize here that the Appellate Body concluded in the *Shrimp/Turtle* case that the United States measure was also 'unjustifiably discriminatory'. The unjustifiable nature of the discrimination was attributed to the failure of the United States to pursue negotiations for consensual means of protection and conservation of sea turtles, resulting in 'unilateral' application of the relevant United States legislation. The Appellate Body further agreed that the United States had applied the measure in an 'arbitrarily discriminatory' manner between countries where the same conditions prevailed, contrary to the requirements of the *chapeau* of Article XX.

The Appellate Body then stressed (in paragraph 185 of its report), that it had *not* decided that the sovereign nations that are members of the WTO cannot adopt effective measures to protect endangered species, such as sea turtles. As they put it, 'Clearly, they can and should.' This I can interpret as underlining what the Singapore Ministerial also referred to: namely, that GATT/WTO Agreements provide significant scope for national environmental protection policies, provided that they are non-discriminatory. This is in my view the jurisprudence that the Appellate Body reference should have set. This is how the CTE should assess the Appellate Body findings and conclusions, rather than in a way that overturns the consensus reached in the CTE after protracted and difficult debate.

The call for a High Level Meeting

The relationship between MEAs and the WTO remains one of the most controversial issues of the trade and environment agenda. The call of the European Commission for a High Level Meeting between trade negotiators and environmentalists finds its roots in this controversy, as the European Commission was unhappy with the results of the debate in the WTO CTE. This dissatisfaction, however, can be attributed to the following reasons.

First, the report of the CTE to the Singapore Ministerial, and its main paragraphs attempting to set straight the relationship between MEAs and the WTO, are open to different interpretations. Developing countries had stood solid against any attempt to inject language that might indicate that WTO provisions 'accommodate the use of trade measures for environmental objectives'. This notion was accepted only when put into perspective, namely by clearly linking any such accommodation with the relevant criteria of the general exceptions provisions of GATT Article XX, which provide a clear safeguard for developing countries in a way that is consistent with the WTO rules and regulations.

Second, the hierarchy between the two was deliberately left vague. Sending out the message that there is recourse to a WTO dispute settlement mechanism as a last resort was not accepted by developing countries. On the other hand, developed countries were in favour of extensive use of compliance mechanisms available under the MEAs before having recourse to the WTO. The resulting language on this issue could be subject to different interpretations, as it encouraged countries to make use of the mechanisms available under MEAs; at the same time, it did not forestall the rights of the WTO members to have recourse to its dispute settlement mechanism. A case in point is the *Shrimp/Turtle* panel, in which developing countries raised the matter directly before the WTO's dispute settlement processes.

Third, developing countries had insisted at the time of its conclusion that the Singapore report is not legally binding, i.e. that it does not create legal obligations or alter the rights and obligations of any WTO member under the WTO Agreements. Thus the point was stressed that the outcome is not a negotiated text of contractual obligations. It was agreed, however, that the report represents a political statement issued largely to appease the concerns of the environmental community.

Eco-labelling

That the Singapore report failed to reach any agreed conclusions on eco-labelling or any resolution of the 'non product-related PPMs' issue was due to the fact that views remained wide apart during the whole debate. The two issues continue to be difficult to resolve and necessitate further work before final conclusions can be negotiated. The question remains open: are we ready and willing to legitimize environmental 'policies' and 'values' in the WTO, which is a rule-setting body? How can we translate environmental preferences into strict rules? Many continue to argue in favour of disciplining eco-labelling schemes on the basis of the concepts of 'equivalence' and 'mutual recognition,'[10] where each country sets its standards according to its own values as stipulated by Agenda 21. Aiming to harmonize or internationalize non-product-related PPMs on the basis of any set of multilateral guidelines means

[10] *Editors' note*: 'Mutual recognition' could involve e.g. recognizing another country's eco-labelling scheme as equivalent to your own so that products awarded under one label would automatically qualify under the other. The notion of 'equivalence' is closely related and could mean e.g. that individual criteria under different schemes were recognized as 'equivalent', or that an individual *product* could meet different but 'equivalent' criteria to those set by a particular scheme and still be recognized as falling within it.

contradicting what the international community agreed upon unanimously in Agenda 21.

One should attempt to answer the question of whether eco-labelling was an end in itself, or whether the whole debate was targeting a much more serious matter, aimed at involving the WTO in domestic policies. Making the WTO a forum to address the non-product-related process and methods of production carries the inherent risk of over-stretching the concept in the future and making it a precedent for incorporation of other non-trade-related goals, such as labour standards, human rights, democratization and good governance. Is eco-labelling as a cover for altering the basis of the entire multilateral trading system? Future debate on eco-labelling should easily be solved on the basis of equivalencies and mutual recognition. We should not attempt to legitimize environmental non-product-related domestic policies and preferences in the WTO.

Market access and competitiveness concerns

The debate on this issue was set from the very start in a North–South context. Developing countries contested the effects of environmental measures and regulations on the competitiveness of domestic producers, in particular with regard to small and medium-size enterprises (SMEs). In contrast, developed countries, especially the EC, insisted on parallel reference to the inappropriateness of relaxing environmental standards in order to attract investment. The EC felt that these two notions represented two sides of the same coin. This has caused more harm than good to the debate.

We continue to encounter false allegations, by firms in countries with high environmental standards and costs of compliance, that they are often undercut by competition from companies based in countries with less strict regulation and lower costs. In theory, this could lead to entire industries departing for countries with lower standards – the so-called 'pollution havens'. So far, however, no evidence has provided the empirical basis for such a theory. Nor has the reverse been experienced on a large scale, i.e. that high environmental standards are a factor in location decisions or lead to relocation of industry.

It has been even noted that, in order to be successful, a firm needs to be seen as being 'green', i.e. that it has to seen to be environmentally responsible and not to alter its standards when settling abroad. The evidence has shown that the TNCs rarely take advantage of lax environmental standards, but use the same production processes as at home, for the following reasons:

1. Theirs is usually the most efficient technology.
2. TNCs find it only normal to anticipate that standards will rise sooner or later in the developing countries, along with the increased rate of growth and higher standards of living.
3. TNCs see public demand at home as requiring this behaviour.

Consequently one cannot conclude that developing countries encourage lax environmental standards to attract foreign direct investment.

On the other hand, case studies have justified the developing countries' arguments on the negative effects of stringent environmental regulations on their competitiveness in the world market. These effects were particularly pronounced in sectors such as textiles and clothing, leather, footwear, furniture, plastics, etc. Furthermore, these effects are often evident where industry and large transnational corporations are able to shift the costs associated with environmental protection and pollution control onto the suppliers of the raw materials, causing a significant change in the distribution of returns to trade. A case in point is the Malaysian experience with environmental regulation in the palm oil industry.[11] The distributional effects of environmental measures and regulations and their implications internationally should be studied in depth to provide input into any future agenda on the relationship between investment and environment and its implications on the competitiveness of developing countries in the world market.

[11] UNCTAD Secretariat, 'Effects of Environmental Policies, Standards and Regulations on Market Access and Competitiveness, with Special Reference to Developing Countries, Including with Least Developed Among Them, and in the Light of UNCTAD Empirical Studies', *Environmental Policies, Trade and Competitiveness: Conceptual and Empirical Issues,* UNCTAD, TD/B/WG.6/6, 28 March 1995.

The point stressed by developing countries was that substantial financial and technological resources as well as technical and administrative expertise were required to adapt to new regulations and standards in export markets, and that these were frequently not available to developing-country producers or were usually at high cost and with significant trade effects.

With regard to competitiveness issues, it is worth noting that attention was drawn in the conclusions of the Singapore report to the concern that environmental measures and requirements could adversely affect the competitiveness and market access opportunities of small and medium-sized enterprises, especially in developing countries.

It is certainly to be expected that transfer of technology through investment will figure high on future agendas. It is well known that it is private firms in developed countries that develop the new technologies, including the environmentally friendly technologies. These new technologies are normally protected by private intellectual property rights, and can replace technologies that were previously in the public domain. If the new technologies are subsequently imposed unilaterally through PPM standards by developed countries – or even through a multilaterally agreed standard – but without taking such aspects as the financing needs into account, the net result will on balance be unfavourable to developing countries. Developing countries lack the financing, the expertise and the training to acquire and adapt to such new technologies, and this by definition works against protection and preservation of the environment in the developing countries.

There is certainly an urgent need for future work in this domain to develop a common interpretation of the relationship of the relevant provisions of the Agreement on Trade-Related Aspects of Intellectual Property Rights to the protection of the environment. Any investment agreement, whether bilateral, regional or even multilateral, should incorporate environment considerations and requirements with a view to easing transfer of technology as a necessary condition to protect and preserve the environment.

UNCTAD has clearly stressed that the problems of adjustment to new technology based on environmental considerations are higher for

SMEs.[12] These enterprises, however, are important players in the export promotion strategy of many developing countries, especially for sectors such as textiles and footwear. Thus, it becomes all the more relevant in future work to examine the possible congruences and conflicts between the export promotion strategies of developing countries, the need to comply with environmental requirements, and their effects on competitiveness.

Furthermore, empirical and case studies conducted at the request of UNCTAD in a series of developing countries[13] have shown that environmental policies and regulations in the various sectors of export interest to developing countries have had a significant effect on the competitiveness of the developing countries. A number of reasons have been put forward, including the following:

1. the possibility of compensating losses of competitiveness in some sectors by gains in others is greater in diversified and dynamic economies, whereas diversity and dynamism do not necessarily form the main characteristics of developing-country economies;
2. developing-country exporters are normally 'price-takers', as they compete on price rather than on the basis of non-price factors, such as technology and ideas. Consequently, any environmental requirement resulting in cost increases reduces export competitiveness. It nevertheless may vary from one industry to another, as well as among different developing countries with different stages of development and capabilities to integrate innovative approaches;
3. the variable cost component of complying with environmental standards is higher in some sectors than others. Again, evidence has shown that it is higher in sectors of interest to developing countries, especially the leather and footwear, textiles and garment sectors. For example, in the leather tanning industry, the costs of chemicals required to meet international standards were approximately three times the costs of conventional chemicals.

---

[12] Ibid.
[13] Ibid.

I will refrain from going into the internalization of environmental costs and the effects on competitiveness, as this would raise the question of who would decide what and when to internalize. This remains a highly contentious area and one with a bearing on competitiveness, notably that of developing countries. The question of the proper basis for decision-making on internalization of environmental externalities remains very complex; nevertheless it continues to be relevant to many. Most recognize the difficulties in quantifying the benefits of environmental measures, as well as the difficulties and expenses in conducting risk assessments prior to implementing environmental measures. This is also why we encounter on a large scale the precautionary principle replacing risk assessments and scientific evidences to undertake bans or impose stringent environmental regulations, many of which remain unjustified. While protection of the environment is essential for both environmental and long-term economic reasons, such protection does not have infinite value. Therefore, environmental policies should be submitted, like other policies, to a rigorous cost–benefit analysis.

In fact, GATT does not so far endorse the concept of internalizing environmental costs. The concept of internalization remains contested, on the ground that it interferes with the efficiency of the principle of comparative advantage, which is central to the free trading system. Furthermore, environmental externalities are in principle not distinguishable from other factors that contribute to the comparative advantage and thus to the competitiveness edge of an economy, such as education, infrastructure, social policy and so on. Are we to conclude that the costs of all these factors are to be integrated into production processes under the auspices of the multilateral trading system? The fact that domestic producers internalize their environmental costs in no way conflicts with GATT principles. However, when countries start implementing trade policies on the basis of whether or not foreign producers have internalized their environmental costs, this becomes problematic under the GATT. The GATT is more concerned with the trade-distorting or discriminatory effect of such a policy, its necessity and its effectiveness than with its environmental objectives.

Another topic that will have to be debated extensively when the market access and competitiveness issue is addressed in the future is charges and taxes for environmental purposes and their relationship with the multilateral trading system. In terms of economic instruments, no one can deny the validity and effectiveness of imposing such taxes. But what is here at play is the imposition of taxes on a phenomenon that is not quantitative. Forcing producers to incorporate environmental externalities by imposing taxes on products made with pollution processes is based on an assumption that the costs of the polluting firm and the damage function of the polluted firm are known. This is on the one hand. On the other hand, if this is true at the national level, it can only be more complex and difficult if an importing country aims at adjusting such a cost at its borders by imposing a border tax adjustment on its 'like' imports. And the question of what would be the appropriate tax for pollution and would be accepted internationally should also be addressed.

Border tax adjustments should pass tests of 'necessity' and 'effectiveness' to identify how necessary, useful and pertinent they are to the environment, before even beginning the debate on how to adjust them at the border. The effectiveness of border tax adjustment is doubted and goes against the fact – widely acknowledged by developing and developed countries alike – that environmental problems should be addressed at source. So how can a tax imposed on final products, such as a border tax adjustment, be effective for problems that should be dealt with as far upstream in the production process as possible?[14] UNCTAD has rightly suggested that it is in general better if the tax is levied on the production and extraction process causing the environmental problem, rather than on the resulting product. In other words, a tax levied internally by the producing country would be more effective in dealing with environmental problems at their source.

The GATT neither prohibits nor prevents any country from pursuing a policy of taxation or regulation with regard to environmental protection as long as these policies apply to its domestic consumers and producers. In fact, one can even go one step further. For a border tax on imports to pass a test of compatibility with the GATT, it has to respond to the following conditions:

---

[14] Ibid.

1. The tax levied should be product-related.
2. The imported product should not have been taxed in the country of origin (i.e. to avoid double taxation).
3. The imported product should have caused transboundary pollution and the polluting input should not have been consumed domestically.

In the run-up to the Singapore Report, it was agreed in the light of the width and depth of the existing gap between negotiators that further analysis and examination was needed in the future before any consensual decision could be taken. Developing countries had insisted throughout the debate that there should be an explicit reference to addressing charges and taxes that relate only to product or product characteristics that are covered by WTO provisions. Owing to resistance, mainly from the United States and the European Community, reference was made to the need for WTO members to apply environmental charges and taxes in line with the 'existing scope' of WTO provisions. The debate on this issue remains wide open to the results of further study of the environmental effectiveness and potential trade effects of environmental taxes and charges, particularly their effects on market access and competitiveness.

Conclusion

The future will carry with it an interesting and a multifaceted debate on the interlinkages between trade, investment, the environment and development. There is readiness as well as willingness on the part of the majority of countries to enter into an open-ended negotiation, if necessary, for applying WTO rules and regulations to promote environmental protection, but also to discipline the use of trade measures for environmental purposes. The case, as we have seen, is far from settled. Developmental concerns will have to be brought into the debate through the front door and cannot be treated as a trickle-down effect of investment or trade. How to ensure that developmental aspects are part and parcel of the overall consideration of this complex relationship must not be overlooked. This should be carefully considered in advance, especially in the light of the expected power struggle between international institutions dealing with trade, environment and development issues – a struggle in which the WTO could become the most powerful institution, to the detriment of development concerns.

In the light of the Panel and Appellate Body Reports in the *Shrimp/Turtle* dispute, developing countries will have to stress new elements in the future debate with a view to capitalizing on the achievements of the Singapore Report. They should continue to ensure that a balanced approach to the issues is preserved. To this end, they should not shy away from questioning Appellate Body findings and conclusions in the Committee on Trade and Environment so as to clarify certain matters, questioning, if need be, the Appellate Body's processes, and finally mainstreaming the environment debate in a balanced and fair manner in all relevant WTO Agreements, if this is the objective. If environment is to be dealt with in the Agreement on Agriculture, it has equally to be negotiated in the framework of the TRIPs Agreement, the Agreement on Textiles and Clothing, and so on. And, last but not least, it should also be exhaustive, in the sense of addressing equally all the aspects of the environment, including market access, competitiveness and technology.

Multilateral Environmental Agreements

An overview

Duncan Brack

Introduction

The aim of this paper is to explore the interrelationship between multilateral environmental agreements (MEAs) and the multilateral trading system (MTS), the complex of trade agreements centred around the General Agreement on Tariffs and Trade (GATT) and overseen by the World Trade Organization (WTO). The paper provides an outline proposal for a way forward in the context of the forthcoming High Level Meeting of trade and environment ministers and the subsequent Millennium Round of trade negotiations.

The paper starts from the assumption that the removal of barriers to international trade, and the protection of the global environment, are *both* desirable objectives. It is further assumed that in certain cases these two objectives do, or are likely to, come into conflict, and that it is desirable to derive a way to reach the optimal balance of trade liberalization and environmental protection in these instances.

Nearly 200 MEAs currently exist, with memberships varying from a relatively small group to about 170 countries – which means, effectively, the whole world. Over 20 of these incorporate trade measures, i.e. restraints on the trade in particular substances or products, either between parties to the treaty and/or between parties and non-parties. Although this is a relatively small number, it includes some of the most important, such as the 1973 Convention on International Trade in Endangered Species (CITES), the 1987 Montreal Protocol on Substances that Deplete the Ozone Layer and the 1989 Basel Convention on the Control of Transboundary Movements of Hazardous Waste. A series of MEAs recently signed or currently under negotiation, including the 1997 Kyoto Protocol on Climate Change, the Rotterdam Convention on the Application of the Prior Informed Consent Procedure for Certain Hazardous Chemicals and Pesticides in International Trade, the Convention on the Control of Persistent Organic Pollutants and the Biosafety Protocol to the Convention on Biological Diversity, may in due course come to contain trade measures.

Trade provisions in MEAs have been designed to realize four major objectives:

1. to restrict markets for environmentally hazardous products or goods produced unsustainably;
2. to increase the coverage of the Agreement's provisions by encouraging governments to join and/or comply with the MEA;
3. to prevent free-riding (where non-participants enjoy the advantages of the MEA without incurring its costs) by encouraging governments to join and/or comply with the MEA;
4. to ensure the MEA's effectiveness by preventing 'leakage' – the situation where non-participants increase their emissions, or other unsustainable behaviour, as a result of the control measures taken by signatories.

The experience of three of the major MEAs concerned – CITES, the Montreal Protocol and the Basel Convention – shows the value of trade measures. CITES and the Basel Convention are treaties aimed explicitly at controlling trade, which is identified as the source of the environmental harm in question; trade measures are thus the entire point of the treaties. In the case of CITES, no species listed in the appendices to the treaty have become extinct since their listing, and a few – notably, the African elephant – have moved further away from extinction. Since the Basel Convention entered into force, the worst forms of hazardous waste dumping on developing countries have largely ended. In the case of the Montreal Protocol, trade measures were adopted as an enforcement mechanism, providing an incentive for non-parties to join the MEA and ensuring that the production of ozone-depleting substances did not migrate to non-parties to evade the controls adopted by parties. In either case, uncontrolled production would undermine the implementation of the Protocol. There is direct evidence from some countries that the trade provisions were indeed an important factor in persuading them to accede to the treaty; and in general the Montreal Protocol has proved to be a highly effective MEA, with its aim – the recovery of the stratospheric ozone layer to its pre-industrial state – likely to be achieved in the next century.

There are a limited number of routes by which countries can affect the actions of other countries: political/diplomatic pressure; provision of financial and technological assistance; trade sanctions; and military force. While the first two of these are clearly preferable, they have obvious limits. One can assume that use of the military option is unlikely to be helpful. Trade measures are therefore likely to continue to play a role as one component of effective environmental agreements, particularly where trade itself is identified as the source of the environmental harm, and/or where effective enforcement mechanisms are essential to their success, for example by preventing industrial migration or encouraging universal participation. The growing scope and importance of MEAs such as the Kyoto Protocol means that effective methods of implementation have to be found – which in turn means that the inclusion of trade measures at the very least has to be contemplated.

Can the use of trade measures in this way be regarded as an infringement of national sovereignty? The classical doctrines of sovereignty, originating in the seventeenth century, have little of use to say about relations between states, or of the 'rights' of states to expect other states to engage in international trade with them. It is clear, however, that the unrestrained output of pollution that is transboundary or global in scope *does* constitute an infringement of sovereignty, in that it inflicts direct physical harm on the populations and/or territories of other states. The unrestrained depletion of the global commons, for example, or of non-territorial species can, though more arguably, be regarded similarly. The responsibility of individual nations for the protection of the global environment and for the promotion of development that is environmentally sustainable have of course been accepted in many international agreements, most notably Agenda 21. Once again, the use of trade measures in MEAs must be contemplated if the global environment is to be protected effectively.

Interrelationship with the multilateral trading system

Disregarding these more general considerations, and accepting the value of trade measures, the next question is whether the use of MEA trade measures against WTO members can be regarded as an infringement of their rights under the MTS. It seems fairly clear that there is a potential for conflict.

In the first place, GATT Articles I ('Most Favoured Nation' Treatment) and III (National Treatment) outlaw discrimination in trade: WTO Members are not permitted to discriminate between traded 'like products' produced by other WTO members, or between domestic and international 'like products'. Yet all the three major MEAs referred to above discriminate between countries on the basis of their environmental performance, requiring parties to restrict trade to a greater extent with non-parties than they do with parties; indeed, such discrimination is one of the points of these MEAs, since they are aimed to promote sustainable activities while punishing unsustainable behaviour.

Second, GATT Article XI (Elimination of Quantitative Restrictions) forbids any restrictions other than duties, taxes or other charges on imports from and exports to other WTO members; yet each of the three MEAs requires precisely such quantitative restrictions.

Third, Article III requires imported and domestic 'like products' to be treated identically. The meaning of the term 'like product' has become one of the most difficult issues in the trade–environment arena. Originally incorporated into the GATT in order to prevent discrimination on the grounds of national origin, GATT and WTO dispute panels have interpreted the term more broadly to prevent discrimination in cases where process methods, rather than product characteristics, have been the distinguishing characteristic of the product and the justification for trade measures – for example the US embargo on imports of shrimp caught by methods that kill sea turtles. Yet the Montreal Protocol envisages restrictions on trade in products made with but not containing ozone-depleting substances (originating from non-parties), while domestic products produced in this way are not subject to such regulation – although so far this provision has not been put into practice.

It is possible, however, that an MEA trade measure could be 'saved' by the General Exceptions clause of the GATT, Article XX, which states that:

> Subject to the requirement that such measures are not applied in a manner which would constitute a means of arbitrary or unjustifiable discrimination between countries where the same conditions prevail, or a disguised restriction on international trade, nothing in this Agreement shall be construed to prevent the adoption or enforcement by any contracting party of measures:
> … (b) necessary to protect human, animal or plant life or health …
> … (g) relating to the conservation of exhaustible natural resources if such measures are made effective in conjunction with restrictions on domestic production or consumption.

Unlike many MEAs, where terms tend to be defined in the treaty or in subsequent decisions of conferences of the parties, interpretation of the MTS usually proceeds through a case-law-type approach, relying on the findings of dispute panels in particular cases. Since there has never been a dispute case brought before a GATT or WTO panel involving an MEA trade measure, it is impossible to say for certain whether it would be found to be incompatible with the MTS.

It is possible, however, to extrapolate from the arguments and findings in a series of trade–environment disputes that were brought before panels – involving, in this case, unilaterally imposed trade measures. In each of these cases, the panel found the environmental measures in question not to be justifiable, because either:

- the measures were not 'necessary' (Article XX(b)) to the achievement of the environmental goal, because the panel believed that there were less trade-restrictive or GATT-inconsistent measures also available; or
- the measures did not 'relate to the conservation of exhaustible natural resources' (Article XX(g)), because the policies in question were extra-jurisdictional: they attempted to modify the behaviour of other WTO members and could not therefore be considered to be primarily aimed at conserving the natural resources of the country applying the trade measures; or
- the measures represented 'arbitrary or unjustifiable discrimination' (Article XX headnote), in that there were less discriminatory methods available that could have been employed.

It is of course dangerous to extrapolate from arguments used in cases of trade measures imposed *unilaterally* to those involving the application of trade measures mandated by or in pursuance of the requirements of *multilateral* agreements. In any case, it is difficult, even from an environmental viewpoint, to defend most of the measures taken in the relevant disputes. The way in which the United States applied its embargo on shrimp imports from a number of South Asian and Southeast Asian countries, for instance, does appear to be 'arbitrary and unjustifiable discrimination' when compared with the much more gradual and participatory way in which it applied measures to protect sea turtles in the Caribbean region.

Furthermore, WTO dispute panels, and the WTO Appellate Body, have become steadily more sophisticated in their arguments, and more conscious of the environmental debate. The recent Appellate Body decision in the *Shrimp/Turtle* dispute, for example, used the reference in the Preamble to the Marrakesh Agreement establishing the WTO – 'allowing for the optimal use of the world's resources in accordance with the objective of sustainable development, seeking both to protect and preserve the environment and to enhance the means for doing so …' – to dispose of the argument that species protection was not a legitimate objective for trade measures.[1] It also stressed, as have several panels before it, the desirability of multilateral agreements as opposed to unilateral measures.[2]

Unsurprisingly, however, neither panels nor the Appellate Body have ever speculated as to the acceptability of trade measures taken under such agreements under the MTS. It is therefore still not clear as to how panels would rule. Even some of the arguments used in the *Shrimp/Turtle* Appellate Body finding suggest that they might rule against an MEA trade measure:

> Perhaps the most conspicuous flaw in this measure's application relates to its intended and actual coercive effect on the specific policy decisions made by foreign governments …[3]

[1] *United States – Import Prohibition of Certain Shrimp and Shrimp Products*, paras. 131–4 WT/DS58/AB/R, 12 October 1998.

[2] Ibid., paras. 166–72.

[3] Ibid., para. 161.

> However, it is not acceptable, in international trade relations, for one WTO Member to use an economic embargo to require other Members to adopt essentially the same comprehensive regulatory program, to achieve a certain policy goal, as that in force within that Member's territory.[4]

Trade measures employed under the three main MEAs cited above are now unlikely to be challenged in the WTO because of the wide international acceptability they enjoy – though this is perhaps less true of the Basel Convention, where the amendment banning trade in waste between OECD and non-OECD countries (not yet in force) has aroused hostility among some of the industries involved. The possible MTS incompatibility of the amendment has been raised explicitly by those opposed to the principle as an argument against adopting or ratifying it.

This 'political chill' argument is also relevant to other MEAs. Attempts to include trade provisions in the International Convention for the Conservation of Atlantic Tuna, and in agreements to control driftnet fishing, were shelved because of a fear that they would be inconsistent with GATT rules. The same issue was raised in last year's negotiations over the Kyoto Protocol and in discussions this year over the Rotterdam Convention on Prior Informed Consent.

The continuation of this potential conflict between the MTS and MEAs is undesirable for a number of reasons including the following:

- the fact that is not known for certain how a dispute panel would rule on an MEA trade measure creates an unstable and uncertain situation. On the face of it, it does appear absurd that the operation of an important element of international law should be subject to a panel of three individuals deciding what they think ten lines of printed text (the relevant sections of GATT Article XX) written fifty years ago could mean in a vastly changed international environment;
- it creates the spectre of a potential challenge to an existing MEA, bringing the two international regimes of trade liberalization and environmental protection directly into conflict;

[4] Ibid., para. 165.

- it increases the likelihood of conflict over the negotiation of future MEAs with trade measures, potentially weakening their effectiveness – the 'political chill' argument;
- finally, the perception that the WTO threatens environmental sustainability, already widespread in some quarters, assists neither the growth of the MTS nor the further spread of trade liberalization, even where this would have environmental benefit.

Resolution of the problem is therefore required.

Resolving the conflict

When two systems of law come into conflict, actually or potentially, there are three potential methods of dealing with the situation:

1. create some superior balancing mechanism;
2. determine that one legal system is superior to another, either wholly or in part;
3. modify either or both legal systems to bring them into harmony.

The first option, the creation of a balancing mechanism, would be the most desirable solution in a perfect world. This is effectively the system that operates inside the European Union, where trade liberalization and environmental protection are both objectives of the Treaty of Rome. Any conflict between the two objectives can be resolved by the European Court of Justice, which has the power to rule on the appropriate balance between trade and environmental measures in any particular case. In the well-known Danish bottles dispute of 1986, for example, the Court upheld the core of the Danish law requiring a collection system for returnable drinks containers while striking down some of the details of the regulations as unnecessarily trade-restrictive, given the environmental objective in question.

The creation of an equivalent system at a global level would require substantial reform of the entire system of international institutions, however, and is not a realistic prospect in the short term. Having said that, there have been calls for such a reform, perhaps using the International

Court of Justice as the superior body. Proposals for a new World Environmental Organization (for instance by Chancellor Kohl at the UN General Assembly Special Session, 'Earth Summit 2', in June 1997) have had at least partly in mind the objective of creating a balancing institution to the WTO, though the interrelationship between such a WEO and the WTO was not, and has not been, explored in any detail. It is interesting to note that the 1948 Charter for the International Trade Organization (ITO) (the intended third leg of the Bretton Woods tripod, never in fact adopted because of US opposition) did provide that a member prejudiced by an ITO decision could seek an advisory opinion from the ICJ, whose opinion would then bind the ITO. If Thomas Cottier's analysis of the WTO as increasingly assuming 'constitutional functions in a globalising economy' (WTO Symposium, 17–18 March 1998) is accurate, then this argument may need to be addressed sooner rather than later.

The second option, determining that one legal system is superior to the other, is *de facto,* even if not *de jure*, the position as it stands at present. As noted above, the validity of trade measures in MEAs could be challenged under the WTO, and a WTO dispute panel would then rule on their compatibility with the MTS. Although panels have become steadily more aware of and more open to environmental arguments (the decision of the Appellate Body in the *Shrimp/Turtle* case to accept 'non-requested information from non-governmental sources'[5] is a useful step forward), they are nevertheless composed of international trade experts who reach decisions in accordance with a body of international trade law – indeed, they cannot do otherwise, since this is the function of the WTO. The MTS has been constructed by trade negotiators with relatively little awareness of environmental requirements and policies, and, despite a number of references to environmental objectives in some of the WTO agreements, it is not well attuned to environmental imperatives even though it cannot avoid interacting with policies for environmental protection.

Equally, of course, it could be argued that MEAs are constructed by environmental negotiators with little awareness of trade law and the

[5] Ibid, paras. 104–10.

desirability of liberalized trade. But that would be unfair. Many delegations to MEA negotiations routinely include trade department representatives, and in a number of instances (including the Montreal Protocol and Basel Convention) negotiators have sought advice from the GATT/WTO Secretariat in designing particular features of their treaties. Some MEAs, including the UN Framework Convention on Climate Change, contain text drawn more or less straight from the GATT.

More generally, trade departments tend to wield greater political clout within national governments than do environmental departments and agencies; environmental policy objectives are not well integrated into policy across the board; and at the international level the MTS and the WTO (and in particular its dispute settlement system) are considerably more powerful and influential than are MEAs and the various environmental institutions such as the UN Environment Programme and the UN Commission on Sustainable Development. The trade implications of particular MEA requirements can in theory be subject to scrutiny by the institutions of the MTS, but there is no provision anywhere for the environmental implications of the MTS – or, for example, of the agreements likely to be reached in the forthcoming Millennium Round of trade negotiations – to be subjected to scrutiny by environmental institutions.

The existing hierarchy of international law therefore favours, in practice even if not in theory, the MTS over MEAs. For the reasons described above, this is an undesirable situation if one accepts that the two objectives of trade liberalization and environmental protection are of equal validity. The conclusion reached, therefore, is that the third option – modification of one of both of the existing systems of international law, for which priority should be given to the modification of the MTS – is required.

Resolution through the Millennium Round

The approach of the Millennium Round, due to begin at the end of 1999, and the proposed High Level Meeting between trade and environment ministers, provisionally scheduled for spring or early summer 1999, lends urgency to this analysis. And out of the very wide range of issues that could be considered under the 'trade–environment' heading, resolution of the MEAs–MTS conflict has always been regarded as one of the most pressing – as evidenced by the attention given to it by the WTO Committee on Trade and Environment (CTE) during the preparation of its first report, to the Singapore WTO Ministerial Meeting in December 1996.

It is important, however, to avoid a repeat of that sterile and long drawn-out debate. Although it was kicked off mainly by the EU's proposal for an amendment to GATT Article XX, proposals put forward by other WTO members became successively more and more restrictive. Increasingly, they aimed to limit the scope for trade measures in existing and future MEAs, by adding extra requirements to the trade measures under scrutiny. Any or all of 'necessity', 'effectiveness', 'least trade-restrictiveness', 'proportionality' or 'sound scientific basis' were suggested as criteria that trade measures would have to fulfil, and which WTO panels would judge whether they satisfied. In practice, this would have reinforced the existing international hierarchy, rendering MEAs even more subject to WTO scrutiny, and tilting the balance even further towards the MTS and away from MEAs.

Any solution to the conflict needs to satisfy the following criteria:

- There must be certainty about the MTS-compatibility of trade measures under existing MEAs, both those specifically mandated by the MEA in question ('specific measures') and those not specifically required by the MEA but taken in pursuance of its aims ('non-specific measures'). (The Montreal Protocol, for example, leads to both: the bans on trade with non-parties are specific measures mandated by the treaty, whereas parties have introduced a range of controls on trade with other parties in order to meet the requirements of the control measures ('non-specific measures').)
- There must be certainty over the MTS-compatibility of trade measures that might be incorporated in future MEAs or those currently under negotiation.
- There must be flexibility for MEA negotiators to incorporate trade measures in future MEAs where they consider them necessary to the fulfilment of their objectives.

- If trade measures are required by MEA negotiators, they must be applied in as non-discriminatory a way as possible; i.e., they should employ only such discrimination as is required to fulfil the aims of the MEA, and should not provide an opportunity for trade protectionism which is unrelated to environmental objectives.
- If disputes arise, it must be clear in which forum they can be resolved.

There are four main possible routes to resolving the issue:

1. a waiver from the obligations of the existing MTS;
2. modification of the MTS to create an 'agreement-specific' exemption from MTS provisions;
3. & 4. modification of the MTS to create a 'criteria-specific' exemption from MTS provisions; this could be achieved either via amendment of the GATT itself and/or through a new WTO Agreement on MEAs.

The use of waivers has been referred to as the *ex post* approach. Article XXV of the GATT provides for the granting of a waiver from other GATT obligations 'in exceptional circumstances'; Article IX of the WTO Agreement extends this to the MTS as a whole. Such waivers, however, are usually time-limited, can be considered only on a case-by-case basis, and require a three-quarters majority of WTO members to vote for them. Once again, they reinforce the existing hierarchy, firmly placing the WTO in judgment over MEAs; they cannot contribute to certainty about the relationship between MEAs and the MTS; and they do not fulfil any of the criteria set out above.

In contrast, the so-called *ex ante* approach implies modification of the MTS in some way. One possible method is a 'listing' of those particular MEAs whose provisions are deemed to be compatible with the MTS. This is similar to the approach taken by the North American Free Trade Agreement (NAFTA), which provides that, in the event of conflict between itself and CITES, the Montreal Protocol or the Basel Convention (or other MEAs where all NAFTA parties agree), the provisions of the MEA should take precedence over the MTS – though it also adds that parties must use the means least inconsistent with the NAFTA in implementing the MEAs. While more attractive than the waiver approach, this nevertheless involves the WTO in reaching a decision over which MEAs it considers acceptable and which it does not; it still does not create any certainty over the relationship with MEAs in general.

A broader solution is preferred, dealing with MEAs as a category rather than one by one. This implies a 'criteria-specific' modification of the MTS. The clearest political message would be to achieve this via amendment of the GATT. The EU proposal in the CTE, for example, was for a new sub-paragraph of Article XX, covering measures 'taken pursuant to specific provisions of an MEA complying with the "Understanding on the relationship between measures taken pursuant to MEAs and the WTO rules"'.[6] The proposed Understanding included a simple definition of an MEA and stated that measures taken pursuant to the specific provisions of the MEA should be presumed to be 'necessary' for the achievement of its environmental objectives, though they still remained subject to the requirements of the *chapeau* to Article XX.

This particular approach now looks a little dated; since the EU proposal was put together, a number of WTO panels have found trade measures in unilateral trade–environment cases to be justified under either paragraphs (b) or (g) of Article XX, but then failed them under the *chapeau*. (Earlier panels had failed them under (b) and (g), and never reached the *chapeau*.) If it is accepted that MEA trade measures would be likely to be treated similarly, then there is little point in adding a new paragraph: what would be required is amendment of the headnote itself. Since this would have implications for every category of exceptions to the GATT, and for unilateral as well as multilateral trade measures, it would be exceptionally difficult – to put it mildly – to negotiate. Finally, the procedures for amendment of the GATT are themselves quite stringent and time-consuming.

[6] WTO CTE, Non-paper by the European Community, 19 February 1996.

A new WTO Agreement on MEAs

The alternative route for 'criteria-specific' modification of the MTS is through a new WTO Agreement, similar in status to other WTO Agreements such as those on Subsidies and Countervailing Measures, on Technical Barriers to Trade or on Agriculture. The advantages of this approach are that it avoids attempting to amend existing rules, with probable implications for a wide range of topics; it creates a very clear set of rules which apply only to MEAs (i.e. which would not encourage further unilateral actions); and it is probably easier to negotiate.

What would the new Agreement need to cover? An outline of topics is provided here; further work would of course be necessary to develop detailed proposals.

- *The definition of an 'MEA'*, including criteria for its subject matter (possibilities include the promotion of sustainable development, the conservation of natural resources, the avoidance of transboundary pollution and/or the protection of human, animal plant life or health) and for its openness to participation by all parties affected and concerned.
- *The definition of trade measures*, and treatment of different categories of measures. It would seem logical that specific measures – for example the bans on trade with non-parties mandated by the Montreal Protocol, or the import and export licences required by CITES – should fall within the scope of the Agreement and thereby be exempted completely from the other requirements of the MTS.
- *Non-specific measures*, on the other hand, such as the controls on trade with parties implemented by Montreal Protocol parties (including measures such as taxation, labelling requirements, and total or partial import bans), could be covered by the *chapeau* to Article XX, as there seems little reason to think that they would need to be discriminatory to achieve their objectives. If discriminatory measures are required, it seems reasonable to insist that they should be specific, i.e. included in the text of the MEA. What is decided here therefore would have implications for the design of future MEAs.
- *Linkage of burdens and offsets*. Developing countries have tended, as a whole, to be most vociferously opposed to any modification of

the MTS for environmental purposes, including in the context of the MEAs debate. Given the record of Western protectionism against developing country exports, still enshrined in parts of the MTS (such as the Agreement on Textiles and Clothing), one can hardly blame them. It is important that trade measures are not used to force countries into implementing an agreement that unfairly retards their development – bearing in mind, of course, that in many cases the environmental harm at which the MEA is aimed may well retard their development anyway if it proceeds unchecked. The presence of trade measures *as one component* of a range of implementing measures in a particular MEA (including, for example, provisions for finance and technology transfer) is therefore an important feature of MEA design. To what extent this should be specified in a WTO Agreement is questionable, however; one would wish to avoid a situation in which a WTO panel found against the use of trade measures because the MEA's financial provisions were not working well.

- *Dispute settlement.* Finally, the Agreement would need to be clear about where disputes over the application of MEA trade measures should be resolved. In line with earlier CTE discussions, it seems logical for disputes between MEA parties to be resolved by the MEA, and for disputes between an MEA party and a non-party that is a WTO member to be resolved by the WTO. (This in turn has implications for WTO dispute settlement procedures and their ability to consider adequately environmental issues.) There also needs to be some agreed procedure for cases where it is not completely clear whether a trade measure is MEA-related or not; the US actions in the *Shrimp/Turtle* case, for example, could arguably be considered to be justified by a range of MEAs, including CITES, the Biodiversity Convention and the Bonn Convention on the Conservation of Migratory Species of Wild Animals.

Conclusion

The Millennium Round offers an excellent opportunity for the resolution of the potential conflict between the MTS and MEAs with trade provisions. It creates the wider political and negotiating environment, notably lacking within the CTE discussions, within which trade-offs can be reached, and all participants in the debate end up with perceived gains to offset perceived losses. It is the conclusion of this paper that the opportunity should be taken to open negotiations on a new WTO Agreement on MEAs with Trade Provisions. The High Level Meeting of trade and environment ministers provides an initial forum in which this idea can be tested and refined.

The biggest danger in this debate is that no political impetus will be given to it and nothing will in the end be resolved. It is entirely possible to argue, for example, that most MEAs do not contain trade provisions, that there has never been a WTO dispute involving an MEA, and that recent panel and Appellate Body findings have shown that the WTO is sensitive to the environmental imperative; therefore, no action is required. This would be a profound mistake. MEAs are growing in number, in scope and in importance, matching the growing evidence of global environmental degradation. In some cases they will need to impact international trade if they are to be implemented effectively. There have already been instances of MTS incompatibility arguments being used as weapons in MEA negotiations.

Trade liberalization and environmental protection are both desirable objectives. But the legal regimes that govern them are developing largely in isolation. A failure to resolve the *potential* conflict between them can only lead to actual conflict, undermining both. The time to act is now.

An OECD perspective

Michel Potier

We have been debating in the OECD about the relationship between MEAs and trade for the last six or seven years. Although there has been a perception that progress has been very slow, there have been some clear signals about this relationship on both the trade and environment sides. The WTO report of the Singapore ministerial meeting in December 1996 emphasized the importance of multilateral approaches to shared environmental problems, as well as the preference for WTO members in a particular MEA dispute to seek recourse within the dispute settlement provision of that MEA. In the recent *Shrimp/Turtle* Appellate Body report, there was a strong reiteration of the preference within the trade community for multilateral approaches.

Although there has been less systematic analysis within the MEAs themselves about their relationship to the WTO, there are also signs that this is changing; for example, at the last conference of the parties to the Convention on Biological Diversity (CBD), governments underlined the importance of assessing the links between biodiversity issues and trade liberalization. They also instructed the Secretariat of the CBD to follow closely the work of the WTO.

All the evidence points to the fact that knowledge among trade officials about MEAs and vice versa has improved a lot. The question now is, where do we go from here?

A first key issue relates to the importance of trade restrictions in MEAs. The work we have been carrying out in the OECD in relation to CITES, the Montreal Protocol and the Basel Convention shows that the trade measures included in MEAs cover a variety of tools which are applied for different and fairly specific reasons. One very important role for trade measures in MEAs is that of increasing the comprehensiveness of a set of policy responses to very complex environmental problems: preventing trans-shipment through non-participating countries, encouraging participation by increasing the cost of staying outside the regulatory regime, discouraging industrial relocation and discouraging free-riders, closing the loop on domestic production and consumption by monitoring trade – these are all policies that move towards making MEAs more comprehensive and more effective.

In summer 1998 the G7 Ministers' Summit identified illegal trade connected with the environment as a criminal area of growing concern. In September of that year the Solicitor-General of Canada released a study showing that the value of illegal trade in hazardous waste, endangered species and ozone-depleting substances ranked second only to the international drug trade. Therefore a key question is that of the overall environmental effectiveness of MEAs.

A second key issue is how negative impacts on developing countries can be avoided. There has generally been a perception that trade measures in MEAs have consistently been to the disadvantage of developing countries. My experience in dealing with MEAs is that such generalizations are not particularly helpful. The question of potential economic and environmental policy distortion has been raised, especially in the context of the export ban under the Basel Convention; and yet, as noted earlier, trade measures from one part of the package of measures relate to to MEAs, while there are other measures, including additional finance or technical assistance, that would benefit developing countries. It is generally a lack of technical and financial resources that makes the implementation of MEAs particularly difficult for developing countries. Our work at the OECD has clearly stressed that a key factor contributing to the success of MEAs lies with the funding in developing countries of ways to establish the technical and scientific capacity to implement MEAs' obligations.

A third issue deals with the compatibility of MEAs with the multilateral trading system. In the past few years discussions have focused on theoretical situations revolving around WTO law compatibility issues. Many are focused on a single question: what would happen if a WTO member that was not a party to an MEA brought to the WTO a formal dispute regarding discriminatory trade measures between parties and non-parties? There have been various possible solutions to this question, and I am sure we will hear more.

There has never been a formal dispute, or even informal discussion potentially leading to a dispute, between a MEA and the WTO. However, that does not mean that none will arise in the future. Also, membership in high-profile MEAs is generally larger than it is for the WTO. However, the question of legal amendments generates potentially thorny questions about universal coverage. For example, as the Montreal Protocol has evolved through amendments, there are fewer countries signing up to these amendments than signed up to the original 1987 Protocol. Are they considered to be non-parties in this case?

As I already mentioned, the real question in looking at trade measures in MEAs is less about their WTO compatibility than about their actual working. Are there ways to strengthen these agreements and ensure they work well, either by using existing approaches or by examining new approaches? How can the trade system contribute to that?

A fourth question concerns the interrelationship between the Kyoto Protocol on climate change and the multilateral trading system. This is an important issue given that, while much of the trade–environment debate has looked at the use of trade measures, considerably less attention has been focused on the trade effects more generally that can arise for MEAs.

If we turn to the Kyoto Protocol, we can see that implementation of the Kyoto commitments could have profound economic effects. Certainly many key economic sectors, including energy, transport, agriculture and tourism, will be affected. In all likelihood, new markets will emerge in such areas as international emission trading and the extended use of activities implemented jointly.

In addition to the economic and trade implications arising from these measures, questions arising under WTO rules will need to be proved. For instance, will emission trading fall under WTO disciplines including the General Agreement on Trade in Services (GATS)? Will implementation of the Kyoto Protocol mean in practice the adoption of energy efficiency and also climate-related standards? And will these standards be verified through the expanded use of labelling and certification schemes? How will the WTO deal with climate-related policies that differentiate energy-related activity based on production standards?

In conclusion, I would ask if we should not look for new approaches when reviewing the relationship between MEAs and trade. Put another way, has the debate over the last seven years made for more effective MEAs, and if so, why? Has the debate made for more stable and transparent expectations in the multilateral trading system, and if so, why?

There is now a sense that, since we are all convinced about how to make better policies, the MEA and trade question might need to be shifted. There has been an endless series of proposals regarding potential amendments to GATT Article XX to accommodate MEAs as a general exception. Are there other options that should be explored? Recently the suggestion has been made for a kind of cooperative arrangement on a functional basis to be struck between the WTO and individual MEAs.

The UN Environment Programme (UNEP) in a recent study also suggested that the WTO should engage in a formal agreement with other institutions, such as the World Bank or the International Monetary Fund (IMF), in pursuit of better policies. Is this an option for MEAs? Along these lines, both the WTO Director-General and UNEP's Executive Director have acknowledged the need for a framework to work out the initial relationship between MEAs and the WTO. This behaviour seems to be gaining momentum in Geneva, particularly against the backdrop of the proposed High Level Meeting on trade, environment and sustainable development. I think this signals that the old approaches to MEA trade rules issues have not been as fruitful as possible, and that new approaches may need to be explored.

An industry perspective

Reinhard Quick[1]

Overview

European industry considers that the relationship between trade measures contained in multilateral environmental agreements (MEAs) and the WTO should be resolved at the 1999 WTO High Level Meeting on trade and the environment. The WTO needs to make a clear statement in support of multilateral solutions to global environmental problems.

European industry considers that trade measures taken pursuant to MEAs should be accommodated by the WTO. The accommodation of these trade measures could be achieved by introducing into GATT Article XX(b) the words 'and the environment' and by adding to this amendment an Understanding on the relationship between trade measures taken pursuant to MEAs and the WTO rules.

The Understanding needs to set out certain basic criteria that MEAs have to meet in order to benefit from the WTO accommodation, in particular a test as to whether the trade measure is necessary to achieve the environmental objective of the MEA. If the MEA meets the criteria, the trade measures will be presumed to be necessary within the meaning of GATT Article XX(b). A challenge remains possible, but the challenger needs to rebut the presumption of necessity. Thus, European industry favours an *ex ante* approach combined with the possibility of very limited *ex post* WTO review of the trade measure.

[1] *Editors' note*: This paper is an annotated and updated version of the UNICE Position Paper, 'UNICE Position on the Relationship between the Provisions of the Multilateral Trading System and Trade Measures for Environmental Purposes, including those Pursuant to Multilateral Environmental Agreements', dated 22 July 1996.

Introduction

The key issue is whether the WTO should judge trade measures taken pursuant to MEAs more leniently than trade measures taken unilaterally – in other words, whether GATT Article XX should be less rigorously applied in trade disputes involving trade provisions taken pursuant to an MEA than it is normally applied.

The main problem with trade measures allowed by MEAs is discrimination. Some MEAs allow trade measures to be taken against non-parties. These measures are allegedly considered necessary to achieve the environmental aims of the MEAs concerned. But one of the pillars of the WTO, and its predecessor the GATT, is most favoured nation treatment and the associated principle of non-discrimination. Trade measures against non-parties to an MEA that are members of the WTO can be accepted only if they meet the conditions of GATT Article XX.

MEAs and the WTO are international agreements which bind their members. The WTO does not take priority over MEAs and MEAs do not take priority over the WTO: the WTO and MEAs exist in parallel. The WTO is the multilateral agreement dealing with trade issues and is therefore, and rightly so, the ultimate forum for deciding on trade issues. MEAs rule on international environmental issues. If a WTO member attacks a trade measure taken by a party to an MEA, the WTO dispute settlement system could rule that the measure was inconsistent with WTO rules. Such a ruling could put into question the objectives of the MEA and could subject the WTO to criticism in so far as the WTO should not second-guess the decisions taken by the members of an MEA. While for the time being no trade measure taken pursuant to an MEA has been attacked in the WTO, the issue of the relationship between the WTO and MEAs needs to be resolved.

Should Article XX, therefore, be changed in order to accommodate trade measures taken pursuant to MEAs? Industry's short answer to this question is a conditional 'yes'.

European industry considers that the WTO is not the right body to deal with environmental issues. Some environmental issues could, however, become important in case of a WTO dispute, such as the question of whether it is necessary to achieve the environmental aim of the agreement or whether the trade measure is the least trade-restrictive. Many problems would not have to be addressed if environmental negotiators had a clear answer to the environmental problem. So if the environmental foundations of the MEA are doubtful, one cannot attack the WTO for second-guessing the trade measures contained in an MEA, but one has to live with the consequences of the outcome of a WTO dispute settlement.

The Basel Convention is a case in point. The European employers' union UNICE holds that the Basel Convention's ban on exports of dangerous waste to non-OECD countries for recycling is neither ecologically nor economically sustainable. The Basel ban does not address the issue of whether a country or a company is capable, in an ecological sense, of recycling the dangerous waste: it just discriminates between OECD and non-OECD members. One cannot expect the WTO to handle a trade dispute arising from a trade measure taken pursuant to an MEA if the MEA in question disregards both the ecological necessity of the trade measure and the basic concepts of the international trading system. Article 4A in conjunction with Annex VII of the Basel Convention cannot be justified in WTO terms. The distinction between OECD and non-OECD members constitutes arbitrary and unjustifiable discrimination. Environmental negotiators cannot expect the international trading system to be silent on a specific trade issue if they are not able to solve the environmental issue at stake in a coherent and sustainable manner.

Industry's basic position

UNICE supports the United Nations Conference on Environment and Development (UNCED) position that multilateral solutions to global or cross-border environmental problems are more effective and more durable than unilateral actions. Given the fact that the effectiveness of trade measures needs to be carefully analysed, UNICE is of the view that trade measures of MEAs that are considered necessary to achieve the environmental aim of the agreement should be accommodated by the WTO.

Of all the suggestions that have been put forward so far, UNICE prefers the so-called *ex ante* approach, i.e. whereby the WTO develops a set of criteria that MEAs containing trade measures have to respect, coupled with a very limited *ex post* review of the trade measure in question.

UNICE favours an amendment of GATT Article XX(b) together with an Understanding on the relationship between trade measures taken pursuant to MEAs and the WTO rules. The Understanding would set out the basic criteria that the MEA has to meet and would spell out that trade measures taken pursuant to an MEA meeting the criteria would be presumed to be necessary within the meaning of GATT Article XX(b).

In the Understanding, the WTO should elaborate on the following criteria:

- the necessity test of Article XX(b), namely an analysis as to whether the trade measure is indeed necessary to achieve the non-trade aim of the MEA, including proportionality, and the concept of least trade restrictive measure;
- the *chapeau* of Article XX, including arbitrary and unjustifiable discrimination or disguised restrictions of international trade;
- the fact that the environmental objective of the MEA needs to be justified scientifically;
- the need for the agreement to be truly global and to address a global environmental problem;
- the necessity for WTO dispute settlement to apply not only in disputes between signatories and non-signatories but, as a last resort, also in a dispute between signatories of the MEA.

The position of the European Union and the question of necessity

The European Union has presented a position in Geneva on how to accommodate trade measures taken pursuant to MEAs in the WTO. The European Union suggested (a) an amendment of GATT Article XX and (b), in addition to the amended Article XX, the adoption of an 'Understanding on the relationship between trade measures taken pursuant to MEAs and the WTO rules' which would lay down certain criteria that would have to be respected by MEAs.

According to the European Commission, in case of a dispute arising from a trade measure of a MEA, the WTO panel would have a limited review, checking whether:

- the measure is taken pursuant to specific provisions of an MEA;
- the MEA meets the parameters of the Understanding and is therefore taken for the achievement of a legitimate environmental objective;
- the measure has been complied with in conformity with the requirements of the headnote to Article XX.

The panel would check whether:

- the measure was necessary to achieve the environmental objective of the MEA, including proportionality;
- the measure was the least trade-restrictive;
- the environmental objective of the agreement was based on sound science;
- the MEA was global and dealt with a global environmental problem.

According to the European Commission, the WTO should accept the views embodied in the MEA and should check only the three above-mentioned criteria. The Commission argues that, if the agreement is global and addresses a global environmental problem, the WTO should accept the environmental wisdom of the signatories of the MEA.

Originally European industry was rather critial of this position, as can be seen from the following passages in the 1996 UNICE position paper:

> UNICE and other business organisations have repeatedly stated that the issue of scientific evidence, the necessity test, the least-trade-restrictive test are indispensable requirements which also have to be respected by the negotiators of an MEA.
>
> The concept of necessity is viewed as fundamental in the interpretation of GATT Article XX. GATT has been an agreement on trade which provided for its Contracting Parties to take measures for non-trade purposes which were inconsistent with the GATT obligations only if the measures were necessary to achieve the stated non-trade objective. This approach is contin-

ued in the WTO and is reflected not only in Article XX but also in the WTO Agreement on Technical Barriers to Trade (TBT) and the Agreement on the Application of Sanitary and Phytosanitary Measures (SPS).

UNICE is concerned that the Commission's proposal gives environmental negotiators a carte blanche to deviate from the most fundamental principles of the WTO. The scope of WTO review of trade measures taken pursuant to an MEA cannot be limited in such a drastic way as proposed by the Commission.

At stake is the issue of how the WTO should handle disputes brought by non-signatories of the MEA against trade measures decided by the signatories of an MEA, in other words, the issue of most-favoured-nation treatment and the principle of non-discrimination. In such a situation, the fundamental WTO principles cannot be given up without strong evidence that the measure is really necessary to protect the environment.

The Commission itself has stated in its Communication on Trade and Environment that 'the use of trade restrictions within MEAs should not go beyond what is necessary to ensure the effectiveness of such agreements and the achievement of their environmental objectives'. UNICE is somewhat puzzled that this statement has not been introduced by the Commission as a prerequisite for the Understanding as well.

UNICE therefore suggests that trade measures taken pursuant to MEAs should only be accommodated by WTO if the Understanding contains at least the necessity criterion. The application of the Commission's concept without this safeguard would leave WTO members defenceless against trade measures provided for in an MEA whose purpose is not guided by environmental, but by socio-economic, political, or moral considerations. It would be an open invitation for protectionism if signatories of an MEA could take trade measures against non-signatories without having to justify the necessity of the trade measure. Such a far-reaching deviation from traditional WTO principles has to be resisted.

The adoption of the report of the WTO Appellate Body in the *Reformulated Gasoline* case brought both the industry's and the European Community's positions closer together in respect of the necessity argument. The Community had suggested that trade measures contained in MEAs should be checked only in relation to the *chapeau* of GATT Article XX and not with respect to the other tests contained in Article XX. However, at that time the *chapeau* had never been interpreted by a panel.

In the *Reformulated Gasoline* case, the Appellate Body interpreted the *chapeau* of GATT Article XX in a way that was remarkably similar to the necessity requirements of earlier GATT dispute settlement cases. Industry's concerns with respect to 'necessity' have thus been taken into account by the Appellate Body's ruling on the *chapeau* of Article XX. On the basis of the Appellate Body's reasoning, the Community's position that a panel should check the headnote of GATT Article XX only in a WTO case concerning a trade measure contained in an MEA has become acceptable to industry.

Industry furthermore welcomes the much closer coordination of trade and environmental policies at national level, which it sees as a positive consequence of the WTO's discussion on trade and environment. As a result of this coordination, industry is confident that issues such as sound science, global participation, proportionality and least trade restrictiveness will be satisfactorily addressed by the negotiators of an MEA. Therefore it will not be for the WTO to decide on these issues, but the negotiators of the MEA.

Further issues that should be addressed in an Understanding on the relationship between trade measures taken pursuant to MEAs and the WTO rules, include the following:

- *Sound science* The rationale for the MEA should be based on sound science. This issue, as such, has no relation to trade. The necessity of a trade measure can, however, be demonstrated only with scientific evidence. The specific provisions of the WTO SPS and the TBT Agreements can serve as a reference for MEA negotiators.
- *Global participation* The MEA should be global and should deal with a global environmental problem. MEAs should be negotiated in a transparent way. They should encourage participation by all interested and potentially affected parties. Global participation should be defined as participation by countries that account for a substantial proportion of the activity giving rise to the agreement.
- *Regional agreements* Industry is reluctant to give trade measures taken pursuant to regional environmental agreements the same WTO accommodation as trade measures taken pursuant to a true MEA. The reason for this position is simple: a minority of countries

should not be able to impose on a majority of countries a deviation from the WTO rules without giving the majority the possibility to challenge the trade measure taken by the minority.

- *Dispute settlement* Dispute settlement will occur mainly in the case of a trade measure taken by a WTO member and signatory of a MEA against a WTO member, that is a non-signatory of the MEA. The WTO dispute settlement mechanism could probably also apply, as a last resort, between members of the MEA once they have exhausted the dispute settlement possibilities of the MEA. (The latter case will rarely occur.) One could furthermore argue that recourse to the WTO dispute settlement in case of a dispute between two members of the WTO should not be possible. The member attacking the MEA trade measure has accepted the MEA in question, and thus also the trade measure of the MEA. An attack could be considered as a violation of the general principle '*pacta sunt servanda*'. Article 26 of the Vienna Convention of the Law of Treaties states: 'Every treaty in force is binding upon the parties to it and must be performed by them in good faith.' A WTO attack against an MEA trade measure could be considered a violation of the good faith obligation.

Practical suggestions for amending Article XX

European industry suggests the following amendment to Article XX(b):

> Subject to the requirement that such measures are not applied in a manner which would constitute a means of arbitrary and unjustifiable discrimination between countries where the same conditions prevail, or a disguised restriction on international trade, nothing in this agreement shall be construed to prevent the adoption or enforcement by any contracting party of measures:
>
> (b) necessary to protect human, animal, plant life or health or *the environment…*

The addition of the word 'environment' into Article XX(b) should not cause any difficulties for WTO members. The WTO preamble refers to the protection and preservation of the environment. It is therefore a logical consequence to introduce into the exceptions contained in Article XX the notion that the protection and preservation of the environment can be used to justify measures that would otherwise be inconsistent with the WTO.

Addition of the word 'environment' is not sufficient to address the relationship between WTO and MEAs. Therefore industry follows the Commission's concept of an Understanding on the relationship between trade measures taken pursuant to MEAs and the WTO rules.

The WTO's accommodation of trade measures taken pursuant to an MEA which meet the criteria of the Understanding would be effected by means of a rebuttable presumption. These trade measures would be presumed necessary in the meaning of Article XX(b). In other words, if the prerequisites of the Understanding are met, the trade measure taken pursuant to the MEA would be accorded the benefit of the doubt. A WTO challenge would remain possible, but the challenger would have to overcome a higher procedural threshold than if a unilateral measure were being challenged. Given the notions of sustainable development and the protection and preservation of the environment in the preamble to the Agreement establishing the WTO, industry considers that a challenger of the trade measure would not be able to rebut the presumption unless it could demonstrate that the negotiators of the MEA had not met the criteria laid down in the Understanding.

Finally, there are some practical suggestions concerning the implementation of this approach:

- the WTO needs to establish the criteria to be incorporated into the Understanding;
- negotiators of an MEA need to coordinate their policies with trade negotiators at a national level. They need to have completed an environmental analysis from both a scientific and a result-based perspective before envisaging the use of trade measures;
- negotiators of an MEA that contains trade measures should, upon conclusion of the negotiations, send a written statement to the WTO with an explanation that the criteria mentioned in the Understanding have been met. They could also consult with the WTO during the negotiations of the MEA. Given the fact that the WTO Secretariat cannot make an authoritative statement on the compatibility

of a certain trade measure with the WTO, the WTO should, upon request of the negotiators of an MEA, ask a member of the WTO Appellate Body to advise the MEA negotiators.

Process and Production Methods

Sizing up the issues from the South

René Vossenaar

Introduction

The impact of environmental standards on market access and the possibility that they could become non-tariff barriers to trade has been an issue of special concern for developing countries.[1] At the same time, there has been growing interest in new trading opportunities that may arise for companies in both developed and developing countries that are moving towards higher environmental performance in terms of both products and production processes.

Traditionally attention has focused on product standards. More recently, however, increased attention has been paid to standards relating to process and production methods (known as PPMs).[2] One reason is

[1] This paper updates an earlier paper by René Vossenaar and Veena Jha, 'Environmentally Based Process and Production: Some Implications for Developing Countries', in Veena Jha, Grant Hewison and Maree Underhill (eds), *Trade, Environment and Sustainable Development: A South Asian Perspective,* 1997. It also draws from UNCTAD, *Integrating Trade, Environment and Development, Recent Progress and Outstanding Issues*, TD/B/COM.1/3, December 1996.

[2] This paper focuses on measures targeting non-product-related PPMs, which do not address a product's final characteristics, but are intended only to control environmental effects caused during production. It excludes PPMs that are related to the product. When PPMs are related to the product, the use of PPM standards may have practical advantages over product standards. In certain cases it may be more efficient and more economic to control the process rather than the product itself to ensure product quality. Sometimes it may be technically difficult or even impossible to control product characteristics by inspecting the product. For example, the ISO 9000 quality system uses the term 'special processes' to describe processes that cannot be fully verified by subsequent testing of the product, and where process deficiencies may become apparent only after the product is in use. An example can be founded in plastic moulding; the ability of a moulded product to withstand stress may depend on the uniformity of dispersion of additives, moulding temperature and other factors in the production process.

that environmental problems are more often associated with the production process, than with the product itself. PPM-related standards are becoming more stringent and comprehensive, particularly in developed countries, in response to improved understanding of environmental risk and public preference for tighter environmental protection.

The use of PPM-based standards, which is essential for environmental purposes, should in most cases not result in conflicts with trade rules. To the extent that environmental externalities are limited to the exporting country, with their effects not being transmitted through the product to the environment of the importing country, there is little justification for applying PPM-based standards to imported products. Furthermore, current international trade rules do not restrict the right of countries to set PPM standards appropriate to their own environment and development. The international community generally recognizes that global environmental problems caused by PPMs should be addressed on the basis of multilateral cooperation, preferably through multilateral environmental agreements (MEAs).

Some issues have nevertheless been put forward. One is the competitiveness issue. Although rigorous process standards generally have positive effects on sustainable development, by requiring the internalization of external environmental costs and by removing inefficiency, concerns about maintaining competitiveness dissuade a country from applying rigorous PPM standards. Concerns here include friction over 'hidden' environmental subsidies, 'eco-dumping', and pressures for harmonization of PPM-based standards which may be inappropriate for developing countries. It would appear, however, that progress has been made on these issues and that some early pressures for trade measures, which some perceived as being necessary to 'level the competitive playing field', have now largely been set aside.

An issue of major concern, in particular to developing countries, is that PPM-based standards may result in the unilateral use of extra-territorial trade restrictions. This issue has been at the centre of the trade–environment debate, ever since the GATT panel in the first *Tuna/Dolphin* case. In general, WTO rules do not permit the application of non-product-related PPMs to imported products. The question is then the extent to which conditioning market access on exporting countries' compliance with environmental policies and measures unilaterally described by the importing country could be justified under Article XX of GATT 1994. This issue was also raised in the *Shrimp/Turtle* case, first by the panel and subsequently by the Appellate Body. The need to avoid unilateralism remains a priority issue in the trade–environment agenda.

Another issue is that of the use of PPM-based criteria in the context of voluntary mechanisms such as eco-labelling, and international standards for environmental management systems (EMS). In the case of eco-labelling, there is a risk that criteria based solely on the priorities of developed countries will discriminate against developing countries. There is also concern that certification against international EMS standards, despite being a voluntary instrument, may become a *de facto* condition for doing business, at least in some sectors, and a barrier to trade to the extent that companies in developing countries may find it difficult and costly to install an EMS and obtain certification. Some progress has been made in the WTO and the International Organization for Standardization (ISO), for example in terms of promoting transparency; but the issue of how to deal with PPM-related criteria in the context of international trade and the multilateral trading system remains largely unresolved.

The treatment of PPM standards in the context of trade rules is an issue that is very difficult to resolve in a generalized manner. The approach of this paper is that trade restrictions are not the right way to promote the use of more 'environment-friendly' PPMs in developing countries. Instead, it examines how incentives and supportive measures can assist developing countries to move towards more 'environment-friendly' PPMs and promote sustainable trade. It also considers how developing countries themselves may design packages of measures, based on multi-stakeholder approaches, to promote synergies between trade liberalization and sustainable development.[3]

[3] UNEP, with the cooperation of UNCTAD, is undertaking work in this area. Discussions in the WWF Expert Panel on Trade and Sustainable Development (EPTSD) are also relevant in this context.

The concept of 'like products'

The rules of the Multilateral Trading System incorporate a concept of 'like products'. The WTO does not allow discrimination between 'like products' imported from different countries or between imported and 'like' domestic products. The 'like product' issue has become relatively important in the context of trade and the environment. Some years ago, Austria announced a mandatory labelling programme for tropical timber and tropical timber products. It was intended that all commercial timber would bear a label displaying the inscription 'made from tropical timber' or 'contains tropical timber'. The ASEAN countries argued strongly that the label requirements were inconsistent with the provisions of the GATT, as the regulations applied only to tropical and not to other types of wood, which were 'like products'.[4]

The issue may also arise in the context of genetically modified organisms (GMOs), which are genetically engineered and in this sense are different from naturally grown organisms. There are a number of issues that arise in the context of WTO rules with respect to such products. The first is whether naturally grown fruits and genetically engineered fruits should be regarded as 'like products' in the context of WTO rules. One argument advanced is that, as genetically engineered products may not reproduce themselves at the end of their life span, the final product characteristics are affected by the process and production method (PPM); therefore they cannot be regarded as 'like products'. At the same time, however, as their end use may be the same as naturally grown products, they could be regarded as 'like products'.[5]

---

[4] There is no definition of 'like products' in the GATT, and the practice has been for dispute panels to determine what constitutes a 'like product' on a case-by-case basis, taking into account the objective and purposes of the chided regulation or measure. Dispute panels have generally taken the view that, while tariff classification could be one of the criteria, the final determination should not be made solely on this basis. Other criteria, such as the nature of the product, its intended use, its commercial value, price and substitutability, should also be taken into account when determining what is or is not a 'like' product. See Vinod Rege, *GATT Law and Environment Related Issues Affecting Trade of Developing Countries*, 1994.

[5] A slightly different problem may arise in the case of transgenics and genetically engineered species. An interesting case in point, which emerged in India, is that of Monsanto, which tried to register a patent for a gene code-named 'terminator'. The special

Another related issue that is particularly relevant in the context of the Biosafety Protocol relates to the labelling of products using GMOs. While some countries take the view that such labelling would be entirely consistent with WTO rules on grounds of public health concerns, other countries may argue that their exports may be affected by such labelling, as this would allegedly increase handling, storage and transport costs.

PPM standards in the context of international trade

The use of PPM standards in the context of international trade has raised a number of issues. They include:

- issues related to the competitiveness effects of differences in environmental stringency across countries;
- the use of trade measures to influence environmental policies of trading partners;
- the use of PPM-related requirements in business-to-business operations.

The competitiveness issue

The debate about the competitiveness effects of environmental regulations has focused on the costs of compliance and the variations between environmental regulatory systems in different countries. Although more stringent process standards and regulations may produce economic benefits in terms of improved human health and efficient use of resources, they may also adversely affect competitiveness at the sectoral or enterprise level. While the compliance costs at this level appear higher in a static analysis, a dynamic analysis shows lower costs since incentives for innovation and the use of 'clean technolo-

[5] (cont)
... property of this gene is that it mutates at the end of its life span. Cross-pollination with plants using this gene could have serious deleterious effects on the environment. Thus, India, on grounds of public health and the environment, rejected Monsanto's application to patent this gene.

gies' may result in cost savings over the long term. In addition, some sectors will actually benefit if large markets exist for their particular 'environmental goods and services'.

Studies have shown that on average environmental costs amount to only one to two per cent of total production costs. However, they have a more significant impact on capital costs, particularly in pollution-intensive industries. In addition, most of these studies have considered only part of the environmental protection costs, such as specific industrial pollution control costs.[6] Moreover, these studies have not picked up micro impacts; for instance, in particular sectors or firms, differences in process standards and regulations may have more serious cost impacts if environmental externalities are more fully internalized.

In expanding sectors, differences in environmental standards between countries should not raise problems for competitiveness. However, in sectors that are intensive in natural resources, and are heavily dependent on price as a factor of competitiveness, even small differences in standards may have a significant impact. This applies especially to low value added products, which constitute the bulk of the exports from developing countries. The ability of developing countries to implement higher environmental standards will also be limited by financial and technological constraints, and they may find it difficult to subsidize the development of environmentally sound production methods.

1. Do 'dirty' industries migrate? The issue of whether 'dirty' industries migrate in response to differences in PPM regulations raises two concerns. First, the 'push effect' of stringent regulations can lead to an exodus of polluting industries; and, second, the 'pull effect' of laxer environmental policies can lead to a 'pollution haven' effect.

Studies do indicate that pollution-intensive industries are growing faster in developing than in developed countries. Whether this can be

---

[6] One shortcoming of many studies is that they focus almost exclusively on industrial pollution control costs. For a summary of limitations of different studies, see Congress of the United States, Office of Technology Assessment (OTA), *Trade and Environment, Conflicts and Opportunities*, Appendix E. OTA-BP-ITE-94, US Government Printing Office, Washington, DC, May 1992.

attributed, at least in part, to the migration of polluting industries because of differences in PPM standards remains inconclusive. In some sectors, such as asbestos, heavy metals and leather tanning, some relocation of dirty processes does seem to have occurred. Migrating industries, however, are generally those that are relatively less competitive, and environmental regulations may be only one of many reasons why they migrate. Arguments that differences in PPM-based standards lead to production migration and employment loss in OECD countries have not yet been confirmed, either.

2. Is eco-dumping an issue? What does seem clear, however, is that developing countries are unlikely to use lower standards as part of their 'strategic policy' to gain competitiveness.[7] Maintaining lax environmental standards and weak enforcement procedures may entail greater costs in abatement, resource degradation and depletion in the future. Lax domestic environmental regulations may also encourage more inward-oriented and uncompetitive industries, which are economically as well as environmentally inefficient. In addition, products manufactured by these industries may not find markets in countries with high environmental standards, and these migrating industries are typically stagnant or declining.[8]

3. Do globalization and liberalization result in a race to the bottom? One concern, particularly in the early trade and environment debate, was that globalization and trade liberalization would lead to competitive deregulation and a 'race to the bottom' in environmental standards. It has not been possible to find much evidence to substantiate such fears. Some have refined this hypothesis by stating that, rather than a 'race to the bottom', heightened competition for global markets

---

[7] On the contrary, experience shows that developing-country firms that sell in external markets where environmental requirements are stringent tend to make relatively larger investments in environmental management than firms that operate predominantly in the domestic market. Thus, firms tend to raise rather than lower environmental standards to enter international markets.

[8] Lyuba Zarsky, *Trade-Environment Linkages and Sustainable Development*, Report of the Department of Arts, Sports, Environment, Tourism and Territories, Nautilus Pacific Research, North Fitzroy, Australia, October 1991.

causes environmental policy to be 'stuck in the mud'.[9] Industries in different countries, it is argued, are pulled towards environmental policy convergence by market-driven and political pressures, primarily to gain competitiveness. In the balance, and over time, the effect of convergence pressures on the average level of national environmental policy may be positive. Without effective international policy coordination, however, the terms of convergence will be 'too low' and 'too slow' to point development towards sustainablility.

Another view, however, is that trade and investment links with markets where environmental requirements are stringent results in a convergence of standards. Convergence of environmental product standards, for example, is driven by import requirements in large import markets. For developing countries, the primary export markets are OECD countries. Product standards are therefore pulled towards the OECD average.

In a recent study, Lyuba Zarsky notes that, while this may be true for product standards, environmental standards for PPMs and resource management are less likely to be subject to policy transmissions than product standards are. She argues that in the short run PPM standards are likely to converge not to towards the OECD, but towards some kind of benchmark set by the relatively more advanced developing countries. However, Zarsky herself qualifies this statement. To some extent, environmental performance in the context of globalization, in both OECD and developing countries, is nevertheless propelled upward by other forces, including consumer trends, industry self-regulation and the advocacy efforts of citizen groups (both internal and external). In addition, transnational corporations (TNCs) often apply the corporate or home-country standards in their affiliates or joint ventures in developing countries (see further below).

In the long run, as the environmental management capacities of developing-countries improve, or as market forces themselves bring new norms, developing-country environmental production standards may increasingly be pulled towards OECD average.[10]

---

[9] Lyuba Zarksy, Nautilus Institute for Security and Sustainable Development, Berkely, California, 'Stuck in the Mud? Nation-States, Globalisation, and Environment', in *Globalisation and Environment, Preliminary Perspectives,* OECD, Paris, 1997.

[10] Zarksy, *Globalisation and Environment.*

4. Conclusions with regard to trade rules. In UNCTAD, the OECD and the WTO, governments have strongly rejected WTO inconsistent or protectionist trade restrictions (such as 'green' countervailing duties) to offset any real or perceived adverse competitiveness effect of applying environmental policies. At the same time, it has been widely recognized that it would be inappropriate to relax existing environmental standards or their enforcement to promote trade and investment.[11]

Unilateral measures

A major concern in the area of PPMs is that making access to the domestic market of the importing country subject to compliance with unilaterally determined PPM standards can easily result in protectionism and could undermine the WTO multilateral trading system.[12] As mentioned above, so long as there are no transboundary environmental effects, the environment of the importing country will not be affected by PPMs used in the exporting country. In these cases, protection of the importing country's domestic environment does not require that products imported into that country meet its own product-related PPM standards.

In some cases, unilateral measures are used to deal with issues of global environmental concern. However, the United Nations Confer-

[11] See, e.g., Commission on Sustainable Development, fourth session, Decision 4/1 on Trade, Environment and Sustainable Development, para. 4.c: Commission on Sustainable Development, *Report on the Fourth Session*, E/1996/28 and E/CN.17/1996/38.

[12] The Business and Industry Advisory Committee of the OECD (BIAC) has observed that 'Unilateral trade measures imposed on the basis of the process or production method used to make a product are unacceptable. Such measures assume that importing countries have the right to pass judgements on the domestic policies of their trading partners, and to impose their judgements through trade instruments. There is no limit to the extent to which such unilateral measures could be used because no two countries have (nor should they necessarily be expected to have) equivalent environmental policies and standards in all areas. The use of trade measures in such circumstances would tend to lead to their imposition for any difference between national environmental policies and standards (not to mention policies in the areas of labour, tax competition law, etc.) and to rapid decline in international law.' Business and Industry Advisory Committee of the OECD, *BIAC Statement to the Special Session of the OECD Environmental Policy Committee*, Paris, 7–8 December 1993, p. 3.

ence on Environment and Development (UNCED), through Principle 12 of the Rio Declaration, states that 'Environmental measures addressing transboundary and global environmental measures should as far as possible be based on international consensus.' Thus, unilateral measures are again difficult to justify.

The WTO Panel in the *Shrimp/Turtle* case found that conditioning access to a WTO member's domestic market on the adoption by exporting countries of certain conservation measures unilaterally prescribed by the importing country cannot be justified under the *chapeau* of Article XX. The Appellate Body reversed this finding by concluding that the US measure in question qualified for provisional justification under Article XX(g). However, it found that it had been applied in a manner constituting both unjustifiable and arbitrary discrimination between countries where the same conditions prevail.[13] Therefore, the measure failed to meet the requirements of the *chapeau* of Article XX.

The intention of this paper is not to go into a legal analysis. However, some lessons may be drawn from the findings of the Panel and the Appellate Body which could be taken into account in the use of PPM-related measures, including those of a voluntary nature:

- Countries should engage in serious, across-the-board negotiations with the objective of concluding bilateral or multilateral agreements to address environmental issues of mutual interest. In other words, countries should not impose unilaterally determined conservation measures through restrictions on trade, but should work cooperatively with other countries to identify internationally shared concerns and consider ways to address them.
- Account should be taken of the fact that exporting countries may use policies that are appropriate for their circumstances, yet different from those of importing countries, even though they yield com-

[13] With regard to unilateral measures, in its report the Appellate Body mentioned some issues that it had not been required to address. First, it did not address the question whether there is an implied jurisdictional limitation in Article XX(g), and, if so, the nature or extent of that limitation. Second, it did not address the question whether the importing country would have been entitled to adopt unilateral measures in case efforts to achieve international cooperation were not successful.

parable results.[14] Thus, there would be a need to examine the appropriateness of the importing country's regulatory framework measures for the conditions prevailing in the exporting country. According to the Appellate Body, it is not acceptable, in international trade relations, for one WTO Member to use an economic embargo to *require* other Members to adopt essentially the same comprehensive regulatory program, to achieve a certain policy goal, as that in force within that Member's territory, *without* taking into consideration different conditions which may occur in the territories of those other Members.[15]

- Discrimination may arise from the application of certain requirements to all exporters from a particular country. For example, according to the Appellate Body, the United States did not permit imports of shrimp harvested by certain commercial vessels, even when they were using approved turtle excluder devices (TEDs), solely because they had been caught in waters of countries that had not been certified by the United States.

PPM-related trade measures in multilateral environmental agreements

PPM-related measures have on occasion been considered for inclusion within the framework of multilateral environmental agreements (MEAs). But in these circumstances PPM-related trade measures may in practice prove quite difficult to implement. For instance, in the case of the Montreal Protocol, it has not been considered feasible to implement provisions on products that are made with, but do not contain, CFCs. This was partly been due to the fact that there are problems with inspection of PPMs that are not detectable in the traded product. The

[14] In this context, Australia, in its submission to the Appellate Body, argued that the United States had refused to certify Australia even though Australia's sea turtle conservation regime 'extends well beyond protecting turtles from shrimping nets and includes cooperative programs with the shrimp industry to limit turtle bycatch'.

[15] *United States – Import Prohibition of Certain Shrimp and Shrimp Products*, WT/DS58/AB/R at 164, 12 October 1998.

accelerated phase-out of CFCs by the signatories to the Protocol also meant that this trade measure did not become necessary.

Market forces

Apart from the question of trade rules, PPM-related standards may play a role in overall consumer acceptance of a product. Both product and process-related environmental 'virtues' of a product may become factors of competitiveness in environmentally conscious consumer markets.

Thus, producers may incur costs for environmental investments because of demands arising in export markets. For example, it is believed that part of the investment costs incurred by Canadian and Swedish pulp and paper industries are a result of consumer pressure in Europe, particularly Germany, for chlorine-free paper, and are not solely a result of higher standards.[16]

Environmentally related consumer preferences in overseas markets may have effects on processes and raw material usage in developing countries. Retailers may give instructions to their suppliers on how a product should be made or which raw materials should be used. For example, a number of Turkish exporters reported that importing companies require detailed information on the manufacturing process and/or undertake plant inspections.[17]

More research is needed to analyse the true extent to which the above mentioned factors affect market access and competitiveness. Consumers in OECD countries may show a preference for specific PPMs favouring domestic products over imported ones. For example, if sustainable forest management is an important element in the choice of wooden furniture in OECD countries, then temperate wood products may automatically be substituted for tropical wood products.

[16] See OTA, *Trade, Technology and the Environment*, p. 199.

[17] Celik Aruoba (Research on Trade and Environment Linkages in Turkey), 'Report I: Environment–Trade Link: Impact of Environmental Regulations and Standards in European and North American Markets on Turkish Exports', in V. Jha, A. Markandya and R. Vossenaar (eds), *Reconciling Trade and Environment,* Edward Elgar, Cheltenham, forthcoming.

Often consumer preferences for specific PPMs may be related to familiarity and knowledge of the environmental characteristics of certain domestic processes, thus forcing developing countries that use different but equally environmentally friendly PPMs to obtain international certification to testify that their products are environmentally friendly; otherwise, they may be unable to capitalize on the environmental virtues of their products.

Some traditional policy responses

This section examines advantages and disadvantages of some measures that have traditionally been proposed to deal with the use of PPMs in the context of international trade.

Is harmonization of PPM standards desirable?

It is sometimes suggested that harmonization of PPMs could be a mechanism for alleviating competitiveness concerns as well as being beneficial to the environment. Environmentalists at times favour harmonization of process standards as a guarantee against deregulation. From an environmental point of view, harmonization guarantees a commitment to specified environmental objectives.[18] Some industry groups and certain labour groups have also favoured harmonization as a means of combating import competition and to avoid migration of pollution-intensive industries. There are, however, several arguments against harmonization, particularly because of the fact that assimilative capacities and social preferences vary between countries.[19]

When dealing with intrinsically domestic environmental problems, each country should be allowed to adopt standards that reflect its own environment and development conditions. Developing countries must build up an adequate framework of environmental rules and regulations which can be effectively enforced in order to encourage the

[18] See, e.g., Latin American Economic System (SELA), *Trade, Environment and the Developing Countries,* SP/LC/XVIII.O/Di No. 2.

[19] The 'polluter pays' principle, while encouraging harmonization, does not require it: indeed, it recognizes that differences in standards may be justified by a variety of factors.

switch to environmentally more friendly processes and technologies and the orientation of technology transfers towards more environmentally sound technologies. The implementation of environmental standards may require careful adjustment, allowing for different levels of technological and socioeconomic development and taking into account the uniqueness of countries.[20]

Upgrading standards is often intimately linked with a gradual and long-term process of capacity building, involving the formation of skills and the building of institutional and firm-level capacities. Thus, it can be argued that any imposition of standards that does not take into account the long-term nature of this process would penalize low levels of technological development.

While strict harmonization of PPM standards across countries where different conditions prevail may not be appropriate, incentives, supportive measures and the building of environmental infrastructure may be useful in moving towards greater convergence of standards, including through international trade links.

Is there a case for minimum standards?

While harmonization of standards might be encouraged where the same environmental and economic conditions prevail, minimum standards could be useful in other cases. They could, for instance, be a possible means of avoiding trade friction arising from differences in environmental standards.[21] For example, there are minimum standards relating to CFCs under the Montreal Protocol; there are also codes of conduct, which represent accepted minimum standards for air pollution emissions.

Internationally agreed minimum standards might also be linked with supportive measures, such as the transfer of finance, technology and general environmental support. A case in point is the Montreal Protocol, where special and differential treatment was accorded to developing

[20] UNCTAD and the Government of Norway, *Report of the Workshop on the Transfer and Development of Environmentally Sound Technologies*, Oslo, 13–15 October 1993, p. 22, UNCTAD, Geneva, 1993.

[21] Latin American Economic System (SELA), op. cit.

countries and a Multilateral Fund was established to meet their financial and technological requirements in order to encourage them to meet reduction targets.

Subsidies

Direct financial assistance provided by governments to producers in order to assist them in complying with environmental regulations is considered a subsidy by the GATT. However, under the Uruguay Round Agreement on Subsidies and Countervailing Measures, some environmental subsidies are exempted from the general rule that 'specific' subsidies are 'actionable'. Assistance made available to firms for the adaptation of their existing facilities to conform with new environmental regulations which results in a greater financial burden is 'non-actionable', provided that certain other conditions are met.

Some subsidies eliminate external costs or capture environmental benefits, and these should not be actionable, in principle, under the GATT.[22] Developing countries may have special needs in the field of subsidies; for example, it may be worth exploring the needs of small and medium-sized enterprises (SMEs) in developing countries. However, because of competing financial priorities, developing countries often cannot provide compensating subsidies for environmental standards.

PPM-related measures with potential positive impacts on trade

A promising way forward on the PPM issue is to identify 'win–win' situations, where improved market access for developing country exports can be achieved simultaneously with environmental and developmental gains. Supportive mechanisms for addressing PPM-related issues, such as technology transfer and financial and technical assistance, could be sought through international cooperation. Well-designed

[22] C.S. Pearson and R. Repetto, 'Reconciling Trade and Environment: the Next Steps', paper prepared for the Trade and Environment Committee of the US Environmental Protection Agency, 1992.

eco-labelling programmes and environmental certification pursued at an international level may also help developing countries capture the rents associated with environmental concerns in industrialized countries. At the same time, such measures might enable developing countries to upgrade their PPM-based standards. Proposals to move towards more 'environment-friendly' PPMs can also be put forward.

Financial assistance and transfer of ESTs

The need for the international community to provide funds for the so-called 'incremental costs of technology switching' to address global environmental problems has already been recognized with the creation of the Global Environment Facility and the Multilateral Fund under the Montreal Protocol. However, there are no comparable international mechanisms for facilitating the transfer of environmentally sound technologies (ESTs) that are appropriate for local environmental problems. In issues such as poverty alleviation, where the concerns are simultaneously of an environmental and developmental nature, the transfer of ESTs urgently calls for facilitating mechanisms.[23]

Measures that induce trade in environmental protection goods, services and technology should also contribute to the upgrading of environmental standards in developing countries, combining commercial and foreign policy environmental objectives in a complementary way.[24]

Improved market access for exports from developing countries

As progress in providing developing countries with financial resources and access to and transfer of technology has not as yet fulfilled the

---

23 UNCTAD and the Government of Norway, op. cit.

24 For example, in the United States the Overseas Private Investment Corporation has proposed an environmental Investment Fund to stimulate environmental investment in developing countries. The Energy Policy Act of 1992 directs the Secretary of Energy, through AID, 'to create a technology transfer program aimed at reducing the US trade deficit through the export of innovative environmental technologies'. The Export Enhancement Act of 1992 seeks to encourage exports of environmental goods and services. See Pearson and Repetto, *Reconciling Trade* op. cit.

expectations of Agenda 21, trade liberalization and improved market access have become even more necessary as a means of generating sources of financing for sustainable development.

Win–win situations arise when the removal or reduction of trade restrictions (tariff peaks, tariff escalation and remaining non-tariff obstacles to trade) and distortions have positive effects on both trade and the environment. This issue is of key interest to developing countries, for example in the context of the deliberations in the Committee on Trade and Environment. A WTO report[25] examines possible environmental effects of removing trade restrictions and distortions in sectors such as agriculture, energy, fisheries, forestry, non-ferrous metals, textiles and clothing and leather. Of course, the environmental benefits of improved market access are not automatic: they depend on whether or not sound environmental policies are in place. Therefore there is a need to promote a process in which trade liberalization is complemented by sound environmental policies.

Investment and sustainable development

Foreign direct investment (FDI) holds the promise of contributing to sustainable development in so far as (a) it provides a source of long-term finance to developing countries; and (b) the integration of economies encourages the transfer and greater convergence of environmentally friendly technologies across borders.

Major emerging issues with respect to international investment and the need for sustainable development therefore concern (a) the incorporation of countries and regions that have not benefited from the FDI boom of the 1990s, (b) the potential positive role that TNCs could play in conjunction with governments in achieving global goals on emission standards, and (c) the continued competition among developing countries for foreign capital.

FDI has an important role to play in providing host countries, particularly developing countries, with easier access to ESTs. The early debate on the relationship between FDI and the environment focused

---

[25] WT/CTE/W/67.

largely on the issue of 'dirty industry migration' (see above). More recently, discussions have focused on the issue of technologies and management practices associated with FDI. A widely held view is that TNCs tend to apply the environmental standards and management practices of the corporation or the home country, which often go beyond local legal requirements in the host country. According to another hypothesis, however, trade liberalization and FDI can at times result in the transfer (to developing countries) of technologies and products that have become 'obsolete' as a result of increasingly stringent environmental policies and regulations in developed countries. An important question concerns the extent to which foreign investors have contributed sufficient leadership with respect to fulfilling local and global environmental targets.

In many respects, the answer to these questions depends on the extent to which TNCs have devised environmental management policies, procedures and practices for their subsidiaries in developing countries (labelled as 'cross-border environmental management'). UNCTAD, through its Division on Investment, Technology and Enterprise Development (DITE), jointly with the Department of Intercultural Communication and Management (DICM) of the Copenhagen Business School (CBS), is carrying out a project comprising a number of case studies on cross-border environmental management of TNCs.[26]

Building on these activities, UNCTAD is initiating a new project which focuses on the contribution that investment could make to achieving the objectives of selected multilateral environmental agreements, as well as the role that TNCs could play in disseminating high environmental standards and environmental management systems to local companies in developing countries. The emphasis is on technology dissemination and spillovers on host countries. Building on the findings of the DANIDA project, this project focuses on MEAs. The government of Germany is providing funding to the project. The German government is also funding a parallel project, executed by the Institute for Environmental Management and Business Administration at the European Business School in Germany.

[26] This project is funded by the Danish International Development Administration (DANIDA).

'Premiums' for 'environment-friendly' PPMs

Under certain conditions, green consumerism in OECD countries might also help developing countries upgrade their PPM standards. Premiums could provide a means of recovering the higher costs of producing a product in an environmentally friendly way, compared with the older production technique.

Some developing countries have indeed expanded exports of several products with environmental and health advantages and thus have profited from changes in consumption patterns in developed countries. The challenge now is to broaden the number of developing countries and their enterprises that can turn this potential into practical financial, social and environmental gains. A range of policy, market and technical obstacles need to be overcome, such as insufficient access to information, lack of technical capacity, continuing trade barriers, an absence of supportive policies at home and abroad and weak business partnerships. These obstacles are particularly acute for small and medium-sized enterprises and the least developed countries.

UNCTAD's activities in this area are commodity and country-focused and aim to assist in developing a proactive strategy among exporting firms in developing countries. The objectives are:

- to encourage company or (industry) association partnerships between eco-pioneers in developed and developing countries;
- to improve access to and the review of existing and emerging environmental requirements in target markets;
- to encourage exporting firms in exploring the use of environmental management systems, such as ISO 14001.

It is important to promote partnerships and proactive approaches between developing-country producers and their clients, retailers, environment and development organizations and government agencies in developed countries for promoting the export of environmentally friendly products of developing countries. UNCTAD, under its technical cooperation programme, intends to hold a series of workshops between the relevant partners, preferably on a bilateral basis, between a source developing country and a target developed nation. Workshops will be confined to one or two sectors.

Environmental management standards

1. Eco-labelling Developing countries have expressed concern over the use of PPMs in the context of eco-labelling and have questioned the legitimacy of using a range of PPM-related criteria in product categories that are predominantly supplied by imports from developing countries. PPM-related criteria that are based on environmental and technological conditions and priorities of the OECD countries may be difficult for developing countries to meet, or environmentally inappropriate. PPM-related criteria need to be used carefully. Focusing on a few criteria in areas where developing countries can make meaningful improvements may be preferable. Compatibility between eco-labelling and the trade and sustainable development interests of developing countries could also be increased through concepts such as equivalence and mutual recognition.

2. Environmental management systems International EMS standards can bring important benefits for both companies and governments. Although the implementation of the ISO 14001 standard[27] is still relatively recent and the full implications are not yet fully understood, it may be a useful tool, at the company level, in promoting a move towards the use of more environment-friendly PPMs. It is recognized, however, that ISO 14001 may create obstacles to trade, to the extent that companies in developing countries may find it difficult and/or expensive to implement and certify an EMS. More work is needed on the trade implications of ISO 14001 and on national implementation issues with an impact on trade.

[27] With regard to the issue of PPMs in the context of international trade, ISO 14001 has the advantage over other policy instruments, such as eco-labelling, of not having specific PPM-related criteria or requirements set by the importing country, thus avoiding the issue of extra-territoriality. The commitment to comply with applicable laws and regulations refers to the regulatory requirements relevant to the site or country and the company's environmental policy and targets. On the other hand, it should be noted that the establishment and operation of ISO 14001 does not, by itself, guarantee enhanced environmental performance.

Governments can play an important role in providing an 'enabling' environment for the implementation of ISO 14001, particularly in developing countries. For example, governments in the export-orientated economies of Asia have taken significant steps to promote ISO 14001 standards by establishing infrastructure and providing incentives, as well as comprehensive support programmes for SMEs and financial assistance. Governments could also play an important role in promoting awareness and capacity-building.

In addition, policies and measures at the bilateral and/or multilateral levels, including cooperation in the area of technical assistance and capacity-building, may assist developing-country companies and their governments in setting up EMSs. The private sector, in particular TNCs, can play an important role in promoting the implementation and improvement of EMS in developing countries, e.g. through cooperation between companies in developed and developing countries. Of particular relevance is cooperation between companies in developed countries and their suppliers in developing countries, and between subsidiaries of TNCs and their local suppliers, in particular SMEs.

Certification of 'environment-friendly' PPMs

In assessing the potential of developing countries to take advantage of trading opportunities for products made using 'environment-friendly' PPMs, certification is a key issue. It is important to ensure that certification is objective, transparent and affordable. Building and strengthening capacities of developing-country certification bodies as well as promoting mutual recognition is of key importance. International aid agencies also have a role to play here.

Sustainable production of commodities

The introduction of sustainable practices for the production of internationally traded commodities may require innovative forms of cooperation between producers and consumers. In fact, studies are already under way regarding the possibility of facilitating the internalization of environmental externalities in the production of commodities with the help of International Commodity Related Environmental Agreements (ICREAS). Various options are being analysed to determine how financial transfers or environmental premiums might be provided and whether or not they need to be combined with preferential market access.

Small and medium-sized enterprises

Discussions and analysis so far have recognized the special situation of small and medium-sized enterprises (SMEs) in the trade–environment interface. At the same time, there is great potential for improving environmental management and PPMs used in SMEs provided that proper supporting infrastructure is set up. Many practices that are cleaner than present methods of production are feasible for SMEs, but one important obstacle is the lack of knowledge of available options. UNCTAD studies have proposed several measures aimed at improving the access of SMEs to information, ESTs and required input materials, such as dyes and chemicals. This is certainly an area where win–win situations can be created through appropriate measures at both national and international level.

Conclusions and recommendations

PPM-related measures can be essential instruments of environmental policy. However, to the extent that environmental effects are intrinsically local, using the same standard across countries or regions, or even within a country, may not be appropriate. Thus, using trade measures based on PPMs may not meet the environmental objectives for which the PPMs are designed. Additionally, compliance with specific non-product-related PPMs in the context of either eco-labelling or other similar standards could require the use of specific technologies.[28]

From a trade point of view, there is concern that harmonization of PPMs could undermine comparative advantage, which is the very ba-

---

[28] Some have expressed the view that concerns about the possible discriminatory character of PPM-based standards could be magnified, depending on the degree of patent protection of specific technologies.

sis of welfare gains derived from international trade. Applying PPM-based standards to imported products could also involve the extra-territorial application of domestic environmental law. For these reasons, making market access conditional on the use of particular PPMs is generally considered incompatible with existing trade rules.

It seems reasonable that, from a development perspective, PPM-based standards should be commensurate with a country's environmental problems, environmental absorptive capacity, economic resources and social preferences. In this context, it is also worth noting that certain instruments that are used in developed countries to influence PPMs may be less effective in many developing countries. Policies and measures aimed directly at increasing the capacity of firms to improve their environmental performance, such as building environmental infrastructure for SMEs, may yield greater benefits in economic and in environmental terms.

Consumer preferences may affect market access conditions and the competitiveness of specific products based on the PPM used in their production. These forces have the potential to work either as an obstacle to trade or as a means to help improve PPMs through trade, by providing premiums to environmentally friendly products. Measures that have a certain degree of government involvement, such as eco-labelling systems, should be notified to the GATT. Wide adherence by local and non-governmental bodies to the new Code of Good Practices for the Preparation, Adoption and Application of Standards under the Agreement on Technical Barriers to Trade also appears to be essential. Efforts by developing-country exporters to obtain environmental premiums for environmentally friendly products available in OECD markets should be encouraged. This could best be achieved when initiatives involving products of export interest to developing countries are based on an international process with their fullest possible participation.

Experience from UNCTAD studies shows that trade and investment links with countries where environmental requirements are relatively stringent may have positive effects on environmental characteristics of PPMs in the exporting country. Thus, trade and investment can play a role in promoting environmentally preferable PPMs worldwide, provided that PPMs are also useful in the context of the environmental and developmental conditions in the country of production.

Future work on PPMs could include analysis of the relationship between PPMs and trade, including consideration of trade principles which could ensure that the application of PPM-based instruments does not result in arbitrary discrimination or unjustified restrictions on trade. A second issue is whether international standards developed for instruments and measures that extend to PPMs, such as the ISO 14000 series, could provide sufficient guarantees to this effect. A third issue that arises is this: if there is a consensus on the need to move towards greater convergence of PPMs, what would be an appropriate mechanism, and what would be the role of FDI, taking into account the interests of all parties with different environmental endowments and at different levels of development?

Reassessing 'like products'

Konrad von Moltke

Introduction

The issue of process and production methods (PPMs) in the trade regime has vexed the environmental community since the first *Tuna/ Dolphin* panel claimed that distinctions between products based on their production methods were not permitted under the GATT. The reason for its distress is straightforward: an open trading system, which does not provide for distinctions between products produced sustainably and those produced unsustainably, is unacceptable from an environmental perspective.

Unless the issue of PPMs is resolved in a reasonable manner, the environmental community will ultimately oppose trade liberalization. It is up to those interested in trade policy to decide whether they are willing to pursue their goals against environmental opposition – in essence, whether they can persuade voters in democratic societies that the economic benefits they promise outweigh not only the inevitable economic costs to those who do not enjoy comparative advantage, but also the risks to the environment, and to communities.

'Like products' in WTO dispute settlement

Before addressing possible solutions to the issue of PPMs within the trading system, it is necessary to dispose of the myth that no such distinctions are possible, either because this is contrary to fundamental principles of the trading system or simply because the current text of the GATT forbids it. Frequent repetition of this error, including repetition by those responsible for managing the trading system and by many eminent commentators, makes it no more correct than it was to begin with.

The issue of PPMs in the GATT/WTO revolves around the interpretation of the word 'like', as in 'like products'. The concept of 'like' products is in many ways the linchpin of the GATT/WTO system. Its two central principles, most favoured nation treatment (MFN) and national treatment, are critically dependent on this concept. The key passages in the GATT read as follows:

> any advantage, favour, privilege or immunity granted by any contracting party to any product originating in or destined for any other country shall be accorded immediately and unconditionally to the like product originating in or destined for the territories of all other contracting parties. (Article I.1)
> The products of the territory of any contracting party imported into the territory of any other contracting party shall not be subject, directly or indirectly, to internal taxes or other internal charges of any kind in excess of those applied, directly or indirectly, to the like domestic products. (Article III.2)

The English word 'like' has no perfect counterpart in French or Spanish. The French version of the GATT speaks of 'equivalent', which actually expresses something different again, since it derives from 'value' rather than focusing, as the word 'like' does, on the inherent characteristics of a product. Consequently 'equivalent' expresses more clearly the valuation of products, and of distinctions between products, by certain economic actors.

The drafters of the original GATT text (in practice, those drafting the Havana Charter) were presumably well aware of the ambiguities of the term 'like' and of the inherent dangers in using such an ambiguous term in passages so critical to the text. They chose the word 'like' precisely because its ambiguities reflected a problem in the real world. Some products are equivalent but not like (for example whiskey and sake). Some products are like but not equivalent (for example wild caught salmon and the ranched version). In the modern trading system, some products are identical but not alike (for example genetic and branded pharmaceuticals). In short, the term 'like' requires careful interpretation to ensure that the GATT does not produce unacceptable results.

Given its importance, it is reasonable to expect extensive analysis of the concept of 'like' products in dispute settlement proceedings of the GATT and in the general literature. In fact, there is not much to be found, presumably because the significance of the ambiguity appeared intuitively obvious and because, surprisingly, countries have rarely attempted to use criteria viewed as spurious by other countries to distinguish between otherwise like products.

The most important dispute to date revolving around interpretation of 'like' concerned liquor taxes in Japan. The dispute panel struggled hard with the problem, not least because the equivalence of sake and many liquors imported to Japan was intuitively obvious, the protectionist intent of Japanese tax rules was hard to overlook, and still it was difficult to develop an argument that was free from internal contradictions and did not open the door to a Pandora's box of other problems. The Appellate Body, reviewing the panel report on appeal, was seduced by the outlandish view that Article III.1 should be read as a *chapeau* to the entire Article III, possibly because a more obvious distinction between Articles III.1 and III.2 seemed unpalatable since it opened the door wide to PPMs, including PPMs in other countries: that Article III.1 deals with production while Article III.2 addresses products in trade.

At the very least, it should be clear that the GATT contains no explicit prohibition on the use of PPMs in general. This view is the result of a process of interpretation, which sometimes resembles the rule-making committee of a club rather than that of an international body with global responsibilities. There is, however, a more direct way in which to approach the issue of PPMs in the trading system. To prove that PPMs are possible within the GATT, it is sufficient to show that they are currently being utilized.

'Like products' and intellectual property rights

It may come as a surprise to some observers that there are several areas in which the GATT handles PPMs without apparent difficulty. The most dramatic application of PPMs in the GATT/WTO to date is in the field of intellectual property rights. The Agreement on Trade Related Aspects of Intellectual Property Rights (TRIPS Agreement) is, in effect, an agreement on PPMs. It distinguishes between products in trade not on the basis of their inherent characteristics, but on whether certain rules have been observed in the production process – namely, whether the rights of the holders of intellectual property have been respected.

A compact disk with a pirated version of music, a film or computer software is indistinguishable from a disk with the same (not 'like'!) materials: otherwise, as often as not, it would not function properly. A generic pharmaceutical product can be identical with its branded equivalent; in some cases it is legally required to be identical so as not to endanger the health of users. Indeed, some generic pharmaceuticals are manufactured on the same machines as their branded equivalents, yet they are clearly distinguished in the trade regime. The difference between PPMs arising from intellectual property rights and those needed for environmental purposes is that the former benefit the most powerful interests in the global economy while the latter appear to benefit nobody in particular, merely 'the environment'.

The economic effect of intellectual property rights (IPRs) is to assign a temporary monopoly to the holder of these rights. Most of these monopolies are of course worthless because there is no market demand for the vast majority of patents, manuscripts, recordings or software. When such demand exists, however, the profits can be staggering, and many major multinational corporations derive a significant proportion of their income from IPRs, most dramatically companies like Microsoft, Philips or Toyota.

It is interesting to note that only one environmental dispute has arisen concerning the products of producers such as these: the dispute over CAFE standards and the gas guzzler tax, which pitted Daimler-Benz and BMW against the US automobile industry, one of the more unusual GATT disputes in terms of its outcome. The vast majority of environmental disputes in the GATT/WTO concern commodities, that is products, that are produced and traded to a non-proprietary standard. The environmental concern for PPMs focuses primarily on the need to segment commodity markets in such a manner that the environmental impact of the extraction process becomes transparent to subsequent users, and the environmental costs can be successfully internalized: tuna, shrimp, forest products, fish, gasoline, soya beans, beef. One way to test the free trade fervour of those who deny the possibility of introducing necessary environmental PPM distinctions is to suggest that all products currently being traded with IPR protection should be traded as commodities, i.e. to a single, universally accepted specification.

This brief discussion is not the occasion to discuss the role of commodity markets in pricing the environment or in promoting (or obstructing) the internalization of environmental costs in products traded on international markets. This is a matter requiring much more research and public debate than it has received to date.

Taking the debate forwards

Since 'like' products are at the heart of the GATT/WTO system, changing the definition of what will be recognized as valid distinctions between otherwise 'like' products is a matter of great concern to those responsible for managing the trading system. In particular, it raises the spectre of disguised forms of protectionism, precisely because it relates to the central principles of the regime designed to keep protectionists at bay. What worries many proponents of trade liberalization is the prospect of disguised forms of protection, which are particularly insidious when wedded to seemingly legitimate environmental goals, such as protecting dolphins, improving air quality or strengthening the ecological management of forests – alliances that David Vogel has called baptist/bootlegger coalitions.

It is important for those concerned primarily with the environment to recognize the legitimacy of such fears. Indeed, the *Shrimp/Turtle* dispute is the only one where I am unaware of any significant commercial interest allied with the surface environmental concern. On the other hand, the existence of some protectionist effect of a measure must not in and of itself invalidate it. Sometimes the environmental need clearly outweighs the economic costs of protectionism.

It seems to me that it is in the interests of everyone concerned that we move beyond the absurd debate about PPMs, as if they were some form of original sin in the trade regime. We must seek a way to ensure that the use of environmental PPMs occurs in a rule-based manner. That, after all, is what the trading system is supposed to be about. So the correct question in relation to environmental PPMs is not whether they are permissible, but whether they are needed – and, if they are needed, what rules should apply.

The importance of PPMs for the attainment of sustainability has not yet been conclusively demonstrated. The significance of PPMs in this context is highly intuitive; nevertheless it resides on a critical notion related to the characteristics of commodity markets: namely that without certain PPMs producers of commodities will be confronted with an invidious choice: degrade the environment or lose market share.

This is a restatement of one of the most persistent of all ideas in the environment–trade debate: namely, that rules are required to avoid the creation of 'pollution havens'. No clear evidence has yet been adduced to show that pollution havens exist. In part, this is attributable to the fact that researchers have been asking the wrong question: is there any risk of a general move of production from 'high-regulation' to 'low-regulation' jurisdictions? Enterprises with significant profit margins, in particular those benefiting from IPRs, will not make location decisions based on the cost of environmental protection. The reasons are complex, ranging from the modest cost of environmental measures, relative to other factors of production, to the importance of proximity to major markets to the need to protect a brand's image. On the other hand, there is some evidence that the production of commodities, and to a lesser degree of certain commodity manufactures, has shifted away from high-regulation jurisdictions to those with lower regulation. The reasons are again complex, ranging from the availability of higher-value uses of scarce environmental resources in locations close to the value added centres of the world, to the resistance of highly urbanized societies in Europe and Japan to further destruction of the landscape, and to the availability of cheap labour for labour-intensive phases of the product chain. With these few observations, we are again in the relatively unexplored area of commodity production and the environment, which also happens to be the prime domain for environmental PPMs.

Interestingly, viewing the TRIPS Agreement for what it is – an agreement on the application of certain PPMs – provides some guidelines on how to address PPMs in the trading system. It is true that national environmental protection measures are the first step towards any international structure. It is also so obvious as to be trite that national measures alone cannot suffice. Consequently the GATT/WTO needs an agreement on how to develop and apply environmental PPMs at all levels where they are needed: local, regional, national, international and global.

This is not a task for the GATT/WTO. Just as the TRIPS Agreement rests on a broad base of preparatory work undertaken by those whose concern is the development of IPR, so an environmental PPMs Agreement must originate with those whose primary concern is the environment. They must specify what is needed, and how they plan to go about putting it in place. The role of the GATT is then to insert such an agreement into the rule-based structure of the trading system in a manner that respects the needs of both those concerned with the environment and those whose focus is trade liberalization.

It sounds simple. It is not. But it is straightforward, and may contribute to shortening a debate that seems to be going nowhere even while the underlying issues become more urgent with every environmentally related trade dispute.

The impact of the *Shrimp/Turtle* dispute

Charles Arden-Clarke

The *Shrimp/Turtle* dispute has changed the face of the issue of process and production methods (PPMs) and trade. There are still problems with the outcome. The final decision went the wrong way in the end for the environmental community, and that will create political problems in the United States for the Administration's efforts to secure 'fast track' negotiating authority, as well as for the WTO more generally in other parts of the globe.

Shrimp/Turtle was also the irrefutable proof that the multilateral trading system has to, and is beginning to, come to terms with the issues surrounding processing and production methods. The Appellate Body found that the US measure requiring the fitting of turtle excluder devices (TEDs) to shrimp nets did in principle qualify it for exception under Article XX(g), which means that discrimination based on PPMs is acceptable under WTO rules. The Appellate Body ruling also began to come to terms with other civil society concerns about the WTO in that it used a fairly liberal interpretation of WTO rules to accept unsolicited *amicus* briefs from non-governmental organizations. Third, the Appellate Body began to enact something that first appeared in the *Venezuela Gasoline* Appellate Body report, in beginning to take account of other public international law; in particular, the Appellate Body took account of multilateral environmental agreements (MEAs).

The World Wide Fund For Nature (WWF) was among the NGOs that submitted *amicus* briefs to this panel, and we called for these three things to be done. We also called for the measure to be upheld given the endangered status of turtles and their protection under MEAs; but the Appellate Body still struck the measure down on the grounds that it was arbitrary and unjustifiable on seven separate counts.

That is a lot of hurdles to get over before a trade measure can be held compatible with WTO rules. Some of the hurdles look like reasonable ones, others may be construed as less reasonable. To take one example, the Appellate Body in the *Shrimp/Turtle* case found that the United States gave more technical assistance to some countries than to others, and that amounted to unfair discrimination. It is important to be careful in assessing the implications of this interpretation: presumably, if the United States had given no technical assistance to anyone, it would not have failed on that hurdle. There are other important elements too. The Appellate Body did not look at the question of whether or not the US measure was a 'disguised restriction on trade'; and it pointed to the fact that the measure was 'coercive in intent and effect' without saying whether that might amount to a test that would have to be met by any future measures.

The core of the problem with PPMs arises when they result in transboundary and/or global effects. I would never advocate unilateral trade measures as a tool of first resort, but *Shrimp/Turtle* came close to presenting a factual situation where they could and should be allowed as a last resort – an endangered species being pushed much closer to extinction by a clearly identified threat, which the technology required by the measure could reduce. Those points at least were recognized by the panel.

Better adherence to existing MEAs is also needed. One of the most interesting points that came out of the *Shrimp/Turtle* case was a footnote which noted that the country with the worst record on signature and ratification of MEAs out of the five countries involved in the dispute was the United States. Some countries are setting themselves up as environmental policemen, but that role is not necessarily reflected in their signature of the multilateral legal instruments that exist for the protection of the environment. This is something that governments, NGOs and civil society as a whole must address.

The question now is, how can the WTO evolve further? There seem to be two ways for it to evolve. One is through the dispute settlement process. Dispute settlement in the WTO on trade and environment matters has improved fairly steadily since the first *Tuna/Dolphin* Panel back in 1991, through the second *Tuna/Dolphin* Panel and the *Automobile Tax* dispute in 1994, and on to the *Venezuela Gasoline* Appellate Body ruling in 1996. Dispute settlement has been getting better from an environmental perspective, and, while I hope that *Shrimp/Turtle* is not the peak of that trend, it is the peak so far.

The second way for the WTO to evolve is through renegotiation and reinterpretation of WTO rules, and this is still likely to be necessary. If we settle these things purely through a dispute settlement process, which is a very closed process, it is risky. These issues will need to be settled, and they will need to be settled in the open. PPMs – the most controversial subject, which has destroyed consensus in the WTO on a regular basis – will have to be addressed as a central and systemic issue. More than that, it will need to be mainstreamed into the WTO. It is not just a question of dealing with it in the context of individual specific issues: any deal on PPMs has to be part of a bigger trade deal. This may sound like an argument for the Millennium Round. It is not: it is an argument for mainstreaming environment in the next Millennium Round.

This brings me to the proposed High Level Meeting on trade and environment. This is a litmus test of government commitment: whether or not that High Level Meeting takes place; whether it is about substance; and whether there is serious preparation beforehand. The High Level Meeting should be preparation for mainstreaming the environment, including the PPM issue.

I agree that the environmental community will also have to articulate better what we want on PPMs, and that the process of securing this will have to be an open and inclusive one. We also need a real-life discussion with real-life issues that involve both the World Trade Organization and existing MEAs, because otherwise the discussion will become very oblique and abstruse. *Shrimp/Turtle* was just that. We could do worse than take the example offered by the *Shrimp/Turtle* case as a starting point from which to begin building lasting solutions. It has all the elements. It is about PPMs and it involves MEAs and the WTO. It does not perhaps involve MEAs as much as it should have, but that is a question of political will for governments, and also a job for NGOs. But we have to do this outside the WTO; it has to be done in a forum that encompasses trade, environment and development. We need to escape the 'WTO decides' factor, and we also need to escape the national-level 'chill factor' that WTO rules apply to the development of effective environmental policies.

Finally, we also need a multi-stakeholder approach. In the case of shrimps and turtles, we do not want just the vociferous NGOs: we also want the fishermen whose livelihoods are affected by the trade embargo, and who depend on a healthy marine eco-system for those livelihoods. We need the appellants in the case and the respondents; we need the United States and the four countries involved in the dispute. We need anybody else who is interested as a third party. We need representatives of the WTO and of the MEAs. We need the environment and the development NGOs, and we need the independent experts who often have a key role to play, because even NGOs can have vested interests.

Conflict Resolution in the World Trade Organization

Assessing the story so far: hope on the horizon?

Thomas Cottier and Krista Nadakavukaren Schefer

Introduction

The World Trade Organization is dedicated to improving the standard of living of people in its member states by establishing legally binding rules to liberalize international trade. WTO rules affect trade in goods, services and the trade-related aspects of intellectual property rights. The structures of liberalized trade, in turn, often impact on the environment. When they do, non-governmental organizations (NGOs) may attempt to sway public opinion so as to limit the measure's negative impacts on the environment.

Environmental protection rules are dedicated to conserving resources and maintaining the health of the natural environment and its inhabitants. Environmental rules affect the use of resources, the consumption of products and services, and the production of services. In addition, however, environmental rules sometimes affect the trade of goods, services and the trade-related aspects of intellectual property rights. When they do, conflicts often arise, and, in the absence of other formal dispute settlement forums, WTO Members often turn to the processes contained within the WTO Understanding on the Rules and Procedures Governing the Settlement of Disputes (DSU) to protect their rights under the various WTO Agreements.

Conflict resolution and dispute settlement are becoming increasingly important at this intersection of the trade and environment fields. In part this is due to the public's attention being captured on this problem more than on any other topic relating to the WTO. In part it is because the severity of environmental problems is becoming more pressing in the developed as well as in the developing nations of the world, and the WTO is perceived as standing in the way of achieving the increased cooperation required to solve environmental problems. Another reason for the increasing importance of conflict resolution in the trade and environment areas lies with the interests of the trade system (or, more specifically, the WTO system) in proving its legitimacy as an international rule-maker. Should global or national environmental concerns be made subsidiary to the profit motives of private industries, the authority of the WTO could be seriously damaged.

This paper addresses the trade–environment issue in relation to the WTO dispute settlement system. First, it gives a brief overview of the dispute settlement process itself. Next, it highlights the past cases brought before the WTO implicating environmental concerns. Finally, it makes some recommendations and speculates on what the future of the trade–environment interface in the WTO may bring.

The WTO's dispute settlement system

The dispute settlement mechanism of the WTO is one of the major achievements of the Uruguay Round of negotiation, and it differs substantially from the diplomacy-oriented resolution of conflicts that characterized the first forty years of the GATT system.

The WTO mechanism set out in the DSU, like GATT dispute settlement practice, is still based on the principle of mutually acceptable resolution of disputes. But now, after mandatory consultations between disputing Members have taken place, the disputing parties may invoke formal procedures for deciding which Member's interpretation of the relevant agreement is legally correct. The formal procedure consists of an exchange of evidence and legal arguments in a hearing, with a resulting report issued by a three-person panel of decision-makers. Each stage of this process occurs according to rules set out in the DSU and its annexes. Adoption of the report is virtually automatic: the entire membership of the Dispute Settlement Body (the Members of the WTO acting as dispute settlement bodies), including the 'winner' of the case, would have to reject the report in order for it not to be considered accepted. Prior to adoption, however, the disputing Members have the right to appeal the legal findings of the panel's opinion. The Appellate

Body, a seven-person standing body, is called upon to issue a final opinion on the dispute, giving the authoritative interpretation of the WTO Agreements.

Although the Dispute Settlement Understanding will be under reconsideration over the course of the next year, proposals for change thus far have been mainly on technical aspects of the process. There have been strong calls for increased transparency in the various dispute settlement steps, but the authority to give the ultimate interpretation of agreement provisions will most likely remain firmly with the Appellate Body.

The trade and environment conflict

The main goals of the WTO system of rules are to improve market access; to support non-discriminatory treatment of imports *vis-à-vis* other imports and *vis-à-vis* domestic products; to reduce competition-distorting non-tariff measures such as subsidies, and to increase the transparency of domestic regulatory regimes. The main goals of environmental protection are to maintain or improve our physical surroundings and to conserve a varied flora and fauna in order to improve the health and happiness of the Earth's inhabitants. Importantly, besides the economic benefits of healthy populations and eco-systems, there is a strong philosophical aspect to environmentalism which does not lend itself readily to being monetized.

There is a difference of opinion among scholars and practitioners as to whether or not there is actually an ultimate conflict between the goals of the trading system and those of environmental protection.[1]

[1] See Sanford E. Gaines, 'Rethinking Environmental Protection, Competitiveness, and International Trade', *U.Chic.Legal F.* 231, 238–48 (1997) (presenting a short history of the attitudinal changes as regards trade and environment), and especially 231 ('With specific reference to the environment and international trade, Agenda 21 contains the affirmation that environment and trade policies should be mutually supportive' [citing Agenda 2 1, UN Doc A/CONF 151126 (1992)] but neither before nor after Rio have governments or analysts been able to agree on how (or even whether) such a mutually supportive relationship can be achieved'); David A. Wirth, 'The Rio Declaration on Environment and Development: Two Steps Forward and One Back, or Vice Versa', 29 *Ga.L.Rev.* 599 (1995) (fearing that economic development necessarily entails environmental damage).

The traditional idea that trade and environment were inevitably at odds with one another gave way in the late 1980s to the teachings of those who emphasized the compatibility of the two systems: trade, they said, leads to increased growth, which in turn leads to wealth, which in turn leads to an interest in environmental protection. Environmental rules, moreover, need not collide with the principles of non-discrimination and economic liberalization enshrined in the WTO (then GATT) Agreements. A decade later, scholars began to question this new thinking.[2] Today, while the trade community generally still adheres to the theory of trade and environmental compatibility, many environmentalists are rediscovering the potential for conflict: they emphasize that, although it may indeed be true that the goals of trade and environmental protection do not generally conflict in practice, there is an inherent potential for conflict between the two that needs to be addressed (in part at least because of an inability to translate the value of a healthy environment into quantifiable economic units).[3]

The WTO officially supports the idea that trade and environment goals are mutually supportive. Whether or not this is a correct view at the level of philosophical fundamentals of the two systems will not be further analysed here. Practical experience would indicate that there is a potential for certain of the rules of the two systems to conflict, but that this conflict is not intrinsic to all of the rules.

What is important to the immediate issue of trade–environment conflict resolution is that almost every agreement within the WTO system contains exceptions from the trade liberalization rules in order to provide for Members' efforts to protect the environment, thus supposedly lowering the likelihood of direct conflicts between trade rules and en-

[2] See, e.g., Paul Brietzke, 'Insurgents in the New International Law', 13 *Wis.Int'l L.J.* 1 (1994) (discussing the different perspectives of 'classical' international law views and the views of 'insurgents', 'without lapsing into the polemics of the conflict models that rival those of a consensus'); Jeffrey L. Dunoff, 'Rethinking International Trade', 19 *U. Pa. J. Int'l Econ. L.* 347 (1998) (examining 'linkage' issues, such as trade and the environment, and concluding that a new way of thinking about these issues must be developed).

[3] To borrow a term from international trade expert John H. Jackson, this is the 'clash of cultures' idea. See John H. Jackson, 'Greening the GATT: Trade Rules and Environmental Policy' in James Cameron, Paul Demaret and Damien Geradin, eds., *Trade & the Environment: The Search for Balance*, Chapter 2 (Cameron May, London, 1994).

vironmental rules. These various provisions include the Preamble to the Marrakesh Agreement Establishing the World Trade Organization; the General Agreement on Tariffs and Trade (GATT) Article XX; the General Agreement on Trade in Services (GATS) Article XIV; the Trade-Related Aspects of Intellectual Property (TRIPs) Agreement Article 27(2); the Agreement on the Application of Sanitary and Phytosanitary Measures (SPS) Agreement Article 2; the Agreement on Technical Barriers to Trade (TBT) Agreement Article2.2; and the Agreement on Subsidies and Countervailing Measures (SCM Agreement) Article 8.2.[4] In terms of usage in dispute settlement, the most prominent among these are the Preamble to the Marrakesh Agreement,[5] GATT Article XX,[6] and Article 2 of the SPS Agreement.[7]

Before beginning the categorization of trade and environment conflicts, four basic observations about trade and environment conflicts should be noted.

---

[4] The text of these Agreements can be found in WTO Secretariat, *The Results of the Uruguay Round of Multilateral Trade Negotiations: Legal Texts*, WTO, Geneva, 1995.

[5] The text of the Preamble states, in relevant part: 'The Parties to this Agreement, *Recognizing* that their relations in the field of trade and economic endeavour should be conducted with a view to ... expanding the production of and trade in goods and services, while allowing for the optimal use of the world's resources in accordance with the objective of sustainable development, seeking both to protect and preserve the environment...[agree to the provisions of the Agreement].'

[6] The text of GATT Article XX states in relevant part: 'Subject to the requirement that such measures are not applied in a manner which would constitute a means of arbitrary or unjustifiable discrimination between countries where the same conditions prevail, or a disguised restriction on international trade, nothing in this Agreement shall be construed to prevent the adoption or enforcement by any contracting party of measures... (b) necessary to protect human, animal or plant life or health... (g) relating to the conservation of exhaustible natural resources if such measures are made effective in conjunction with restrictions on domestic production or consumption ...'

[7] The text of Article 2 SPS Agreement states in relevant part:

1. Members have the right to take sanitary and phytosanitary measures necessary for the protection of human, animal or plant life or health, provided that such measures are not inconsistent with the provisions of this Agreement.
2. Members shall ensure that any sanitary or phytosanitary measure is applied only to the extent necessary to protect human, animal or plant life or health, is based on scientific principles, and is not maintained without sufficient scientific evidence, except as provided for in [the risk assessment provisions].
3. Members shall ensure that their sanitary and phytosanitary measures do not arbitrarily or unjustifiably discriminate between Members where identical or similar conditions prevail...

First, the Preamble to the Agreement Establishing the WTO clearly states that environmental concerns should not be ignored by the Organization and its member states, and a recent Appellate Body decision has implicitly supported this language (and, in doing so, overruled a contradictory panel opinion that had held that the Preamble requires that the trade interests of the Members supersede environmental interests).[8] While it often appeared that the priority of trade interests over other interests had been assumed by the trade community, and while it was certainly feared by the environmental community, the panel in the *Shrimp/Turtle* case was the first to put it so bluntly.[9] The Appellate Body's expression of environment's legitimacy is thus a refreshing surprise and may signal the coming of a truly 'greener' WTO at some time in the future.

Second, despite the professed commitment to environmental protection by panels and the Appellate Body[10] as a whole, the dispute settlement system seems to be trailing the public's ideas (in industrial nations

---

[7] (cont)

... Sanitary and phytosanitary measures shall not be applied in a manner which would constitute a disguised restriction on international trade.

4. Sanitary or phytosanitary measures which conform to the relevant provisions of this Agreement shall be presumed to be in accordance with the obligations of the Member... in particular the provisions of Article XX(b) [GATT]'.

[8] *United States – Import Prohibition of Certain Shrimp and Shrimp Products*, WT/DS58/AB/R at para. 116 (12 October 1998) ('Maintaining, rather than undermining, the multilateral trading system is necessarily a fundamental and pervasive premise underlying the WTO Agreement, but it is not a right or an obligation, nor is it an interpretive rule....')

[9] See *United States – Import Prohibition of Certain Shrimp and Shrimp Products*, WT/DS58/AB/R para. 7.42 (15 May 1998) ('While the Preamble confirms that environmental considerations are important for the interpretation of the WTO Agreement, the central focus of that agreement remains the promotion of economic development through trade; and the provisions of the GATT are essentially turned toward liberalization of access to markets on a nondiscriminatory basis.')

[10] See *United States – Import Prohibition of Certain Shrimp and Shrimp Products*, WT/DS58/AB/R at para. 185 (12 October 1998) ('We have *not* decided that the protection and preservation of the environment is of no significance to the Members of the WTO. Clearly, it is. We have *not* decided that the sovereign nations that are Members of the WTO cannot adopt effective measures to protect endangered species.... Clearly, they can and should. And we have *not* decided that sovereign states should not act together bilaterally, plurilaterally or multilaterally, either within the WTO or in other international fora, to protect endangered species or to otherwise protect the environment. Clearly, they should and do.')

at least) on how to address the trade–environment interface. The WTO has recently been yielding to increasing pressure from certain governments and many non-governmental organizations to open the decision-making and dispute resolution processes to outside participation under the rubric of 'transparency'.[11] Yet a consistent refusal to allow trade interests to be infringed upon by environmental interests in the form of national legislation – no matter how compelling the environmental interest – must cast a doubt on the seriousness with which the WTO takes its non-trade commitments. Continued reliance on pure and narrowly defined multilateralism, to the point of excluding measures that protect the environment more strongly than other Members can politically accept, will perpetuate the WTO's image of an anti-environmental organization. The 'constitutionalization' of the WTO as a result of the Organization's ever more intrusive reach into domestic regulations demands a more nuanced approach to a Member's use of unilateral measures to achieve non-trade goals: environmental protection should be able to be pursued legitimately by a Member, just as a Member may unilaterally impose measures to protect its domestic industries from unexpected inflows of competitive imports (under GATT Article XIX; the Agreement on Safeguards and the Agreement on Agriculture); or the health of its consumers (under the SPS Agreement). As of today, however, what would be allowed as a unilateral measure to protect a Member's economic goals is not permitted when a Member's environmental interests are at stake.

Third, in addressing an environmental barrier to trade in goods, the definition of 'like product' is of utmost importance: in order to establish that the barrier is a measure that disadvantages an imported product, it must be shown that the 'like' (domestic or other imported) product is not similarly disadvantaged. The current definition of 'like product' is based on a narrow definition of 'likeness'. The panels and Appellate Body currently use a two-part analysis to determine whether products are 'like' each other: whether there is a 'commonality of end uses' of

[11] See, e.g., the new links installed by the WTO on its Internet home page (www.wto.org) for the benefit of NGOs and the wider public, as well as various speeches by General Director Renato Ruggiero on the issues of transparency and relations with civil society.

the two products, and whether the products have 'essentially the same physical characteristics'.[12] This has two implications for trade and environment problems: first, the chemical or genetic composition of the product at issue must differ from that of the domestic or other foreign product in order for an environmental law to distinguish the treatment given to the product at issue and remain WTO-compatible; and, second, the environmental law may not distinguish between treatment of 'like products' based on the method of production of the product. The WTO's approach to the latter, the so-called process and production methods or PPM problem, is to consider only the product itself as a product, and to reject the use of trade barriers to protect a different product. As we will see, however, the PPM issue has been downplayed in the most recent Appellate Body decision in this area.

Finally, the structure of the commitments in the GATS makes the use of environmental protection measures aimed at trade in services potentially more valuable than does the exception in GATT for environmental barriers to trade in goods. Unlike in their goods sector obligations, WTO Members may attach conditions to their liberalizing concessions in the field of trade in services. These conditions, presumably, could include requirements to meet environmental standards in the production of the service as well as in the marketing or even in the consumption of the service – whether in the Member's territory or outside of it.

Categories of environmental barriers to trade and WTO dispute settlement

There are several basic types of environmental law that might have an impact on trade. Some have already been declared WTO-'illegal' by the dispute settlement authorities at the WTO. These types of law are considered further below. One should be aware however that the trade–environment debate is both highly complex and under intense

12 *Japan – Taxes on Alcoholic Beverages*, WT/DS8/R, WT/DS10R, WT/DS11/R, para. 6.22 (14 February 1997). See also *Japan – Taxes on Alcoholic Beverages*, WT/DS8/AB/R, WT/DS10/AB/R, WT/DS11/AB/R at p. 23 (4 October 1996) (affirming the panel's use of end-use and physical characteristics in testing for 'likeness' analysis under Article III:2 GATT).

scrutiny. Therefore, these are certainly not the only possible WTO–environment conflicts, and, as discussed above, there may be environmentally friendly changes in the WTO's attitude to such conflicts in the not so distant future.

Import prohibitions

First, there are environmental laws that prohibit the importation of certain environmentally unfriendly goods or services in accordance with a multilateral agreement regulating such trade. An example would be a prohibition on the importation of a particular endangered species (or a good produced from the parts of an endangered species) listed in Annex 1 of the Convention on International Trade in Endangered Species (CITES). Although such a law would violate the GATT prohibition on import restrictions,[13] it would certainly be seen as a legitimate exception under the provisions of GATT Article XX. By virtue of the presence of the species on a multilaterally approved list such as the Annex to CITES, the restriction would almost automatically be considered 'necessary' to protect human, animal or plant life or health',[14] or 'relating to' the conservation of an exhaustible natural resource.[15] In addition, the *chapeau* of Article XX requiring that the measure not be a discriminatory restriction or disguised protectionism would be similarly fulfilled.

A modification of this example would be an environmental law that restricts the importation of a product or service on the basis that that product or service is environmentally unfriendly, but without regard to a multilateral environmental agreement. Even if the Member also prohibits the production of the product domestically, such a law is much more likely to be found to violate a Member's WTO obligations than the first example. This is due to the emphasis given to the *chapeau* of Article XX and the concept of multilateralism that has become domi-

[13] See GATT Article XI.

[14] GATT Article XX(b). Virtually the same exception is found in the General Agreement on Trade in Services (GATS) Article XIV(b).

[15] GATT Article XX(g). The GATS has no equivalent provision.

nant in the opinions of the panels and Appellate Body.[16] In the absence of formal multilateral agreements establishing near unanimity on what constitutes an environmental problem, and on the 'correct' approach to solving the problem, Members will face an uphill battle to get the WTO to approve the implementation of its trade-restricting regulation.

If the law treats domestic producers and foreign producers differently, this is almost certain to be found to amount to a disguised restriction on trade, and therefore to be incompatible with the Member's WTO obligations.[17] Thus, a US Clean Air Act provision that omitted the possibility for foreign gas refiners to establish their own baselines was found WTO-illegal despite the Appellate Body's decision that the measure did relate to the conservation of a natural resource (clean air).[18]

---

[16] The Appellate Body's decision in the recent dispute regarding US regulations limiting shrimp imports based on the injury to turtles from the fishing methods used finds the measures an unexcused violation of US GATT obligations based on the *chapeau* of Article XX. The Appellate Body found that the US unilateral imposition of a policy requiring the use of particular fishing methods and the implementation of the law were arbitrary. *United States – Import Prohibition of Certain Shrimp and Shrimp Products*, WT/DS58/AB/R, at para. 184.

[17] Although different treatment for like products may be permitted as long as conditions of competition are not unequal, the difference in treatment raises the suspicion that it had the aim of discriminating or disadvantaging one group of producers. See *United States – Standards for Reformulated and Conventional Gasoline*, WT/DS2/AB/R (20 May 1996), at DD98A/20: 'There is, or course, no textual basis for requiring identical treatment of domestic and imported products, Indeed, where there is identity of treatment – constituting real, not merely formal, equality of treatment – it is difficult to see how inconsistency with Article 111:4 of GATT would have arisen in the first place. On the other hand, if *no* restrictions on domestically produced like products are imposed at all, and all limitations are placed upon imported products alone, the measure ... would simply be naked discrimination for protecting locally produced goods.' See also *EC Measures Concerning Meat and Meat Products (Hormones)*, WT/DS26/AB/R, and WT/DS48/AB/R (16 January 1998), para. 240 (explaining that arbitrarily different sanitary and phytosanitary standards are violations of the Agreement on the Application of Sanitary and Phytosanitary Measures if the difference in fact discriminates between WTO Members or constitutes a disguised restriction on trade).

[18] *United States – Standards for Reformulated and Conventional Gasoline*, WT/DS2/AB/R (20 May 1996).

Regulations on process and production methods

A second type of environmental law is one that targets products or services that are categorized as environmentally unfriendly because they are produced in such a way as to cause environmental damage. This is the problem of process and production method (PPM) regulations. Here, the WTO law seems to be softening from its absolute prohibition on such regulations. The decision of the GATT panel in Mexico's complaint against the tuna import prohibition embodied the traditional rejection of PPMs by the GATT.[19] This case held that a regulation that prohibited Mexican tuna imports on the basis that the Mexican fishermen's methods for catching tuna simultaneously killed numerous members of an endangered species of dolphins violated US GATT obligations.[20] The prohibited product (tuna), said the panel, was physically identical to other allowed products; the only difference was in the production norms. The measure at issue affected trade in tuna, not dolphins, so the exceptions found in GATT Article XX could not be legitimately invoked.

The PPM conflict arose again in the *Shrimp/Turtle* case.[21] Again, the complained-of regulation prohibited imports of the product (here, shrimp) on the basis of the secondary effects of the production of the product (killing of turtles).[22] And again, the regulation was declared illegal by a WTO panel. This panel's emphasis, however, was on the unilateral character of the action rather than on the separation of the product and the process.[23] The Appellate Body's review of the panel's decision was similarly void of mention of the PPM problem, declaring that, although the environmental protection law did relate to the conservation of an exhaustible natural resource, the application of the law was unjustifiably and arbitrarily discriminatory.[24]

[19] *United States – Restrictions of Imports of Tuna*, BISD 39th Supp., 155 (1992) (decision of 16 August 1991).

[20] Ibid.

[21] See generally WT/DS58/R (fn. 12 above).

[22] The regulation in dispute was US Public Law 101–162, section 609. See description of the regulation in the Panel's findings, WT/DS58/R at paras. 7.2–7.5.

[23] WT/DS58/R, para. 7.40: '...[W]e do not suggest that import markets must exist as an incentive for the destruction of natural resources. Rather, we address a particular situation where a Member has taken unilateral measures which, by their nature, could put the multilateral trading system at risk.'

[24] WT/DS58/AB/R at para. 184.

It is not clear if the *Shrimp/Turtle* case signals a move towards acknowledging the close link between environmental protection goals and production standards, or if the PPM issue was simply avoided in the context of this particular case.

Environmental subsidies

A third category of potential trade–environment conflict is that of a WTO Member offering competitive advantages to environmentally friendly products or services. Environmental subsidies – monies given to a producer for using the presumably more expensive methods of production in order to protect the environment – could theoretically cause a distortion in the conditions of competition, as the products subsidized are not physically different from non-subsidized products.[25] Thus, a question arises as to whether the competitive advantage is warranted. No such case has yet been addressed in the WTO, but if or when one is, it will require renewed investigation into how to define a 'like product' (under the GATT) or a 'like service supplier' (under the GATS) as well as an examination of whether the offsetting of the increased costs of environmentally safe production methods through subsidies is fair, recognizing that other producers to a very large extent are able to simply externalize their pollution costs.

Related to this issue, what if a Member used environmental standards – either positively or negatively – in its treatment of foreign investments or to prevent foreign service suppliers from establishing a commercial presence in its territory? Although it would clearly go

[25] There is a provision under the Subsidies Agreement that allows a Member State to offer a one-time subsidy to an industry in order to assist the industry in complying with a new environmental protection regulation. (Subsidy Agreement, Article 8.2(c)). The use of subsidies, including environmental subsidies, under investigation is particularly important for the service sectors. See GATS Article XV; Decision on Trade in Services and the Environment, in WTO Secretariat, *The Results of the Uruguay Round of Multilateral Trade Negotiations: Legal Texts* 457–458, Geneva, 1995. See also 'WTO Completes Framework for Environmental, Regional and R&D Subsidies', *WTO Focus*, No. 32, p. 2 (July 1998) (reporting that the WTO Committee for Subsidies and Countervailing Duties has established rules to govern binding arbitration in the area of environmental, regional and research and development subsidies).

against the ideas of the WTO for a Member to *lower* environmental standards to attract investments, it is as yet unclear whether establishment of a foreign firm could be made conditional (absent any reservations taken) on its abiding by particularly stringent environmental standards (even if the same standards have to be fulfilled by 'like' domestic firms). The ability of a Member to make service-sector liberalizations selectively and conditionally, however, would imply that such standards would be upheld as GATS-compatible.

Environmental safety standards

Finally, the category of conflicts that started with US and Canadian complaints about the EC's prohibition of imports of hormone-treated beef deserves mention.[26] This category is likely to increase as genetic engineering becomes more common. Cases in this category are not all purely 'environmental' (there are ethical and moral aspects in addition to health concerns), but it does raise similar issues of how or whether to acknowledge a Member's right to impose higher standards than are internationally accepted. Issues related to rules on biotechnology fall into this category.

In this context, the US complaint against the EC's prohibition on imports of beef from cattle treated with growth hormones needs to be mentioned, as it might signal a possible avenue for environmental protection within the WTO system. The *Beef Hormones* case was decided not under the GATT, but instead under the rubric of the Agreement on the Application of Sanitary and Phytosanitary Measures. The SPS Agreement encourages harmonization of health standards worldwide by providing preferential procedures to Members with a view to ensuring that their domestic health regulations can withstand WTO scrutiny even if they discriminate among products on the basis of their country of origin. The Appellate Body's approach to the SPS Agreement has differed from its approach to the GATT. Although the European Community's restrictions on imports of hormone-treated beef were

[26] *EC Measures Concerning Meat and Meat Products (Hormones)*, WT/DS26/AB/R and WT/DS48/AB/R (16 January 1998).

considered to violate their obligations,[27] this was due to failures in the risk assessment procedure that had been applied by the EC,[28] rather than to any violation of the conditions allowing a Member to impose trade restrictions based on dangers to human, animal or plant health or safety.[29] Although the panel decision in *Beef Hormones* rested on the principles of multilateral rules (as embodied in the Codex Alimentarius), the Appellate Body gave much more deference to the Member's decision to use trade restrictions in the area of sanitary and phytosanitary measures than in 'regular' environmental areas. Overturning the panel's ruling that a Member's regulation that establishes higher standards than an existing international standard should be treated as an exception to the general rules of the SPS Agreement, the Appellate Body held that the establishment of [peculiar] levels of sanitary or phytosanitary protection is an autonomous right and not an 'exception' from a 'general obligation' under Article 3.1.[30] Such differences must be noted and evaluated individually: one case cannot be the basis for talking about jurisprudential trends, although it could be of future importance.[31]

27 Ibid. at para. 253 (l).

28 Ibid.

29 Ibid. at para. 253(h)

30 Ibid. at para. 172.

31 The *Salmon* case addressed a 'typical' use of sanitary measures rather than one relating to biotechnology. See *Australia – Measures Affecting Importation of Salmon*, WT/DS18/R (12 June 1998); WT/DS18/AB/R (20 October 1998). Here again, however, there seems to be a more deferential attitude of the panel and Appellate Body to a Member's use of trade restrictions for health than there is under the GATT environmental exceptions. In *Salmon*, the Appellate Body found that there was no risk assessment made by the Australian government, as required by Article 5.1 of the SPS Agreement, and thus the import prohibition on fresh, frozen or chilled salmon violated Article 5.1: WT/DS18/AB/R at para. 136. In analysing the compatibility of the import prohibition with Article 5.6 of the SPS Agreement, the Appellate Body comes to no definite conclusions (owing to a lack of sufficient fact-finding by the panel on this issue), but asserts that the Member itself may determine the level of protection it desires. Consequently, the WTO review of the measures used to achieve such a goal is limited to determining whether they are the least trade-restrictive measures to achieve that level of protection: the level of protection itself is not to be questioned. Even a zero-risk level is permissible. See WT/DS18/AB/R at paras. 193–213.

The future of trade and environment dispute settlement

In conclusion, the overall picture of where the WTO will stand one year from now on the issue of environmental regulations that restrict trade is still unclear, but the professed trend towards a more environmentally friendly Organization has not – one hopes – yet neared its apex.[32] The Ministerial Declaration of 20 May 1998 committed Members of the WTO to 'continue to improve ... efforts towards the objectives of sustained economic growth and sustainable development'. However, until the dispute settlement system can internalize such commitments, the words remain empty. This 'internalization' process must begin with a deep conviction within the system of the need to balance Members' trade interests with non-trade interests. Recognizing the legitimacy of environmental interests was a start, but simply voicing this recognition is not enough: the next step should be to act on this conviction by treating environmental interests as equal in the dispute settlement system.

A balanced system also requires the WTO to release its adherence to the principle of 'pure multilateralism'. While one could well argue that multilateral consensus on the need for a high level of environmental protection (or an unwavering adherence to just wages and comfortable working conditions) is an admirable goal, the reality is that the world is far from achieving such an aim. Indeed, the WTO Members cannot even agree on how to treat the much more quantifiable problem of cartelization within an industry. Disallowing environmental protection regulations merely on the basis of their being implemented unilaterally quashes the ability of the most environmentally protective of WTO Members to stimulate the addressing of a particular problem. Allowing only those trade-hindering measures found in multilateral environmental agreements slows the movement towards the goal of a healthy ecosystem. It is entirely possible that the process of arriving at global consensus could take decades – time enough for irreparable damage to

---

32 The future of the trade–environment discussion is evident through further WTO instruments, namely the Decision on Trade and Environment and the Decision on Trade in Services and the Environment. Formally organized discussions such as the one that took place in mid-March 1998 also push the trade–environment agenda forward.

occur. The WTO needs to adopt a more differentiated stance in its evaluation of unilateral trade barriers imposed to further environmental goals.

Hope also lies in the more liberal attitude of the Appellate Body to the Members' use of the SPS Agreement and the potential for Members to attach conditions to their liberalizations in trade in services. Nevertheless, attention to the workings of the WTO dispute settlement process by those outside the WTO and pressure to force the dispute settlement process to recognize non-trade interests as legitimate are both necessary to the future of global environmental protection.

The *Shrimp/Turtle* dispute and the future

James Cameron

Introduction

This short paper addresses the 'how' of dispute settlement. What can be done to change the way the dispute settlement system operates in order better to accommodate environment and development issues? To be even more precise, what kinds of environment and development issues are currently not adequately accommodated in the dispute settlement system?

The *Shrimp/Turtle* dispute

The substantive issues

First, some initial remarks about the substance of the *Shrimp/Turtle* dispute. There are still questions to be resolved about the distinction between multilateral and unilateral measures, which the *Shrimp/Turtle* case does not determine. The relationship between MEAs and the Multilateral Trading System is not settled, and we must put effort into that, distinct from dispute resolution, before we make sense of precisely the sort of constitutional issues that Professor Cottier's paper raises. Indeed, we have to put effort into that relationship before we can deal with the proper integration of environmental policy into the various international agreements we have on economic issues.

The *Shrimp/Turtle* case is, in my view, a significant step forward in the debate on trade and environment. From a legal point of view, it is a significant advance on previous jurisprudence and an enormous leap in respect of the panel decision. It is still a bad decision for turtles. However, as a matter of law it is more rational, more cogently argued, and it is a sensible reference point for trade–environment disputes. The Appellate Body went out of its way to say what it did *not* decide and made a kind of plea for understanding. Much of that language will be very useful for future cases. The way Article XX was interpreted is acceptable, although too much remains loaded onto the *chapeau* – and I do not quite understand why the *chapeau* has anything particular to say about MEAs.

The irony here is that for many years I have argued for a technical fix in Article XX which would involve adding a reference to multilateral environmental agreements in a sub-paragraph, possibly attached to an Understanding which would explain why reference to the MEAs is relevant and how it could be used to settle disputes – including, for example, a definition of what a 'multilateral environmental agreement' is.

However, since WTO cases have loaded more responsibility onto the *chapeau* of Article XX, we have now to pay attention to that line of reasoning. It is not possible to solve the problem technically by adding a new paragraph to Article XX which relates to MEAs. We need something that informs the interpretation of the *chapeau* as well. That might argue for a separate set of negotiations related specifically to that question. There is no simple way of curing the problem relating to MEAs by an amendment of one of the sub-paragraphs of Article XX now that the reasoning in *Shrimp/Turtle* is established.

The procedural issues

Another critical part of the *Shrimp/Turtle* decision is procedural, and it relates to *amicus curiae* briefs.[1] I do not want just to talk about *amicus* briefs, but it is a very important step in a process for procedural reform of WTO's dispute settlement system. The Appellate Body has cleared away opposition to a point that has been made for some years by NGOs and independent experts about the opportunity for submitting additional information to a panel process from outside non-governmental sources. The Appellate Body has said that there is nothing in the rules to prevent that. In their conclusions, they inverted a simple sentence: there is nothing in the WTO's Dispute Settlement Under-

[1] *Editors' note*: literally, 'friend of the court' briefs. These are briefs submitted by a bystander, normally a lawyer, who informs an adjudicator on a point of law or fact on which he or she is doubtful or mistaken (adapted from *Mozley and Whiteley's Law Dictionary*, Butterworths, London, 1977).

standing which prevents non-requested information from being put into the process by non-governmental actors. In one sense, they have simply stated the rules. Nothing very novel about that – but the way it is put is very clear and encourages a positive response.

In this particular case, especially at the Appellate Body stage, the additional information that was not requested by any government was attached to the US arguments that were put into the Appellate Body. It was physically attached, but not attached in terms of argument. The United States did not say it adopted these views; it simply said, 'We think you ought to hear them.' So the consequence is removal of an impediment to putting in information, information that is in fact more in the nature of a legal argument than simply factual information; then an accepted route emerges for attaching that information to a government, with that government being able to distance itself from the substance of the arguments but to endorse the opportunity to put information into the process. By the Appellate Body stage, the 'information' is really only legal argument. So that is a route that people can use now, provided they can get a government to do what the US government did in the *Shrimp/Turtle* case. The US government has said that it will be open to doing this in the future, but that it will of course maintain the discretion not to do it if it does not want to, which is an important qualification. Therefore, the UK government could do the same, or any other government could say, 'All right, come and stick your *amicus curiae* brief on the edge of our submissions, and we will make sure that the Appellate Body understands that it is not our argument but we think they ought to hear it.'

A word of warning for the NGO community, especially for the environment/development NGO community. I would not like to draft a rule that says 'only nice NGOs can put information in, and not wicked business associations'. So this opens up a route for other non-state actors to contribute their views independently of government, which the government can address in precisely the same way. If the government does not like what is there or considers it irrelevant, it does not have to attach it.

There are clearly risks here, because this puts a great deal of power in the hands of the private sector, power that could be mobilized to make sure that additional arguments could be put in which would be persuasive and reflect private-sector interests. On the other hand, I believe there is some value in a distinction being made between what is an avowedly private interest and the public policy expression of a government. So there will be occasions when the government quite likes the idea of being able to separate its view from that of the private sector. It might give governments a little more space to balance other competing public policy objectives, including those related to the environment.

That raises the question: what if what is in your 'information' (I keep using that general phrase, because that is one that has been accepted by the Appellate Body, but it is really something more precise than that) is not what a government wants to hear and is really a counter-argument? In the US situation, although the information contained *different* arguments, they were broadly arguments supportive of the US position, connected to it in some other way and making other points but certainly not on the other side of the case. The Appellate Body has made no ruling on that, and it has not said that there is any other formal route created which will enable submission of an *amicus* brief that is not accepted by a government. However, neither has it been ruled out, and the Appellate Body has certainly not taken away this option. The way I interpret this is as an invitation to governments who are interested in, and want, reform to supply an additional procedure to say 'OK, here is what we could accept'.

The future of conflict resolution in the WTO

What might an additional procedure look like? The first point is that there are real and genuine fears about the process being overwhelmed with lots of *amicus curiae* briefs flowing in. I believe those fears are exaggerated. The whole world is not terribly interested in sending in *amicus curiae* briefs, and the NGO community is perfectly capable of organizing itself to submit fewer documents and deciding who is going to do what – generally controlling the flow, in other words. However, one must recognize these fears and be alive to them.

I would argue for rather strict rules for sending in these pieces of 'information'. They need to be limited in length, for example. At panel stage it is fair enough to put in facts that are of relevance, but at the Appellate Body stage only legal arguments should be permitted. In addition, there is a value in creating what in the UK we call 'your day in court'. People who are involved with disputes really want to say to someone what it is that makes them angry. They want a platform to say: 'This is my view; you have to listen to it.' I would be in favour of creating within the panel process – and also within the Appellate Body process, for an even shorter period of time – a 'day in court', an opportunity for NGOs or indeed business associations to come along and present their arguments very briefly – if you cannot make your main point in 15 minutes, you are not really worth listening to. The US Supreme Court has very tight time limits; the House of Lords in the UK has very tight time limits. So you have an opportunity to come and make your point, but it is a limited-time opportunity and you organize your public relations and your media coverage around the debate and get some publicity for it. The panel is informed, it comes to understand this weird counter-view that it has never really been confronted with face-to-face, but at a certain point that is it – your time is up; the proceedings continue.

There are some other changes that also need to be made in order to make the process more open and accountable generally, but with particular benefit to environment and development organizations.

First, panel and Appellate Body reports are far too long. It is just not sensible to be sending out 400-page reports to people around the world, even if you can get them on the Internet – in itself a very significant innovation in opening up access to information, and one which the NGO community pushed for and achieved. We have to stop governments requiring that all of their arguments be repeated faithfully in the decisions of both the panel and the Appellate Body. It is simply not necessary. If governments want you to know what they have said, then they should publish it, making their arguments public as documents as soon as they feel it is appropriate, and allowing panels and the Appellate Body to make summaries.

I would like to see the system evolve to a point where judgments are really nice, crisp, and written in plain English, so that people can understand why a technical trade rule that has been applied, and that affects a public policy issue, concerns them. That discipline is important if accountability, acceptability, credibility – all these words we work with – are to be the result. So, cut down the length, make the documents public, and allow panels to make succinct decisions and judgments that are clear and can be summarized. Conclusions sections in panel reports are very clear – but there can be 400 pages of unnecessary text leading up to them.

Second, it is important also that there is some way of narrowing the gap between how the Appellate Body reasons and how panels reason. *Shrimp/Turtle* is astonishing. How do you explain to an outsider that the same institution can come to such widely different views about the same rules?

In the European Community we have a function that we give to someone called the 'Advocate General'. The function is to maintain consistency in legal reasoning case by case, and to provide a way whereby panels of judges, which change over time, can receive a regular message about what the law is. It is an opinion that is published and is therefore useful for scholarship, for research for future legal cases. It does not bind the panel or the judge at all but it is relevant. I believe we need something like that for the WTO. So as not to mimic it, I would call it a 'Counsel to the Panel'. A Counsel to the Panel would offer some way of guiding the interpretation of the rules to make them more consistent. A Counsel to the Panel could also be more accessible to other, external, legal arguments, for example by going out and taking part in conferences and meetings, listening and picking up the views and passing them on to inform the panel.

I suggest, therefore, that these sorts of institutional reform would be of benefit to the system as a whole and of particular benefit to those who represent business, environment and development questions, because they would enable them to become users of the system. If you use a system, you can infuse it with your beliefs, attitudes and points of view, and you feel more as if it represents you. That is really the enterprise we should be embarking upon.

Part IV
Environmental regulation and international investment

The Role of Foreign Direct Investment

The case of India

Veena Jha

Introduction

During the 1990s, foreign direct investment (FDI) has come to play an increasingly important role in providing India with sources of long-term capital. Increasing levels of FDI also holds the promise of promoting sustainable development in so far as it encourages the transfer and harmonization of environmentally friendly technologies and practices across borders. In India it is not clear whether FDI and its associated transnational corporations (TNCs) have contributed sufficient leadership in fulfilling local and global environmental targets.

In India, the principal emerging issues with respect to international investment and the need for sustainable development focus first and foremost on the incorporation of a large number of sectors and regions that have not so far benefited from FDI; second, on fostering the positive role that TNCs could play in conjunction with national governments in achieving environmental goals; and, third, on ensuring that the competition between states for FDI should not induce a race-to-the-bottom approach. The national and state governments will increasingly have to consider and weigh policies with a view to encouraging and fostering healthy competition and avoiding policies that seek to attract capital on the basis of lowest-common-denominator variables in terms of health and environmental standards.

The role of FDI in the Indian economy has varied over time, largely as a response to the changing perception and policies of the Indian government. Of late, the increasing and important role of FDI has been recognized by most political parties, both as a source of finance and, more importantly, as a source of top-of-the-line technologies. While there has been a move towards greater liberalization of FDI across the board, certain priority sectors such as infrastructure have been especially identified for investment promotion activities.

FDI has been increasing steadily during the 1990s, but, by comparison with other Asian countries, FDI levels in India are low. In fact, FDI accounts for no more than two per cent of the total investment annually. Recognizing the important role that FDI can play in supplementing domestic savings to achieve the targeted growth rates of GDP, the government has set an ambitious annual target of US$10 billion for FDI inflows by the end of this century.[1] A number of policies, such as tax breaks, permitting FDI in sectors that were earlier reserved for domestic investors, increasing the limits of equity participation, reducing tariffs, etc., have been put in place. It is also hoped that, with declining investment opportunities in a number of Asian countries, some of that investment may be diverted to India.

Simultaneously with growing FDI, concerns for pollution associated with rapid industrialization have increased. An interesting dilemma emerges in the Indian context, out of the twin objectives of attracting investment and protecting the environment. While environmental laws and regulations do not discriminate between foreign and domestic investors, pragmatic considerations arising from capital shortages and technological needs may *de facto* result in a more favourable treatment being granted to the foreign investor. Whether this results in tax breaks or indirect subsidies or easier environmental clearance procedures remains an open and largely empirical question. Another important question is whether some environmental safeguards may be needed in view of India's emphasis on promoting large-scale projects in sectors such as mining and power, a number of which are intensive in the use of environmental resources.

To the extent that there is a trade-off between better environmental performance and more FDI, it is important to resolve this trade-off to make the two goals mutually reinforcing. There may however also be a number of cases where FDI can be environmentally benign or may

[1] Considering that average annual inflows in the post-economic reform period have averaged at US$2.5 billion, apart from 1997–8 when it was estimated at US$4.1 billion, this appears to be an ambitious target indeed. See Secretariat for Industrial Assistance (SIA) newsletters, Delhi, various issues.

actually promote better environmental management. It is important to reinforce these synergies through appropriate government policies. If the state is better administered, then implementation of environmental norms and standards may be better, though this is not necessarily the case. The 'dirty industry' migration hypothesis would suggest that states with a lower record of implementation of environmental standards would therefore attract the highest levels of FDI. This theory, however, is not vindicated by actual inflows of FDI to various states. The states that are best administered, and therefore have better track records of implementation of environmental legislation, appear to attract the highest levels of FDI.

Environmental issues, foreign investors and host countries

It is difficult to generalize on the environmental behaviour of the TNCs. Several factors are relevant and while macroeconomic studies reflect the absence of significant 'dirty industry' migration, they do not take account of the projects that have been shelved on account of environmental considerations. While it is difficult to get an estimate of TNCs that are environmental defaulters, or to estimate whether their environmental performance is better or worse than comparable local firms, an analysis of some specific examples will help clarify the rationale behind the environmental behaviour of specific TNCs in specific activities. Both positive and negative examples are considered below.

Environmental concerns

A number of environmental concerns have been voiced about the operations of TNCs in India. NGOs believe that, given the high fiscal deficit as a proportion of total GNP, the national government would be reluctant to control the operations of TNCs, thus leading to ecological disasters. The dominance of TNCs in environmentally harmful sectors is also a matter of concern, as this could mean that a large proportion of TNC investment in India would necessarily focus on these environmentally sensitive sectors.

Indian NGOs have also expressed concern about the depletion and excessive use of India's genetic resources by TNCs. As TNCs control much of the world's genetic seed stocks as well as financing the bulk of biotechnology research worldwide, they can reap large financial rewards from patenting life forms in India.

Other concerns voiced by various stakeholders relate to resource depletion caused by the scale of operation of TNCs, e.g. deep sea fishing, and the transfer of environmentally harmful technologies and products. Still others that have recently come to the fore in the Indian context relate to the implementation of multilateral environmental agreements (MEAs). Some commentators have claimed that, though TNCs have access to the right technologies, MEAs may be conferring double advantages by providing them with a captive market and monopoly prices accruing from the use of patented technologies.[2]

Highly publicized incidents involving TNCs. The most publicized environmental disaster involved Union Carbide in the Bhopal gas disaster. A leakage of a toxic gas from the plant killed thousands and injured as many. It also polluted the water and the soil and caused cancer in a number of victims. The efforts of the Indian government to bring criminal charges against Carbide's top officials were frustrated. When the government of India, representing Bhopal victims, tried to bring this case to the US courts, the judge ruled that the case should be transferred to Indian courts on the grounds of the doctrine of *forum non conveniens*, i.e. the legal doctrine that lawsuits brought in by non-US plaintiffs can be dismissed if it is too inconvenient or improper to try the case in the United States. This doctrine, according to some, gives TNCs strong protection from having to account financially for the damages that they cause outside their home country.[3] To challenge this judgment, a counter-doctrine on 'multilateral enterprise liability', which emphasizes that the parent company has control over its subsidiaries and should have controlled the subsidiaries' affairs, was invoked but was not accepted by the court. The

[2] See J. Watal, 'Technology Transfer in the Context of the Montreal Protocol', paper prepared for the UNEP-UNCTAD Project on the Use of Trade and Positive Measures under MEAs (1997).

[3] See R. Hager, *Bhopal: Courting Disaster*, Covert Action, Summer 1995.

Box 2: Would Du Pont endanger the environment?

- It was feared that Goa would be used as a dumping ground for the hazardous chemicals produced by the proposed plant. These fears were rejected as baseless by the companies on the grounds that both the Central Pollution Control Board and the State Pollution Control Board had granted them 'no objection' certificates. It was also claimed that Du Pont had been running this type of plant in several locations worldwide and all were well within the specified toxic limits.
- Critics argued that Du Pont was bringing in an outdated product, since users all over the world had switched to 'kevalar' which was considered technically superior nylon to 6,6. Du Pont's defence to this was that the superior product would cost more, and in any case nylon 6,6 was superior to nylon 6, which was being widely used in India.
- It was believed that outdated machinery was being brought in by Du Pont from its Richmond, Virginia, plant and that it could endanger the workers at the plant in addition to increasing the possibility of causing environmental damage. Du Pont's counter-claim suggested that only a few machines, not exceeding 5 per cent of the total cost, were being brought from Richmond, and that the rest of the plant would be new.
- No site appraisal or environmental impact or disaster management plan for the project was carried out. Moreover, raw materials like hexamethylene diamine and adipic acid were considered to be hazardous and were classified as hazardous health substances by US health authorities and in both cases extensive care and protection was demanded in their use. Du Pont claimed that in the United States adipic acid was used to make candy and that the economic benefits of the project would be substantial.
- Concerns regarding disposal and handling of wastes, which would be contracted out, were also raised. Du Pont issued a counter-assurance that the contractors would be trained and that, as it had the technology to ensure their safe disposal, it could assure the citizens that wastes would be disposed safely.

case was shifted to Indian courts where, according to some, a settlement about a sixth the size of the original claim was made.[4]

Another highly publicized case which was more successfully resolved involved the US-based chemical giant Du Pont and its joint venture partner Thapar (see Box 2). This joint venture in the mid-1980s applied for permission to build a factory for producing nylon 6,6, a synthetic cord used in tyres. For this purpose they proposed to erect their plant in a remote village in Goa. With a projected investment of US$200 million, this was supposed to become the world's largest producer of nylon 6,6. The project was opposed by citizens' groups, and later an Expert Committee which was appointed to look into the safety

[4] I. Jaising, 'Legal Let-Down', in T.R. Chouhan et al., *Bhopal: The Inside Story*, Apex Press, NY, and the Other India Press, Goa, India, 1994.

aspects of the project rejected it on several grounds. In addition to environmental objections, several other claims regarding the economic benefits of the project were made. It was claimed that the employment generated by the plant would not be comparable to several smaller units with the same overall capacity, and that the benefits being offered by the government in terms of land at near zero cost and infrastructure, i.e. roads, were considered excessive and disproportionate to the economic benefits that would be generated by the project.

Protests against the plant were voiced by environmental groups as early as 1988 and began to arouse concern among local communities located near the project. In response to rising public enquiry, Goa's Legislative Assembly created a House Committee to examine the nylon 6,6 project. The Committee instituted a series of public hearings. After interviewing Du Pont employees as well as many people and organizations in Goa, in late 1990 the Committee recommended, on both environmental and social grounds, that the project be shelved. The Goan state government refused to abide by the Committee's findings, but these findings helped to galvanize public opinion, and three governing councils of villages near the plant passed resolutions against the project. During the following two years several campaigns were held, but Du Pont started construction of the plant in September 1994. At the actual construction site, there was a large rally by citizens in which they pledged to tear down the boundary wall and equipment. There was a wide-scale boycott of those people involved in the project, with shops and hotels refusing to service them. Several anti-nylon protestors were arrested and one activist died during a campaign. This marked a turnaround in Du Pont's attitude. In June Du Pont announced that it would be shifting its plant to another state, Tamil Nadu.[5]

The shifting of the 6,6 nylon plant from Goa to Tamil Nadu could be indicative of two factors: (a) the environmental absorptive capacity of Tamil Nadu may be higher than that of Goa; (b) economic considerations in Tamil Nadu may have been given priority over environmental considerations.

[5] See J. Greer and K. Singh, *TNCs and India*, Public Interest Research Group/Shahdara, Delhi, 1996; also see M. Cabral e Sa, 'Thapar-Du Pont: Troubled Times', in *Business and Finance*, 31 January 1991.

Another case that has been publicized in the media concerns the transfer of a hazardous technology which is banned for domestic use in Norway. The controversial technology was a membrane cell plant whose operations were shut down in Norway in 1992, under pressure from environmental groups against the use of chlorine in pulp bleaching. Norway has a national policy which targets organochlorine chemicals and includes a provision that the technology in question be reduced and ultimately eliminated. In addition, its international commitments for the reduction and elimination of harmful chemicals, such as the North Sea Ministerial Declarations of 1987 and 1990, should have put natural restraints on the transfer of environmentally harmful technologies. In a counter-claim, however, the Norwegian firm claimed that the technology being sold to India was not the outdated variety, and the intermediary (another multinational) through which the deal had been effected claimed that it had not brokered the deal.[6]

Other cases that have been brought up by the media concern distilleries for making alcohol. A number of these companies are foreign-owned, and considerable scepticism has been expressed over claims by a distillery called Kedia Castle Dellon that a distillery could be a 'zero-pollution' plant. A plan submitted by the company to the State Pollution Control Board in Rajasthan claims that about 1,800 cubic metres of spent wash from the distillery would be processed daily to produce cattle feed. About 90–95 per cent of the wash would be evaporated, leading to the claim that effluents and waste water would not be let out onto neighbouring agricultural land. Citizens' groups have, however, raised questions as to how much energy would be required to evaporate such large quantities of water and where the spent wash would go in case of a shutdown of this cattle-feed plant. They object to the granting of a 'no objection' certificate without a proper environmental impact assessment. Apart from the possible pollution by this plant, local residents are also worried about possible groundwater depletion by water-guzzling distilleries.[7]

In another case, an Expert Panel held Century Rayon responsible for 11 deaths from the inhalation of toxic gases emanating from the re-

[6] See P. Seema, 'Norway Ships Banned Technology to India', *Telegraph*, 1 April 1995.

[7] A. Krishna, 'Is Zero-pollution Distillery Really Possible?', *IED*, 20 May 1995.

lease of untreated spin bath solution in an open sewage canal. The Panel suggested that all major hazardous industries should systematically identify the processes used for treating and storing hazardous chemicals, and factories should carry out a consequence analysis in cases where effluents include chemicals beyond threshold safety levels. This would help prevent disasters.[8]

Political views on environmental responsibilities of TNCs There are several divergent views on the impact of FDI on environment and development. Some, notably NGOs, contend that, in a rush to attract foreign investment, environmental regulations are now being violated.[9] Many TNCS which produce products that are hazardous to human health and the environment have been given permission to establish operations in India, including Dow, Atochem, Kumaia Chemicals Limited and Mitsubishi. It is claimed that these companies, faced with shrinking international markets on account of environmental concerns, are setting up plants in India to boost their share in the Indian agrochemicals market.[10]

Many foreign investment projects that have been approved for augmenting foreign exchange earnings, such as fisheries, aquaculture and agribusiness operations, have not been found to be environmentally benign. Foreign companies involved in deep sea fishing and fish processing have been accused of overfishing, leading to a loss of traditional fishermen's livelihood as well as a loss of domestic markets and a depletion of marine resources. According to the National Fish Workers Forum, 100 per cent export-oriented joint ventures are likely to deprive nearly 300 million Indian consumers of fish, as well as displacing 7.5 million fisherfolk.[11]

Foreign corporations involved in shrimp and prawn production including aquaculture have been accused of ignoring the long-term con-

---

[8] See 'Toxic Waste: Action Against Century Rayon Sought', *Hindustan Times*, 13 April 1995.

[9] See Greer and Singh, *TNCs and India*.

[10] See J. Karliner, 'The Bhopal Tragedy: Ten Years After', *The Global Pesticide Campaigner*, December 1994.

[11] See T. Kocherr, 'Campaign against Joint Ventures', *The State of India's Economy 1994–95,* 1995.

sequences on the people and the environment. It is claimed by a number of environmental groups that the state and the central government, in their desire to earn foreign exchange, have ignored the impact of shrimp farming on agricultural land. In just ten years, land used for shrimp farming becomes barren and unproductive; in addition, shrimp farming leads to degradation of coastal mangrove swamps and water pollution.

It is also claimed by environmental NGOs that, further to the liberalization of investment and trade in 1991, concessions on taxes and customs duties have created a boom in the chemicals industry in India. Those same concessions may also have encouraged toxic waste dumping and migration of polluting and hazardous technologies to India. Plants are being set up without proper environmental clearances from pollution control authorities and NGOs have expressed serious concern about the health and safety of workers living near such plants. They view the Bhopal gas tragedy as an example of a TNC walking away from its environmental responsibilities.

The 'liberalizers' argue that TNCs provide enormous financial resources for investment in India, and thus are likely to be more careful of the environment than comparable local firms. In addition, the top-of-the-line technologies available to them, their access to distribution and marketing networks and their export intensities furnish a number of intangible assets which could be directed towards environmental improvements. Their considerable expertise in facets of product development, using brand names for marketing, advertising and R&D, can also be used to enhance their environmental performance. This same expertise would also expose them to a lot of criticism should they renege from their environmental obligations. The liberalizers further argue that in India protection levels are still excessively high, and thus the country is unable to reap the full benefits, including environmental benefits, of FDI. They therefore advocate further liberalization as an effective mechanism for enforcing standards, including environmental ones, both on national companies and on TNCs.[12]

[12] See Sengupta, A. Banik and R. Karthuria, *FDI Inflows to India in the Post Reform Period: An Analysis of the Structural and Policy Impediments*, Occasional Paper no. 3, International Management Institute Research Paper Series, 1996.

There are several differences in the perceptions of different states regarding the problems associated with foreign investment. Their perspectives are also coloured by their ability to influence FDI as well as their ability to attract FDI. Sometimes these perspectives have been at variance with the central government, as was exemplified by the case of Enron in Maharastra.

It is also interesting to note that, while the nylon 6,6 plant was shelved in Goa, negotiations on establishing it in another state, i.e. Tamil Nadu, were immediately undertaken. That states may enter into some kind of competitive deregulation in order to attract FDI, though not impossible, is however unlikely. This is because FDI flows into states that have better infrastructures and markets. Generally speaking, there is a positive correlation between better infrastructure and better governance, with the result that implementation of environmental laws and norms are also better in states with better infrastructure.

Positive environmental contributions by TNCs

While the preceding section has highlighted several examples of TNCs wilfully flouting environmental regulations and Acts, there are equally a number of examples where TNCs have had a positive effect on the environment. The most striking examples are the activities of TNCs in environmental services such as the provision of solar power, waste management consultancies and water cleaning projects. TNCs have also been active in testing and certification, including certification for environmental management.

An opposing view however holds that TNCs have introduced many dynamic changes in the Indian economy. The example of Maruti Udyog, which is a collaboration with Suzuki, is often cited as an important example. Maruti cars were the first to use catalytic converters and unleaded fuel. Today a number of newer vehicles on the road are designed to use unleaded fuel. In the auto-components sector as well, strict quality controls and close cooperation with vendors have changed the market's perception of design and quality and revolutionized the components industry through a philosophy of vendor upgrading. Maruti actively nurtured some critical component industries by establishing 11 joint venture companies for auto parts to help push quality and productivity concerns upstream. It has also pushed up the levels of fuel efficiency so that competing cars are forced to adhere to higher fuel efficiency standards.

Building environmental infrastructures. TNCs are becoming active in the generation of alternative and renewable energy sources. TNCs such as Amoco and Enron are in the process of creating a large solar photovoltaic power project. Another California-based company called Optimum Power International is in the process of generating wind power from the breezy high-altitude locations in Kerala. Agreements to supply electricity from these units to state governments at economic and fixed prices are also being negotiated. Some of these projects are being assisted by funding from the World Bank, the Asian Development Bank and national aid agencies such as DANIDA. It is envisaged that some of the power stations will also test equipment used in wind turbines, will train personnel in the wind energy sector and will provide an information centre on better and alternative sources of energy, including building a library.[13]

A number of Canadian and American TNCs are currently entering into joint ventures in the area of waste management in India. These companies are in the process of negotiating the provision of such services to local municipalities.

Some TNCs such as Philips are also providing training to local companies to implement ISO 14000 standards on environmental management systems (EMSs); 32 companies in India have obtained accreditation under ISO 14000 standards, of which a significant number are Indian companies. Some testing and accreditation bodies that are transnational in nature, e.g. the SGS, are also collaborating with the national standardization bodies, such as the Bureau of Indian Standards, to build the infrastructure required to implement ISO 14000 standards on a wider scale.

The Indo-German Board of Trade has also set up several testing agencies to test for toxic chemicals (such as pentachlorophenol) in

[13] See 'MNCs to Enter Alternative Energy Sector', *Economic Times*, 15 April 1995.

products such as leather and textiles. These testing agencies are either set up by multinationals or funded by them. Multinationals have also taken the lead in manufacturing environmentally friendly substitutes to azo dyes and for providing testing facilities for them. Most of these substitutes and testing facilities, however, can be utilized only by large firms as they are too expensive for small and medium-sized enterprises which comprise about 70 per cent of the textile industry in India.[14]

In response to a ban on the use of azo dyes in Germany, several large firms including TNCs carried out a detailed analysis of the chemical components of the dyes used by them in order to judge their eco-friendliness and to gauge the extent to which they were required to find substitutes. Once this was established, they were able to persuade the dyestuff manufacturers, also dominated by TNCs, to switch to environmentally friendly substitutes. In fact, within a year TNCs and other Indian large firms had switched to environmentally friendly alternative dyestuffs.[15]

In both the leather and textiles sector, some TNCs have not only set up common effluent treatment plants (CETs), but have also provided consultancy services to local companies to set up CETs. These services are beyond the economic capacity of the small and medium-sized enterprises that dominate production in both these sectors. In the leather sector, however, environmental infrastructure is better established locally than in the textiles sector. While testing for environment friendliness of products is carried out both by TNCs and by government-sponsored agencies, often the waiting time for the latter is much longer than that for the former, perhaps because of the much higher prices charged by TNCs.[16]

Another example is that of NOCIL, an agro-chemical-producing TNC which installed on environmental infrastructure following notification by the Central Pollution Control Board that its environmental standards did not meet the requirements. This firm has taken care to

---

[14] See S. Das, *The Differential Impacts of Environmental Policies on Small and Large Enterprises in India – with special reference to the Textile and Clothing and Leather and Footwear Sectors*, report prepared for UNCTAD under project INT/92/A58 1996.

[15] Ibid.

[16] Ibid.

ensure that spills and wastes are minimized, as well as putting up R&D efforts to overcome problems identified in maintaining and operating a common effluent treatment plant. The company has established a well-defined system for environmental management under the managing director. The set-up is designed to emphasize a self-regulatory mechanism. Following these changes the Central Pollution Control Board gave its consent for its operation.[17] Cooperating with authorities on the setting of high environmental standards TNCs have had a much more decisive influence in setting voluntary standards than mandatory environmental standards. Examples of TNCs acting in collaboration with national authorities are to be observed particularly in dyestuffs and in refrigeration in India. Both these industries are dominated by TNCs.

In the dyestuff sector there are no statutory eco-standards. However, European manufacturers of dyes and organic pigments have voluntarily formed the Ecological and Technological Toxicological Association of Dyes and Organic Pigments Manufacturers (ETAD), which recommends certain standards for handling, packaging and labelling dyestuffs. Although ETAD is a voluntary organization and does not have the authority to enforce compliance, it is compulsory for all ETAD members to adhere to ETAD's guidelines and standards. It is nevertheless believed that TNC affiliates of ETAD have been active in getting governments to ban several benzidine-based dyestuffs that are known to be carcinogenic. In India, too, it is believed that the members of ETAD have cooperated actively with the Bureau of Indian Standards in obtaining this ban.[18]

In the pharmaceutical sector, a TNC called Biocon India adheres to the detailed specification for eco-friendly pharmaceuticals laid down by both the United States and the United Kingdom, and latterly these specifications have been adopted by the Bureau of Indian Standards. Guidelines on packaging and the use of the 'recyclable' symbol as well

---

[17] See 'Environmental Audit of NOCIL Agrochemicals conducted by the Central Pollution Control Board', *Programme Objective Series*, Probes/49/1992–3.

[18] See V. Bharucha, 'The Impact of Environmental Regulations and Standards set in Foreign Markets on India's Exports', in V. Jha et al. (eds), *Trade, Environment and Sustainable Development: A South Asian Perspective*, Macmillan Press, New York and Basingstoke, 1997.

as environmental information on products initially begun by TNCs are now widely used for several products. Standards on food exports, particularly marine products, earlier adhered to by Japanese TNCs are now also being followed by local firms. In all these cases, however, a clear economic advantage, in terms of either brand image, premium in export markets or better recognition, is seen to be the driving force behind local firms adopting higher standards. These higher standards may or may not translate into norms advocated by the Bureau of Indian Standards.

In the refrigeration sector, a TNC collaboration established under the Indo-Swiss Collaboration in Ecological Domestic Refrigeration and the German government is investigating options for producing ecological refrigerators. It is hoped that the standards set by these refrigerators will not only address concerns of ozone depletion under the Montreal Protocol, but will also address concerns of climate change. The project is being jointly set up by the governments of the respective countries, TNCs and research institutes. To gain experience in operating under Indian conditions, pilot projects are being established at refrigeration factories of Godrej and Voltas. These pilot plants will be certified by the Technical Safety Inspectorate for Energy and Environment, located in Germany.

Affecting the adoption of EMSs in the local industry Technological upgrades in both the textiles and leather sectors contribute significantly to their better environmental performance. While large companies have been able to form joint ventures and access superior eco-friendly technologies and management systems, smaller firms are unable to do so. Even if the collaborating company is a relatively small TNC, they seek the larger and better established Indian company as a partner. Thus, the dissemination of better technology and environmentally friendly products in these sectors has been limited to the large-scale segment of the producers.[19]

TNCs have been particularly active in helping firms set up EMSs in order to comply with the ISO 14001 group of standards. Four TNCs

[19] See Das, *Differential Impacts.*

have virtually dominated the market for certifying that firms comply with ISO 14001. Nearly 32 firms have obtained ISO 14001 certificates, of which most are local firms. TNCs that were earlier involved in pre-shipment inspections are now also certifying Indian firms against ISO 14001 standards. They also provide training and have organized various seminars to promote the adoption of these standards by firms.

In addition, TNCs have required their suppliers, subcontractors and vendors to adhere to ISO 14001. Auditing and other forms of training are also provided by these TNCs. However, the rates charged by these firms are approximately double those charged by the Bureau of Indian Standards in granting ISO 14001 certification. The Bureau of Indian Standards has so far certified only one firm versus the 30 odd certified by TNCs. This difference can be attributed to several factors, including the late entry of the Bureau of Indian Standards onto the certification scene, the aggressive marketing strategies of the TNCs, and perhaps the wider acceptability of TNC certification by buyers down the supply chain.[20]

India's stance in international debates on TNCs and environment

In the debate on MAI and the WTO discussion group on a Multilateral Framework on Investment (MFI), India has pointed to certain inequities between investor and host-country obligations. Discussions at the OECD on the MAI and environment have placed the entire burden on the host country by insisting that binding language on not lowering environmental standards be included in the text on MAI. A proposal was also floated to include common minimum standards of environmental protection in the host countries. However, this proposal was opposed by some OECD countries themselves on the grounds that the higher environmental standards of the more advanced countries would be uneconomic for others. In India's view, such macro policies will serve no purpose as individual investment contracts are negotiated on the basis of several factors among which environmental performance is one of the less important. India would prefer to legislate in a way in

[20] Information provided by the Bureau of Indian Standards.

which there is a higher level of investor obligation, even though comparable standards cannot be met by domestic firms because of capital and technology deficits.

To ensure that TNCs make the greatest contribution to their economies, host governments may need to institute screening mechanisms that weed out detrimental FDI projects and encourage beneficial ones. They would also need to institute a mechanism of investors' obligations on various economic, social and cultural necessities, protection of the environment, and promotion of sustainable development. A moot point in this regard is whether TNCs should be asked to maintain the same environmental standards in host countries as they have in home countries, even though host-country domestic investors may be unable to maintain the same standards because of a lack of capital, technology or relevant skills. Discussions on MAI at the OECD have not given much thought to these considerations.

Noting that stronger public liability clauses on FDI have a chilling effect on FDI inflows, the requirement of not lowering standards may be difficult both to define and to implement.[21] For example, policies to attract FDI, such as exempting some industries from FDI clearance procedures, including environmental clearance, could be interpreted as a lowering of environmental standards. Similarly, raising the exemption limits on FDI from US$12.5 to US$25 million could be interpreted as a lowering of standards, although strictly speaking these proposals were directed at facilitating the approval of FDI projects. An MAI that allows developing countries little flexibility in balancing competing economic, social and environmental interests may find little support in India. On the other hand, given the vast resources of TNCs to undertake environment protection measures, either a code of good business practices or investor obligations on a case-by-case basis may better meet India's concerns.

Another contentious issue involving TNCs is the Trade-Related Intellectual Property Rights (TRIPS) Agreement of the WTO. According to a number of NGOs, the Indian Patents Act should be amended in

[21] See *FDI and the Environment: An Overview of the Literature*, Note by the Secretariat, OECD, Paris, 1997.

view of developments concerning plant genetic resources, plant breeding and the development of biotechnology. The current TRIPS Agreement may increase the monopolies of TNCs operating in the pharmaceutical and seed sectors. NGOs argue that the Indian Patents Act could exclude patents on life forms, prevent patents on indigenous knowledge from being registered both in India and in foreign countries, and put under compulsory licensing some essential and generic drugs. It is claimed that these developments would reduce the profitability of TNCs, but that they would have a beneficial impact on the preservation of India's biodiversity.[22]

NGOs argue that pressure to enact laws on plant varieties has come from TNCs seeking monopoly rights to global seed companies. However, laws should be drafted to focus on the conservation of biodiversity and on the protection of farmers' rights and innovation, with limited rights being granted to the seed industry. Again, there appears to be a conflict of interests between the protection of indigenous knowledge and the interests of TNCs.

Debates on technology transfer and the role of the TRIPS Agreement in facilitating such transfers have been another subject of public debate in India. India has argued that trade secrets, copyrights and patents awarded to TNCs for environmentally sound technologies should be either reduced or eliminated in order to facilitate the wider dispersion of such technologies.

Summary of findings and implications

Debates on the environment and investment abound in generalities. Little distinction is made between the macro and the micro aspects or between observations and causative factors. On the one hand, it is claimed that companies are transferring production abroad in order to avoid the more stringent environmental legislation at home. On the other hand, it is claimed that TNCs are the main agents of change in host economies, often bringing better technologies and products, par-

---

22 See V. Shiva and C. Alvares, 'BJP on Swadeshi: the great U-turn', in *Third World Network Features – India,* Third World Network, Penang, 1998.

ticularly to developing countries. In India both views may be valid, depending on the sector of operation. Similarly, the level of environmental protection offered by the investor in the host country is determined by several factors including, but not limited to, the regulatory regime of the host country.

The environmental practices of FDI in India have so far had both negative and positive effects on India's environment. However, most FDI is concentrated in the 29 sectors that have been deemed by the Central Pollution Control Board to be highly polluting. It is therefore likely that a number of new investments will take place in these polluting sectors.

FDI policies in India are being increasingly liberalized. The process of trade and investment liberalization appears to be irreversible irrespective of the government in power. The trend in FDI flows also appears to be following an upward path, indicating that foreign investors continue to regard India as a promising market.

Environmental legislation, though of a long-standing nature, has proved to be difficult to implement in the Indian economy. While India has a comprehensive body of environmental legislation, implementation – particularly at the state level – depends crucially on the governance capacity of the executive machinery. The political situation in the country over the past few years has not been conducive to good governance, especially in the environment sector.

This study has shown that urging TNCs to adopt better environmental practices has depended more on community groups and grass-roots NGOs than on government action. The comparative weight given to better environmental performance has been determined by factors that are often case-specific. Thus, generalizations of the kind that show that TNCs have adopted better technologies and environmental practices than comparable local firms are difficult to ascertain empirically. More case studies are needed to ascertain TNC practices. It is also necessary to evaluate TNC performance against specific environmental goals, such as the preservation of biodiversity, which are either of great national or great global significance.

The overall environmental performance of TNCs is difficult to judge in the case of India. This could be attributed in part to the fact that cases of environmental violation receive more publicity than positive practices.

Another issue that is deserving of attention is whether TNCs are spreading environmentally beneficial practices to local industry. There are several examples of model TNC factories, such as Colour Chem or Bayer Dyes. The interesting question to examine would be whether their practices are leading to comparable local firms adopting better environmental standards and performances.

Another issue that assumes great importance in the Indian context is the waste management practices of TNCs. Reports appear to suggest that TNCs contract the management of their wastes to local firms; i.e., they shift their problems to local companies. How these contractors compare with home-country firms would be an interesting question to pursue. It would also be necessary to examine the costs of clean-up if the TNCs were to undertake their own waste management.

In a rush to attract foreign investment, it is likely that some environmental regulations that the government successfully enforced in the past may now be violated. In particular, states may compete for investments, which could induce a race-to-the-bottom approach. It is especially important to analyse the behaviour of TNCs in sectors that are considered 'high priority' for FDI by the Indian government. It might also be useful to explore whether special environmental safeguards would be needed in these sectors in order to promote sustainable development. India's stand in international debates appears to indicate that both the host governments and the investors must have a stake in promoting sustainable development.

Liberalization, privatization and the water sector

David Owen

Introduction

This paper considers the need for private-sector investment and management in the water sector.

The global players in the international water industry are principally European companies – and it is no coincidence that in Europe it is *environmental* legislation that has been a central driver for private-sector funding and operation. The paper examines some of the key driving forces for future private-sector investment as well as the current state of play, arguing that the private sector has a central role to play in addressing the need for potable water and sanitation in towns and cities in developing economies.

Finally, the paper argues that, for private-sector involvement to work effectively, independent regulation is needed to safeguard environment, public health and consumer interests at the same time as ensuring an operating climate that encourages private-sector investment and involvement.

The need for investment

The continuity of Europe's wealth and influence over the past 2,500 to 3,500 years has in part depended upon its access to reliable supplies of potable water – water to drink, to enable the pursuit of settled agriculture, to ease the passage of goods and people and to facilitate the industrial revolution and its ambiguous aftermath. The lack of such resources or their abuse can be regarded as one of the central blockages to the development of many regions.

Globally, there are four broad themes concerning the interaction of water markets with the private sector. (1) In the Middle East and North Africa and sub-Saharan Africa, the need is to get reliable supplies of water to the customer in the first place and ensuring that these are not wasted through leakage and failure to recover wastewaters. (2) North America faces the problem of having to persuade free markets to pay an economic price for water and to unravel an astonishing web of hidden subsidies. (3) In Latin America and Asia, water privatization is seen as a tool for developing and expanding the infrastructure needed for human and economic development. (4) In contrast, the central theme in most of Europe is one of enhancement and service extension within a burgeoning common legal infrastructure laid down by the European Community (EC). The latter difference is a subtle and costly one, since improvements in water quality and sewerage are not as visible as putting in a modern service. Yet they are almost as essential.

Outside Europe, the urban population is set to soar. Forecasts of the rate and extent of population growth remain contentious. What is not open to dispute is the global trend towards urbanization. The most attractive market for the private-sector water players is the operation and upgrading of services in large cities. Mega-cities offer real economies of scale for the operator and the potential to pass these savings on, while smaller cities offer long-term growth potential.

There are currently 14 discrete areas in each of which more than 10 million people are living in close proximity, and water shortages and sanitation problems are one of the central constraints to the development of these areas. Over the next 25 years, at least 12 more such areas will be added to this total, none of which currently has adequate water or sewerage infrastructures. Most will be in Asia, yet there is a relative lack of development of water resources in a number of key economies in Asia at a time of population growth, urbanization and industrialization.

'Water stress' arises where annual water resources fall below 1,570 cubic metres per person per annum, while scarcity is seen as a major problem when a country has less than 1,000 cubic metres of annual water resources per person. This works out at 2,740 litres per person per day. Worldwide, the average of renewable freshwater resources is 8,800 cubic metres per person per annum, of which 545 cubic metres has been developed (see Table 1). By the year 2025, a total of 27 nations is set to be in the 'high water stress' category, all but three in South Asia and the Middle East and North Africa. In addition, perhaps 50 per cent of people worldwide are without access to adequate sanitation facilities. As a result, some 12–25 million people a year die or cease to be economically active because of water-borne diseases.

Table 1: Water resources, their development and application

Country	Water potential p.a.		Developed water p.a.	
	bn m³	m³ per capita	bn m³	m³ per capita
China	2,800	2,350	460	385
Taiwan	67	3,190	18	857
South Korea	63	1,413	10.7	240
India	1,850	1,691	380	415
Pakistan	298	1,730	153	1,214
Vietnam	376	5,151	5.1	70
Thailand	110	1,864	31.9	541
Indonesia	2,530	13,316	16.6	87
Malaysia	456	23,385	9.4	482
Philippines	323	4,894	29.5	45

Sources: David Owen; UNDP, *Human Development Report* 1998, Oxford University Press, Oxford, 1998; World Bank, *World Development Report 1998/99,* Oxford University Press, Oxford, 1998.

Estimates of the global market size for water and wastewater services and hardware range from US$200 billion p.a. (US$33 per capita) to US$300 billion p.a. (US$50 per capita). The figure is notoriously imprecise, however, because of the extent of hidden subsidies and the inefficiencies inherent in the traditional municipal and quasi-private-sector nature of the industry.

Despite the market's size (and US$100 billion being spent during the World Bank's recent 'Water Decade'), the United Nations concluded in 1997 that 25 per cent of the world's population are facing water shortages. This is set to rise to 66 per cent by 2025. Global water consumption is rising by 2.5 per cent per year, twice the rate of population growth, having risen sixfold this century.

Against this background, state-owned and state-operated water and sewerage concerns are finding it increasingly difficult to maintain their levels of service, let alone expand to meet increasing urbanization or to improve service quality. As a result, private water vendor services provide water of dubious quality at five to 65 times the cost of piped water, owing to a lack of viable alternatives (Table 2). The urban population of the less developed regions is set to grow from 0.81 billion in 1975 to 2.02 billion in 2000 and to 4.03 billion by 2025. By that date, the UN believes that 65 per cent of the world's population will be directly affected by water shortages. According to the Global Environmental Facility (GEF), US$700 billion of capital spending is needed to provide a basic level of water and sanitation services (such as access to piped water and a lavatory connected to a sewer in every street) over the next ten years.[1]

Table 2: The cost of scarcity: the price difference between water from vendors and utilities

City	Country	Ratio
Dhaka	Bangladesh	12:1 to 25:1
Istanbul	Turkey	10:1
Jakarta	Indonesia	9:1
Karachi	Pakistan	28:1 to 83:1
Lagos	Nigeria	4:1 to 10:1
Lima	Peru	17:1
Manila	Philippines	16:1

Sources: David Owen; *Water Utilities Data Book*, Asian Development Bank, Manila, 1993; UNDP, *An Urbanising World*, UNDP, Oxford, 1996.

The politics of water privatization

As the UK water sector has demonstrated since 1994, the private sector has the capability of delivering investment programmes well within budget. Most of the figures on investment needs have been drawn up by public-sector institutions and are based upon traditional engineering and financial approaches to water and sewerage. They highlight the need for new sources of finance along with the potential to reduce projected capital costs by 10–25 per cent.

But water provision is very much in the public eye. For municipalities and regional governments, there are a number of fairly cynical reasons why water provision can be turned into a political issue:

[1] Cited in Anglian Water plc Preliminary Results Announcement, 26 May 1999.

- It removes a powerful source of political patronage at the municipal level. The provision of jobs in the local utilities can be related to political affiliations.
- It eliminates a source of municipal revenues for subsidizing other activities. This is especially the case when a degree of price transparency is involved.
- There are a number of cultural and political shibboleths attached to water being free and people being free to use it, irrespective of the concerns of others. These can be mobilized during elections when changes are proposed.

It is also very easy for vested interests to attack privatized water services. You never 'notice' your water or sewerage services when they are functioning perfectly, and thus perfection is taken for granted as the norm: anything less than perfection – including for example the perceived threat of supply limitations as seen in Britain in 1995 – is an outright failure. In some countries, this can be a good reason for private-sector investors to concentrate on areas such as bulk water provision, so that the actual dealings with the public remain in municipal hands.

One of the commonest political arguments against the privatization of water and sewerage services is that it will mean that water will be too costly for poorer people. But this tends to ignore the fact that under the current arrangements it is the poorer people living in urban areas who have to pay over the odds to water vendors for supplies of distinctly dubious quality. In India, for example, it is common for poorer urban households to pay 25 per cent of their income for water services under municipal control or via water vendors.

In fact, people are willing to pay an economic price for water services if it comes with guarantees of quality and availability. Pragmatic pricing policies based upon charging more per unit of water for households who use water for non-essential purposes has made private water provision both affordable and viable. Popular support exists for adequate supplies of water and improved public health at an affordable rate. Opposition is notable among better-off households who are loathe to pay an economic price for piped water supplies for gardens, washing cars and non-essential household uses. The fact that these are also the people with the most political influence means that the political picture is often distorted.

Privatization can be managed in such a way that local sensibilities are catered for. While the 'asset-sale' privatization model (e.g. Britain in 1989) has many fiscal attractions, taking the water and sewerage infrastructure out of public hands has proven politically contentious. A series of intermediate privatization models (operation and maintenance, build–operate–transfer, and concessional) allow private-sector operation with public ownership of the assets. Furthermore, by being responsible for bulk water provision or sewage treatment and disposal, the private-sector player needs to deal only with the municipality and not with the public. Political risk can be managed even in the more challenging markets, and cost and service quality benefits can be delivered directly or indirectly.

The role of the private sector

Private capital and management can help to address water and wastewater infrastructure and service needs where projects can generate enough revenues to cover their operating costs and service debts and offer a competitive rate of return. Private capital can be attracted to these projects where it can also be demonstrated that political and economic risks are capable of being managed. As a natural monopoly, water and sewerage are unique among the utilities undergoing privatization. However, the progressive demand for better service standards and better-quality drinking water create price pressures not seen in other utilities.

There are many different models for private-sector involvement. The private-sector operator can take over the entire utility system (production, transmission, distribution and billing), or it can be unbundled into five discrete areas: (1) bulk water provision, (2) water treatment, (3) water distribution, (4) sewerage (effluent collection and distribution) and (5) waste water treatment and disposal. This allows a company to decide on what level of political risk it wishes to manage. Bulk water provision, water treatment and sewage/wastewater treatment does not entail direct contact with the public, while water distribution and sewerage do. The latter, especially when involving billing and making a service economically viable (for example, World Bank financed projects had water fees covering 35 per cent of the average cost of its supply), are the most politically contentious. In the words of the ASQC (an American service quality monitoring organization), 'the more contact a firm has with its customers, the more it has a chance to screw up'.

Risks and risk management

Municipalities and governments can optimize the quality of a privatization programme through appropriate framing. A transparent bidding process greatly improves the quality of data that companies can use for deciding on prices and returns. This needs appropriate performance targets, the selection of suitably qualified operators for the short list, and the right tariff levels for delivering performance at an acceptable cost. The better the framework, the cheaper the cost of the project, since predictable and fair rules are needed to secure long-term private capital at good rates.

It is often difficult to raise money at reasonable interest rates from local banks and capital markets, and the difference usually has to be made up by international sources of debt and equity finance. A notable exception has been Puncak Niaga, which raised US$250 million from the Malaysian market, putting it on an even keel with its partner Générale des Eaux for the US$600 million Selangor water management concession. International debt is raised via commercial banks, export credit agencies and multilateral institutions such as the World Bank's International Finance Corporation (IFC) to address sovereign risks. Multilateral institutions are more experienced at mitigating and assessing project risks than investors, and can play an important confidence-building role with the government concerned. In turn, the capital markets are better for established water/sewerage concerns.

There is considerable uncertainty in valuing extant water and sewerage assets. These cannot be traded and indeed need to be maintained and replaced. One could argue that, in the case of asset privatizations, these assets have no intrinsic value at all and are best regarded as liabilities. This is one of the reasons why managing assets (via a management company) can make more sense than owning them. For example, following the 1997 privatization of Budapest's sewerage system, Générale des Eaux and Germany's BWB own the management company, which in turn owns 25 per cent of the asset company. The majority of the latter company remains in the hands of the municipality.

Where privatization stands today

According to the IFC, there have been 140 water privatization projects in the developing economies (see Table 3), with US$28.6 billion raised for infrastructure work to date. Some two-thirds of the project costs have been raised by international sources of finance (US$15 billion in debt and equity and US$4 billion via export credit guarantees). Debt–equity ratios have typically ranged from 60:40 to 73:30, which given the experience of the power sector – where an 80:20 ratio is the norm – have involved a lower than expected level of debt.

Table 3: Water and/or wastewater services provided by the private sector

Region	Population served (mn)	% of population
European Union	126	30
Central/Eastern Europe	9	8
Russian Federation and Central Asia	0	0
Middle East and Africa	13	2
Asia and Australasia	72	18
North America	48	12
South America	21	5
Global total	289	5

Source: D.A.L. Owen, P. Hollobone and P. Wilde, *Come On In, the Water's Lovely*, Panmure Gordons, London 1998. See also D.A.L. Owen, *World Water Review 1999,* Masons, London, forthcoming.

Rapid population growth, urbanization and industrialization have made Asia the most compelling of international water and sewerage markets (Table 4). Water is scarce and a modern operating infrastructure is rarer still. Most EC countries, operating within the framework of the EC Urban Wastewater Treatment Directive, will have 75–90 per cent of their wastewater subject to secondary or tertiary treatment by 2002 (in effect meaning that 90–95 per cent of the effluent's pollution load is removed). In contrast, in Asia, putting in sewerage, let alone sewage treatment, is at an early stage (see Table 4). Yet without a functioning sewerage system and a reasonable level of sewage treatment, it is very hard to obtain reliable supplies of water fit for drinking and for industrial and commercial applications – even after treatment.

Table 4: Urban sewerage: current status in Asia (%)

Country	None	Primary	Secondary	Tertiary
Japan	50	0	50	0
China	92	2	6	0
Hong Kong	80	20	0	0
Taiwan	93	2	5	0
South Korea	80	10	10	0
India	90	5	5	0
Thailand	95	5	0	0
Philippines	98	2	0	0
Indonesia	100	0	0	0
Malaysia	90	10	0	0
Singapore	10	40	50	0

Sources: David Owen, *Water Utilities Data Book*, Asian Development Bank, Manila, 1993; and *Managing Water Resources to Meet Megacity Needs,* Asian Development Banks, Manila, 1994. See also D.A.L Owen, *World Water Review 1999,* Masons, London, forthcoming.

Some 5 per cent of the global water and wastewater market are already under private-sector control. But it would be wrong to assume that the entire market is open to the private sector. For example, many construction-related aspects of these markets are proving to be distinctly unpalatable to private-sector service providers. In certain areas, provision of direct customer services (such as billing and metering) is liable to expose a foreign company to local and nationalistic political concerns.

Over the next decade, the *addressable* market, that is the market involving privatization opportunities for municipal drinking water provision and wastewater treatment services in urban areas, can be more reasonably estimated to be in the region of US$25–45 billion per annum (Table 5). Longer-term markets, which will present opportunities for the private sector from 2005 to 2025, include areas such as Japan, where the concept of privatized water services remains somewhat esoteric, along with areas where urbanization remains at an informal stage.

Table 5: Estimates of the value of global water and wastewater markets (US$ bn p.a.)

	Privatized	Target markets	Longer-term	Total market
Water	20–30	10–15	15–20	45–65
Wastewater	15–25	15–30	30–45	60–100
Total	35–55	25–45	45–65	105–165

Sources: Anglian Water International, Vivendi, and David Owen. See also D.A.L. Owen, P. Hollobone, and P. Wilde, *Making Waves Overseas*, West LB, London, 1999, for revised data.

Table 6: Populations served by the global water companies

	People served ('000)			
Global Water Companies	Domestic	International	Global total	% international
Suez-Lyonnaise	16,000	66,760	82,760	81
Générale des Eaux	24,000	38,120	62,120	61
United Utilities	6,880	17,940	24,740	73
Thames Water	11,600	9,060	20,680	44
Severn Trent	8,300	10,250	18,550	55
Aguas de Barcelona	12,137	4,444	16,581	27
FCC	7,110	670	7,680	9
Anglian Water	5,827	1,600	7,427	21
Aguas de Valencia	2,040	150	2,190	7
Biwater	406	500	906	55

Source: D.A.L. Owen, P. Hollobone, and P. Wilde, *Come On In, the Water's Lovely*, Panmure Gordons, London, 1998; see also D.A.L. Owen, P. Hollobone, and P. Wilde, *Making Waves Overseas*, West LB, London, 1999, for revised data.

Over the next two years, industry sources point to 50–70 million people having their water and/or sewerage services privatized. This number refers to services actively being prepared for privatization. The underlying figure is likely to be at least as high over the next two decades. Major players such as Vivendi (Générale des Eaux) are committed to gaining at least 20 per cent of this market.

The need for independent regulation

The point of privatization

Privatization works where businesses are more competent than the public sector at running utility services. The expansion of telecommunications services and the fall in the cost of telephoning is a case in point. In the context of water, privatization is a key element in de-politicizing water services, by liberating it both from national and regional budgetary constraints and from short-term political rhetoric. In essence, water and wastewater privatization is about allowing major capital expenditure projects to be examined on their economic, service and environmental merits. In addition, monetizing water encourages its conservation, along with service efficiencies (staffing levels can be cut by 30–66 per cent) and the adoption of a 'Best Available Techniques' (BAT) approach towards water quality and environmental compliance. The difficulty in meeting the gap between theory and practice is that these ideals all depend on the existence of independent regulators charged with optimizing value and service, water quality and environmental standards.

Many markets are privatizing without an adequate regulatory infrastructure in place from the outset. This in part reflects the fact that, while the French water model has been widely copied, its legal system has not. Water and wastewater services in France are framed by a fairly comprehensive set of laws. As a result, its regulation is of a passive nature, which relies on the judicial system to resolve disputes. This approach has been copied by, for example, New Zealand and Jamaica. The British model is based upon an independent regulator (OFWAT) adopting an activist stance. OFWAT evolved from OFTEL, which has regulated Britain's telecommunications service sector since 1984.

In areas where water scarcity is a more pressing issue, regulation will need to emphasize the conservation of water in a supply-led industry, as opposed to a demand-led approach which could cut costs by encouraging conservation.

The need for independent regulators and their regulation

The need for an independent regulator as a balance between shareholder and stakeholder concerns is paramount. Where such a balance is struck is a political issue. Shareholder concerns must be reflected, so that it is worthwhile for the private sector to invest in and operate these services. There is a clear need for governments to lay out a political agenda for each regulator. This means optimizing the transparency of the pricing process so that shareholder and stakeholder concerns can be balanced against each other.

Incentive-based regulation is essential for the water sector. The overriding obligation for each private-sector water regulator ought to be the need to reward efficiency, especially where its original targets have been exceeded. At the same time, tangible progress in customer service, environmental compliance and drinking water quality need to be rewarded, so that companies that perform strongly in these areas are valued more highly than their competitors. This would bring about a causal relationship between excellence of service and the creation of shareholder value. Efficiency gains can be shared on a sound basis between customers, shareholders and the environment. The latter is arguably a customer benefit, since they gain through the improved quality of their drinking water.

Lessons from the Multilateral Agreement on Investment

A view from the negotiating table

Jan Huner[1]

Introduction

From September 1995, when Frans Engering was elected chairman of the MAI Negotiating Group, until April this year, when he stepped down as chairman, I sat next to him when he conducted the meetings of the Negotiating Group. The leadership of the Negotiating Group was in the hands of a so-called Bureau, consisting of the chairman and two vice-chairmen, one from the United States and one from Japan. The Bureau met before each session of the Negotiating Group. One of its main activities was to prepare the agenda for each session, and to decide on the kind of documentation to be made available to the group. I was the secretary of the Bureau. My work in these two and a half years, and in fact the negotiation process as a whole, has been greatly facilitated by the staff of the OECD Secretariat. Their professionalism, dedication and creativity has been truly impressive.

The negotiators' failure fully to incorporate the environmental dimension from the start of the MAI negotiations is not the main reason why the MAI as envisaged will not come about. The main problem with the MAI is that its negotiators did not expect to have to sell it politically. Most of the MAI negotiators were investment specialists, not used to viewing from a political perspective the concepts that they con-

[1] *Editors' note*: A version of this paper was given as evidence to the House of Commons Environmental Audit Committee Inquiry into the Multilateral Agreement on Investment. See *Multilateral Agreement on Investment*, House of Commons Environmental Audit Committee 1st Report, HC 58, V. II, pp 103–7, January 1999. For an alternative account of the MAI negotions see David Henderson, *The MAI Affair: A Story and its Lessons*, RIIA, London, 1999.

sider logical and essential parts of an investment discipline. Investor–state dispute settlement is one of these concepts; compensation for expropriation is another. They were thus wholly unprepared to defend these concepts *vis-à-vis* opponents who were distorting them to portray the MAI as a threat. Least of all did they expect to see the MAI portrayed as a threat to environmental protection.

This is not to say that the concerns raised by environmental NGOs, or indeed by environment ministries in some OECD capitals, were unjustified. Most of these concerns deserved serious attention, and they eventually got it. But by that time it was too late.

I will first examine how the environment was dealt with in these negotiations, and then try to draw some lessons from this experience.

The MAI story

The idea behind the MAI was to build on existing OECD commitments and create a comprehensive investment discipline, backed up by a dispute settlement mechanism which was to include investor-to-state procedures. Investor–state dispute settlement is unknown in trade agreements, but it is a common feature of the many hundreds of bilateral investment protection agreements that the OECD countries have concluded over the past 40 years, mostly with non-OECD countries. It is also a key feature of the investment chapter of the North American Free Trade Agreement (NAFTA). As in the NAFTA, investor–state dispute settlement in the MAI would cover both establishment ('market access' for the trade people), and treatment post-establishment. In the OECD instruments, compliance is encouraged by peer pressure.

The main discipline of the MAI, as in all investment agreements, is the rule of national treatment, combined with most favoured nation treatment where national treatment is not applicable. In addition, certain performance requirements for investors, such as transfer of technology, are prohibited.

The negotiations formally began in September 1995, but they were preceded by three years of preparatory work in the context of the OECD Investment Committee. These preparations identified the main concepts of the MAI. I myself chaired the working group on 'Non-

Member Countries and Institutional Issues'. It is noteworthy that the environment was not an issue in this group. The focus was almost exclusively on other agreements that contain investment rules. There was much talk about the MAI's relationship with WTO agreements, in particular the General Agreement on Trade in Services (GATS), which also deals with investment in services. Another hot item was taxation: the MAI was not to affect the many bilateral agreements on taxation concluded between OECD countries.

But the issue of how the MAI relates to multilateral environmental agreements (MEAs) was not discussed. This would suggest that it was not a subject for debate in capitals either. That is certainly true for us in The Netherlands. I am quite sure, though, that the environment was debated in Washington in the context of preparing for the MAI negotiations. After all, this issue figured fairly prominently in the NAFTA negotiations, and the NAFTA investment chapter contains explicit provisions on environmental concerns. It is in fact the NAFTA that provided the model for the proposed 'not lowering of standards' provision in the MAI.

In early 1996 the environment community began to wake up to the MAI negotiations. In February of that year, the environment ministers of the OECD consulted NGOs prior to a meeting of the Environmental Policy Committee at ministerial level. They were confronted with questions about the potential impact of the MAI on national and international environmental regulation. More than a few ministers did not know what the MAI was all about. Consequently, upon their return they issued instructions to be advised on this question. The results of this sparked a lively discussion in the next regular meeting of the Environment Policy Committee. The prevailing view was that the Committee should become involved in the MAI negotiations.

Curiously, a similar request had been made by the Trade Committee and the Committee on Fiscal Affairs of the OECD even before the start of the negotiations. The reasoning was that, since the OECD combined various disciplines within its committee structure (and thus within the Secretariat), we should make maximum use of this. However, most delegates to the Negotiating Group, afraid that this might turn into a turf battle, stressed that the Negotiating Group had been made independent precisely to avoid the need for coordination with standing committees. The solution adopted was that delegations could propose subjects for discussion in the Negotiating Group, and that the relevant expertise should be represented as desired in each delegation. Thus, the environment was put on the agenda of the Negotiating Group for the first time in October 1996, a year after the negotiations had started.

Meanwhile, environmental and other NGOs had been building up pressure, both at the OECD in Paris and in capitals. In Paris the NGOs that are regularly consulted in the framework of joint sessions of the Trade and Environment Committees began to ask for similar consultations with the MAI Negotiating Group. In capitals, parliamentarians were approached and briefed about the perceived negative effects of the MAI as envisaged. Of particular concern was, and still is, the compatibility of the MAI with the Rio Declaration and with the emerging system of MEAs.

But in what ultimately proved to be the most effective move of all, NGOs began to exchange information and ideas through the Internet. The apparent strategy was to provoke a public discussion about the MAI. The tactical instrument chosen was a caricature of the MAI as a threat to environmental, labour, cultural and development interests.

The Negotiating Group decided it did not want to meet with NGOs, but it did agree to an informal briefing for NGOs in early December 1996. The discussion of the environment in the Negotiating Group in October 1996 was based on three ideas put forward by the Chairman of the OECD Environment Committee:

1. to place the MAI explicitly in the framework of sustainable development;
2. to prevent promotion of foreign direct investment (FDI) by relaxing environmental standards;
3. to ensure adequate environmental performance by investors.

These three basic themes were retained in the ensuing debates, which led to the so-called ‘three anchor’ approach of the environment in the MAI. The first anchor would be the preamble, which should re-affirm parties’ commitment to the relevant principles of the Rio Declaration and to the relevant multilateral agreements. The second anchor would be a provision built on NAFTA Article 1114, stating that environmental and social standards as contained in national laws and regulations should not be lowered in order to attract an investment. The main debate here has been whether or not this should be a binding provision. NAFTA 1114 only says that such lowering of standards is 'inappropriate'. The third anchor was investor performance on environmental protection: this would have to be ensured by associating the existing OECD Guidelines for Multinational Enterprises. These Guidelines had been supplemented with a chapter on environmental protection in 1991: there is broad agreement that this chapter is in need of updating.[2]

I should signal at this point that the emerging MAI discipline on environment (and labour, which was dealt with in similar fashion) was not based on consensus in the Negotiating Group. The United Kingdom took a very sceptical line towards all of this up until the early spring of 1997. As the parliamentary elections of May 1997 approached, and a Labour victory appeared a near-certainty, the UK delegation became more silent on the issue. After the Labour government took power, the UK became a strong advocate of meaningful MAI provisions on environment and labour issues. It was the UK that, in September 1997, suggested that an environmental review of the MAI was desirable.

Other opponents of labour and environment clauses in the MAI were Australia, New Zealand, Korea and Mexico. Mexico was perhaps the strongest critic, which is not surprising in the light of the NAFTA history.

International business took a dim view of this turn in the debate. Business was regularly consulted through the standing Business and Industry Advisory Committee (BIAC). A similar committee, the Trade Union Advisory Committee (TUAC), was used for consulting trade unions.

BIAC's initial strong support for the MAI had already weakened when it became clear that an almost total carve-out of taxation was inevitable. A binding clause on not lowering standards and on the annexation of the OECD Guidelines on Multinational Enterprises, including reopening the debate on the chapter in the Guidelines on environmen-

[2] *Editors' note*: A process to review the Guidelines is currently under way.

tal protection, were poorly received in business circles, particularly in the United States.

There are doubts as to how representative BIAC's views really are for international business. The only worldwide business organization, the International Chamber of Commerce (ICC), has never been a strong supporter of the MAI. The ICC's view is that a multilateral investment agreement in an era of globalization should necessarily be worldwide. The WTO is clearly the relevant framework for such an agreement. The MAI would at best be a useful intermediate step towards a WTO agreement.

In spite of the negotiators' ongoing efforts to produce something meaningful on labour and environment, the NGO campaign against the MAI further intensified throughout 1997. The fact that the original deadline of May 1997 for concluding the negotiations was not met provided the NGOs with a window of opportunity. One of their strongest weapons was that the negotiations were conducted in secret. They did have a point here. All of the Negotiating Group documents were classified 'confidential'. However, so-called 'sanitized' versions (i.e. with country names removed) of the records of Negotiating Group meetings were made available a few weeks after each such meeting, mostly for the benefit of non-OECD countries. Draft texts were not released.

When the pressure from NGOs began to rise, the chairman of the Negotiating Group suggested that Negotiating Group documents, in particular draft texts, should be declassified. This was not approved by a minority of countries. One of the arguments for not releasing texts was that in doing so we would find ourselves having to negotiate with NGOs about them. This prompted Canada to say that it had already put draft texts on a ministry Internet site, and it would continue to do so.

By the early autumn of 1997 it became clear that some form of direct dialogue between NGOs and the negotiators was inevitable. The chairman managed to persuade the reluctant minority of the Negotiating Group not only that such a meeting should take place, but that to make it meaningful the draft text of the MAI as currently known should be made available.

Thus, a meeting with NGOs was called on 27 October 1997. This was to prove to be a memorable and decisive event, for a variety of reasons. Memorable because some 50 NGO participants took part, representating a wide range of interests and a wide range of intensity of opposition to the MAI. Memorable also because the NGOs, in spite of their differences, managed to agree on a single moderator on their behalf. This had in fact been requested by Frans Engering, because it seemed the only way to conduct an efficient and productive meeting. This set-up largely helped to prevent a planned walkout by some of the more radical American NGOs, who wanted an immediate response to their demand that the negotiations be suspended immediately. Decisive, because some of the points raised by environmental groups convinced many Negotiating Group members that a few draft provisions, particularly those on expropriation and on performance requirements, could be interpreted in unexpected ways. The dispute between the Ethyl Corporation of the United States and the Canadian government illustrated the point that the MAI negotiators should think twice before copying the expropriation provisions of the NAFTA. Ethyl considered that the Canadian ban on a certain additive for petrol amounted to an expropriation, mainly because Ethyl was the only producer of this additive. Canada eventually went for a settlement that reportedly involved the sum of $13 million. This surprised not a few observers, because Canada was expected to win the dispute. This settlement was invoked by NGOs to demonstrate the need for clarity in the MAI as to what expropriation really means. Above all, they insisted that the MAI should clearly state that the expropriation clause can never be interpreted to prevent governments from adopting rules and regulations on environmental protection.

Although everyone agreed on the usefulness of the NGO hearing, this did not bring consensus on how to deal with labour and environment in the MAI any closer. In fact, the negotiations as such began to unravel when the United States announced in February 1998 that in its view the new deadline of April 1998 could not be met. The background for this lay in a combination of factors. Approval by Congress of the MAI was far from secure. Also, there was still no firm view within the government as to how best to deal with the labour–environment issue. The intense campaign by pressure groups was taking its toll.

There were also signals from the French that it would be difficult for them to sell the MAI politically. The artistic and intellectual community had discovered the MAI as yet another American-inspired instrument of ultra-liberalism, posing a threat to artistic and literary freedom and cultural diversity in France. Environment is not the main political concern in France when it comes to investment agreements.

The Chairman of the Negotiating Group made a final attempt in March to bridge the gap by proposing a package of provisions on labour and the environment. He did not succeed. Although there was praise all round for this credible effort, the Europeans saw too many NAFTA-inspired texts, and the Americans opposed making the 'not lowering of standards' clause binding.

At the OECD ministerial meeting in April 1998, France proposed that the negotiations be suspended for six months in order to determine the political viability of MAI. This suited the United States very well, and it was thus agreed. On 14 October 1998 Prime Minister Jospin resolutely delivered the final blow to the MAI by announcing that France had decided to withdraw from the negotiations.

The lessons

At this point, just two weeks after a French torpedo caused the capsizing of the leaky MAI boat, it is too early to tell precisely what made this ship so vulnerable. It would be wrong to blame only the French for sinking it. The truth is that the MAI had become a liability rather than an asset to most OECD countries, but few countries were willing to admit it. And it was not just poor handling of the environmental question that was the main cause.

Let me offer some personal thoughts on what, in hindsight, caused the problems. First of all, I remain convinced that the OECD is the right forum for negotiating an investment agreement. Not only does it have the expertise and the experience in this area, but more importantly, it is an interdisciplinary organization where all other policy areas that were relevant in the MAI debate are represented. In that sense the OECD is unique.

The question is: did we use this to our advantage? My answer is: only very modestly, and far too late. Other committees and Secretariat directorates should have been actively consulted during the preparatory phase between 1992 and 1995. In spite of the OECD dogma of policy integration, the walls between the various disciplines in the OECD can be as high as they are between ministries in capitals. We should have copied the joint discussions on trade and environment, where NGOs are also involved.

We are now, it seems, going to make up for this. In January 1999, an OECD Conference on Foreign Direct Investment and the Environment will be held in The Hague.[3] It will be a joint responsibility of the Environment and Investment Directorates of the OECD Secretariat. The co-sponsors on the Dutch side are my own ministry and the Ministry of the Environment. Here, at least, the walls have come tumbling down.

The second lesson is that the MAI debate and negotiations were dominated by experts who spoke in a language that was impressive and intimidating to the non-initiated. These experts had rarely been challenged by politicians and political activists. The exception here would be the Americans, who had been taught a lesson or two in the NAFTA debate in their country. It remains a mystery to me why they did not raise, or were not forced to raise, the labour–environment issue at an early stage. Instead, the United States was totally preoccupied with the liberalization question. They were caught by the NGO campaign as much as were the Europeans. In my view, the only country that woke up early to potential political problems was Canada, where the cultural issue (not the environment issue!) was recognized as a make-or-break issue at an early stage.

A third lesson is that complex multilateral negotiations in the trade and investment field are likely to raise suspicions. If, on top of that, you create an impression of secrecy, you have a political time bomb. In the case of the MAI, it provoked NGOs to disseminate caricatures of the MAI and press politicians to demand debates in national parliaments. Not surprisingly, those debates were often unrealistic and therefore unhelpful – witness the disastrous discussion in spring 1998

[3] *Editors' note*: The conference was held in The Hague on 28–29 January 1999. See also *Conference on Foreign Direct Investment and the Environment: Summary of the Discussion,* CCNM/EMEF/EPOC/CIME (98) 7, 13 April 1999, which can be found at http://www.oecd.org//daf/env/report.pdf.

in the European Parliament, culminating in an equally disastrous resolution.

The final lesson is the power of the Internet. This medium turned out to be the worst enemy of the MAI. Let us make sure that, in any future multilateral negotiation on investment, in the WTO or elsewhere, the Internet is our best friend.

An industry view

Kristian Ehinger

The objectives of the MAI

How can environmental protection be built in into international investment agreements? My answer is simple: whenever and however this serves the principal purposes of the MAI. Business does not seek an MAI that gives investors scope to weaken their environmental policies. Neither should the MAI restrict the possibility for host-country governments to adopt the non-discriminatory measures they deem necessary to protect their environment and/or to conform to the standards established in multilateral environmental agreements.

But what are the principal purposes of the MAI? In May 1995, after four years of an OECD study on the feasibility of such a project, OECD ministers called for:

> The immediate start of negotiations [on an MAI] which will provide a broad multilateral frame-work for international investment with high standards for the liberalization of investment regimes and investment protection and with effective dispute settlement procedures.

OECD ministers aimed to replace the vast network of more than 1,600 bilateral investment treaties (BITs) with a multilateral treaty that was supposed to grant no less protection to foreign investors than the BITs. BITs generally guarantee national treatment, non-discrimination and most favoured nation status for foreign investors. Many provide not only for state–state but also for investor–state dispute resolution. What is new in the MAI is the element of 'multilateralization' and the aim of significant up-front liberalization. It was not intended to include other policy objectives in the MAI.

It has thus always been the position of international business that the MAI is to be an investment agreement – a place to set high standards for the treatment and protection of investment. An MAI should not and will not affect the behaviour of companies in meeting national laws and regulatory environmental standards of host governments. It simply says that governments should apply any laws or regulations on a non-discriminatory basis. We have said many times that the MAI is not the place to set specific standards on labour or the environment, and we continue to believe that.

Environmental safeguards in the MAI

On the other hand, we recognize that the Agreement can make references and provide appropriate safeguards to ensure that it does not conflict with non-discriminatory domestic rules or agreed international standards that are negotiated separately in specialized forums such as multilateral environmental agreements.

For this reason, we continue to support the so-called 'three-anchor approach', namely:

1. preambular language referring to the positive role that investment should play in encouraging sustainable development;
2. a provision stating that environmental standards should not be relaxed in order to attract an investment; and
3. an appropriate reference taking note of the OECD's voluntary Guidelines for Multinational Enterprises and associating them with the Final Act of the MAI.

In our view, these three provisions are an effective and appropriate means to address the key environmental aspects of the investment agreement.

We have even gone further than the negotiators have so far been willing to go, stating that the MAI could include an Article similar to NAFTA 1114.1:

> that nothing in the Agreement should prevent a signatory from adopting, maintaining or enforcing any measure which it considers appropriate to ensure that investment activity in its territory is undertaken in a manner sensitive to environmental concerns, as long as such measures are consistent with the obligations of the Agreement (i.e. national and most favoured

> nation treatment). We believe these provisions will ensure that the context in which countries liberalize investment regimes and develop investor protection will be consistent with the existing trends toward comprehensive, effective and science-based environmental standards.

We maintain that the MAI is not an appropriate vehicle for setting precise environmental standards. Such standards are more effectively negotiated in multilateral forums established for that purpose. Environmental issues are complex, and they deserve the concentrated attention of government and all other interests in order to achieve comprehensive and workable solutions. Any attempt to use the MAI would duplicate, pre-empt and/or conflict with efforts in the proper, specialized forums. The introduction of protective standards on, for example, toxic chemicals in the MAI would undoubtedly duplicate and potentially conflict with more specialized, multilateral efforts to address environmental management issues.

We are also concerned that more specific text on the environment would introduce considerable uncertainty into binding MAI provisions and could result in disputes in which parties use the language as an excuse for administrative delays or outright discrimination against foreign investors. Moreover, we believe that any effort to establish binding environmental standards in the MAI will preclude the accession by many non-member countries that is a key objective of the business community.

There are many references in international law to the effect that normal, non-discriminatory government actions taken to regulate economic activity cannot be considered to amount to expropriation. This is also reflected in Article 11 of the Multilateral Investment Guarantee Agency Convention, and we understand that an appropriate note to this effect will be added to the MAI. However, it is necessary to include measures 'tantamount to expropriation' so that governments cannot resort to so-called 'creeping expropriation' through discriminatory actions clearly designed to 'take an investment'.

In this context, it is even suggested that the investor-dispute settlement mechanism would give multinationals extraordinary power to challenge in particular smaller governments' regulatory powers. But this is not a new concept. The vast majority of BITs include investor–

state dispute settlement provisions similar to those being considered for the MAI. Most refer to the International Centre for the Settlement of Investment Disputes (ICSID), which has been available for the mediation or conciliation of investment disputes between governments and private investors for over 30 years. There is no evidence that these facilities have resulted in frivolous cases or have been abused by foreign investors to obtain unfair advantages relative to their domestic competitors. Rather, such mechanisms exist to ensure that foreign investors are protected from discriminatory treatment by host governments and domestic courts. Without an effective investor–state dispute resolution mechanism, the MAI would be a clear step backwards from the BITs.

Globalization as a positive force

We fully support OECD ministers' conviction that globalization is a positive force for improving living standards and ensuring sustainable development around the world. Promoting investment through the MAI and other international instruments will thus help to improve standards for environmental protection. Indeed, by introducing international standards consistent with, for example, the ICC Business Charter on Sustainable Development and/or internal codes of conduct, multinational enterprises can and do accelerate the process by applying higher environmental standards than their domestic counterparts.

Our primary objective for this Agreement is that it should truly raise investor confidence by providing clear and strong obligations on non-discrimination, investment protection and dispute settlement. We will thus continue to oppose ambiguous provisions or language that leaves open the possibility for conflicting interpretations of the obligations, and hence increases the risk of unpredictable treatment of foreign investors or their investments.

What went wrong?

What went wrong with the MAI? This question certainly has to be asked following the OECD Ministerial in April 1998 which failed to resolve the MAI controversy, and especially after France officially stepped out of the negotiations a fortnight ago.

I think that nothing went wrong so far in substance with the MAI, since the OECD Secretariat's work throughout the negotiations seemed to stay in line with the main purposes of the task at hand. This is especially true in the context of the environmental relevance of the MAI.

Procedurally, on the other hand, one could argue with the benefit of hindsight that it was not politically wise to concentrate the negotiations of the MAI on governments. From the beginning, however, various consultations have taken place with two NGOs: the Trade Union Advisory Committee to OECD (TUAC) and the Business and Industry Advisory Committee to the OECD (BIAC).

The non-inclusion of other NGOs and of parliamentarians has, in my opinion, resulted in misunderstandings in certain circles. But I cannot avoid the personal impression that some of these misunderstandings appear to be somewhat tactical. I have real difficulties understanding why the MAI was seen to amount simply to a capitalistic and a neo-liberal effort aimed at the suppression of the development of international (core) labour standards and sustainable environmental development. I simply repeat the original aims of the MAI: non-discrimination and national treatment plus liberalization of foreign investment – again, under the auspices of non-discrimination and national treatment.

Would WTO negotiations be better?

Would WTO negotiations be better? This question was considered before the beginning of the negotiations and has been repeatedly raised within the OECD.

One of the key debates at the beginning of the OECD negotiations involved the question of whether it was more important to have broader coverage geographically or higher standards. Supporters of negotiations in the OECD felt it was better to have agreement on higher standards, which could be negotiated more quickly by advanced economies, signed by some non-OECD countries, and then eventually transferred to the WTO. Supporters of the WTO rightly said that the main problems lie outside the OECD, and since non-OECD countries might not be prepared to sign an OECD agreement, it would be better to involve them in the negotiations from the beginning – in the context of the WTO. The compromise has been to push ahead with the OECD effort, and to keep non-member countries informed in the hope that they will want to sign on. The WTO option remains as an ultimate goal.

The good news is that some key countries have been following the negotiations closely and have stated their intention to sign. These include Argentina, Brazil, Chile, Singapore and Taiwan. The bad news is that some key countries, including China, India and Malaysia, have not shown much interest in signing an MAI – whether at the OECD or the WTO.

I continue to believe that the conclusion of an OECD agreement remains the better choice – although France's withdrawal will certainly not improve the chances for such an agreement. Particularly in view of the specific question at hand, i.e. the inclusion of environmental regulation aspects, I would suggest that the chances of success would be even lower in a WTO agreement. The WTO's Singapore ministerial agreement on the ILO's competence on labour issues is a clear indication that almost any coupling of environmental regulations with a 'WTO MAI' would increase the obstacles to success.

Conclusions

In conclusion, let me quote the diplomatic language used by the UK Minister for Trade, Brian Wilson, last week after the OECD meeting in Paris:

> The intention of the MAI negotiating parties had been to present an agreement to OECD ministers for signature in May 1999. This now looks most unlikely. However, the Government – together with our new partners – remains committed in the longer term to promoting the negotiations on investment to the WTO.[1]

The international business community remains committed to the achievement of a broad multilateral framework for international investment

[1] 'Brian Wilson Voices Support for New Rules on Investment', DTI Press Release P/98/799, 21 October 1998.

with high standards for the liberalization of investment regimes and investment protection and with effective dispute settlement procedures. It does not seek a weakening of environmental policies or the restricting of host governments from adopting any non-discriminatory measures they deem necessary to protect their environment and/or to conform to the standards established in multilateral environmental agreements.

A view from the South

Pradeep S. Mehta

Building environmental protection into international investment agreements

Not lowering standards

One of the main demands articulated by the civil society movement in relation to the OECD draft Multilateral Agreement on Investment (MAI) is the incorporation of a clause on 'Not Lowering Standards in the area of Environment and Labour'. This demand is based on a fear that countries will lower or relax their environment and labour standards to attract investment. The fear is partly right and partly wrong.

Assuming that the target for the MAI is the developing countries, it must be admitted that in some of them standards have been lower than those that prevail in developed countries. This is a result of the inherent differential in levels of socioeconomic development in countries where jobs take priority over environment. In these countries, standards are generally never *lowered* as such, but those that exist may be less stringent. And often the standards themselves may be high but their enforcement poor, for reasons ranging from sheer incapacity of the enforcement machinery, in terms of resources, through to corruption, supervisory negligence, or even lack of political will.

The issues relating to environment in the context of transnational investment or a multilateral framework are not limited to this area of lowering standards to attract investment. There are two other major types of issues, both of which smack of double standards. The first concerns 'eco-dumping', and the second concerns operations that are inherently 'dirty'.

Technology transfer or eco-dumping?

To what extent do multinationals follow environmental standards of the highest quality in their developing-country operations? Do they apply the same standards as in their home country or in other developed countries? Similar questions arise in relation to technology transfer: are the technologies applied by multinationals in developing countries clean, or are their investments used as a means of shifting dirty technologies?

In practice, these issues can be raised only if there is sufficient transparency in the host country, so that potentially affected communities can acquire impartial information and influence the siting of plants. The same can be true of government authorities where they are required to allow or not to allow an investment that seeks to transfer dirty technology.

Notwithstanding the infamous memo written by Lawrence Summers when he was at the World Bank, calling for dirty factories to be located in less polluted and poor African countries,[1] often it is actually the high standards of environmental protection in developed countries that result in transfer of polluting industries to less fortunate countries. A few examples will bear this out:

1. In 1987, after synthetic Nylon 6,6 technology had lost out to steel radials in the West, E.I. Du Pont de Nemours, the largest chemical multinational in the United States, decided to shift their outdated 1938-fabricated nylon plant to Goa, a province in western India, in partnership with an Indian company. Contrary to the firm's claim of being safe and clean:
   - the production technology is unknown, and the process uses hexamethylene diamine and adipic acid, which are flammable, toxic and may be carcinogenic;
   - the mandatory Environmental Impact Assessment was not conducted;

[1] *Editors' note*: In 1991, an internal memorandum from Mr Summers was sent to senior staff at the World Bank. One passage infamously asked 'Just between you and me, shouldn't the Bank be encouraging more migration of the dirty industries to the LDCs [less developed countries]? ... the economic logic behind dumping a load of toxic waste in the lowest-wage country is impeccable.' The Bank apologized on behalf of Mr Summers, who explained that the comments were intended as an ironic attempt to stimulate policy debate. See 'Save Planet Earth from Economists', *Financial Times,* 10 February 1992.

- appropriate measures regarding critical areas of groundwater protection, waste water treatment, solid waste recycling and air pollution control were not considered; and
- most shockingly, in spite of a liability law in India spurred by the Bhopal gas tragedy, the government agreed to indemnify Du Pont against any claims resulting from an accident.

Following pressure from a strong citizens' backlash in Goa, Du Pont shifted the plant to Tamil Nadu, a state in southern India. The Indian partner also retired, and now Du Pont is 100 per cent owner. This is a typical example of the 'WIMBY' (welcome in my backyard) syndrome operating at the national and the subnational level in India.

2. Following pressure by the British Health and Safety Executive, Thor Chemical Holdings closed its mercury plant in Margate, Kent, in 1987, while expanding in Carte Ridge, Natal, South Africa. The facts were uncovered in April 1997, when 20 Zulu workers received compensation of US $2million by suing Thor in the UK for poisoning that resulted from working in the mercury plant.
3. Dansk Sojakagefabrik Industries of Denmark shipped a mercury cell chlor-alkali factory to be located in Pakistan in 1991. The Danish company wanted to avoid the costly disposal fees that would have been charged in the European Community, while at the same time providing Pakistani businesses with cheap electricity. Subsequently, Denmark introduced a ban on such exports.

Inherently dirty operations

The second type of problem or issue associated with environmental protection and transnational investment concerns extractive industries. Some of these investments are inherently environmentally unfriendly, even though the installation itself is run in accordance with good environmental management practices. The best example is that of the oil industry.

Studies by the Washington DC-based NGO Conservation International show that oil operations conducted by transnational corporations in Ecuador caused the spillage of an estimated 19 billion gallons of toxic waste between 1972 and 1989.[2] Between 1982 and 1992, Shell's subsidiary in Nigeria spilled about 1.6 million gallons of oil in the Niger Delta, most from leaking pipelines, causing high levels of water pollution and the death of fish, mangroves and tropical forests. In a blatant example of the application of double standards, Greenpeace reported that the construction of a single pipeline in Scotland required Shell to produce 17 environmental surveys and a comprehensive environmental impact assessment.

Similar problems have been observed and catalogued in other major extractive industries such as forestry, mining and fisheries. How far these problems can be resolved through environmental protection measures incorporated in an investment agreement is a moot point. Would such measures lead to investors becoming more benign towards natural resources and the ecology? Or should the problem not be addressed through a raft of policy tools, including promotion of sustainable consumption and production? Much work on this issue is currently under way at the United Nations Commission on Sustainable Development (CSD).

How to address the concerns

Over time, and in particular from the time of the Earth Summit in 1992, the profile of these concerns has been high. The precursor of the CSD, the UN Conference on Environment and Development, led to a plan of action in the form of Agenda 21. This document included policy options for business, and its implementation is being addressed in sectoral forums at the CSD.

Other than what has been catalogued in Agenda 21, businesses (both foreign and domestic) need to follow, and governments need to legislate and enforce, widely recognized fundamental principles of environmental protection. These should include the following basic principles:

---

[2] Ian A. Bowles et al., 'Oil and Gas Development in the Tropical Andes', in *Natural Resource Extraction in the Latin American Tropics* (citing work by Acción Ecológica and the Natural Resources Defence Council), Conservation International Policy Brief no. 1, Spring 1998.

- the *precautionary principle*, which calls for businesses to adopt adequate measures against possible environmental hazards even though full scientific evidence is not available;
- the *polluter and user pays principles*, which call for businesses to pay for environmental harm caused by them in the course of conducting their operations;
- the *principle of transparency*, which calls for businesses to afford easy access to information on their operations by government inspectors or public interest groups;
- the *principle of maintaining the same standards in plants/operations worldwide* and keeping their employees and governments informed about those standards.

There are several other relevant principles, and many are incorporated in a number of voluntary guidelines, such as the OECD Guidelines for Multinational Enterprises or the International Chamber of Commerce's Business Charter for Sustainable Development.

One of the arguments in favour of incorporating these principles in an international investment agreement is that it will lead to the contracting parties' abiding by them through implementation and enforcement of high standards, without running in a race to the bottom.

What went wrong with the MAI?

The OECD MAI aimed to secure increased rights for business and responsibilities for host countries. There were several fatal flaws in this Agreement.

1. While the main *goal* of the MAI was to protect investments from expropriation and nationalization, and if such an event took place to provide for quick redress and compensation, its *target* was the resources and the consumer markets of developing countries who were never even a part of the negotiations.
2. The United States, at the instigation of its big business lobbies, pushed the developed world to launch negotiations on the MAI in early 1995 in the OECD, even though a multilateral forum for trade, the World Trade Organization, had just been established.

3. The European Commission succumbed to the pressure of US business lobbies in spite of a warning that the MAI would not be accepted by developing countries as they were not part of the negotiating forum.
4. Both the WTO and UNCTAD Secretariats were very annoyed by the move to negotiate an MAI within the OECD because the Agreement was being negotiated among a select group of countries, and it was thus incorrect to refer to it as a 'multilateral' agreement. The UNCTAD Secretary General referred to it as the 'plurilateral' agreement on investment, while the WTO Director-General launched a broadside against the MAI by pushing for a discussion on the issue within the WTO.
5. Most developing countries were clearly confused as, on the one hand, the OECD was calling them to sign on to an agreement over which they had had little influence and, on the other, it was nearly those same countries who were pushing it at the WTO. No doubt, to add to the confusion, there was also pressure on regional and bilateral investment treaties.
6. The scope and ambit of the proposed MAI was too great, touching on nearly every aspect of life and governance. Yet a very ambitious (and impractical) target of completing it in less than two years was set. The result was that the negotiators did not even bother to inform and consult the other branches of their own government or parliaments. This lead to the MAI being looked at most suspiciously by civil society representatives and in many countries enraging parliamentarians from both ruling and opposition parties and also subnational entities.
7. While the basic framework draft of the MAI was nearly ready by December 1997, nearly 600 pages of reservations and exceptions were filed by the member nations of the OECD. Half of these were lodged by the United States. The negotiators went too fast in seeking liberal conditions for business to operate in all countries, and with the benefit of hindsight even the powerful USA's knees were shaking.
8. Lastly, the MAI sought to provide increasing *rights* to investors without binding *obligations*, and also placed stronger obligations

on the host countries. There was no consideration of a need for a proper balance of rights and obligations on the investors. This itself was an anathema to most countries.

Would WTO negotiations be better?

At the Singapore Ministerial Conference of the World Trade Organization held in December 1996, it was, somewhat contentiously, resolved to set up two working groups to study and examine the linkages between trade and investment, and between trade and competition policy including anti-competitive practices. There was also agreement that each working group could draw upon the other's work as the issues are closely interlinked.

Both working groups have progressed in terms of examining and understanding the issues. The developing world views both investment and competition policy as the developed world's new tools for increasing market access, and consequently approaches these areas with a degree of suspicion, playing its cards close to its chest.

Some of the key remarks within the Working Group on Trade and Investment, under its item on the Relationship between Trade and Investment for Development and Economic Growth, include the following:

1. The OECD made a submission which analysed the relationship between foreign direct investment (FDI) and economic development through case studies of six developing countries: Argentina, Brazil, Chile, Indonesia, Malaysia and the Philippines. The key point to emerge from the analysis in this submission was that the overall policy framework in host countries was a critical factor in maximizing the gains from FDI. Trade policy was of particular relevance in this regard. Policies pursued in the past by some developing countries with large domestic markets to attract FDI on the basis of a protected home market have lost their effectiveness as they have ran into market saturation and foreign investors have shifted to more dynamic countries and markets. Recent evidence showed that trade liberalization has a positive effect on the volume of FDI inflows.

2. The Philippines, speaking on behalf of the ASEAN WTO members, stated that FDI on the whole played an important positive role in transferring intangible assets to recipient countries, especially developing countries, but that developing countries have sometimes also been confronted with the negative effects of FDI. For example, foreign affiliates were sometimes prevented from undertaking certain activities by restrictions imposed by their parents in technology transfer agreements, which might have an adverse impact on competition and corporate development. Furthermore, some developing countries faced the possibility of becoming locations for simple assembly operations. Referring to analysis of possible negative effects of FDI in the contribution submitted by Japan in WT/WGTI/W/11, a Philippines delegate observed that instability in the balance of trade and balance of payments on account of FDI movements was a very real risk, demonstrated in the recent experience of some ASEAN countries, and that there was also a risk of foreign companies exercising undue political influence.
3. India supported the views expressed by the Philippines and pointed to the need for further analysis of restrictions on transfer of technology in transactions between parents and affiliates and the impact of such transactions on trade and competition.
4. Referring to the text on the relationship between the mobility of capital and the mobility of labour, India pointed to the basic complementarity between capital and labour as production factors and between capital mobility and labour mobility as delivery modes for trade and investment in goods and services. Although this complementary relationship between capital and labour called for a liberal, integrated approach to the mobility of labour as part of the free global flow of capital, goods and services, in reality mobility of capital and mobility of labour had been treated quite differently. The failure to ensure mobility of labour more comprehensively as a complementary and critical factor in the mobility of capital has far-reaching adverse economic consequences, particularly by creating labour shortages which prevent the efficient use of capital.

This is an issue that also occupies UNCTAD, which received a mandate at UNCTAD IX, held in 1996 in Midrand, South Africa, to work on a possible multilateral framework for investment and also to equip developing countries with the necessary knowledge and negotiation skills. UNCTAD has been organizing symposia around the world and in Geneva, and these events have also helped developing countries to understand the dynamics better.

At a symposium in New Delhi in July 1998, the noted trade theorist, Professor Jagdish Bhagwati, denounced the OECD's MAI and lauded the efforts of UNCTAD and developing countries to reform it. Admitting that FDI is a huge and growing phenomenon, he acknowledged the attempt to draft the MAI and its eventual location at the WTO. 'The main problem, however, is that the MAI, as presently conceived and pursued, is fundamentally flawed', he asserted.

In a letter to the *Financial Times* on 22 October 1998, Bhagwati further argued:

> there are powerful reasons to have the matter dropped altogether from the WTO agenda. First, the WTO is now a 'Single undertaking' so that the revised MAI would still be mandatory on all WTO members. The issues it touches are inherently controversial, will take the WTO gratuitously into the politically supercharged domain, and endanger its real mission: to free trade.
>
> Many of us have been arguing that labour and environmental agendas be pursued (proactively) by means other than trade treaties and institutions, leaving the WTO to pursue free trade instead. But it is hard to tell the lobbies seeking to push these agendas into the WTO to get off its back even as the MAI is sought to be worked into the WTO. It was bad enough to work Intellectual Property Protection – an issue of enforcement of asserted property rights against essentially poor nations rather than of trade where all gain – into the WTO as the Uruguay Round closed. But with intellectual property protection and an MAI both in, it would be hard to refute the charge that what is good for capital at the WTO is not good for labour or for nature.

Conclusion

In conclusion, there are three key questions to be considered:

- Is there a need for a multilateral and a comprehensive agreement on investment, given that FDI is growing in the existing framework?
- Would such an agreement change the skewed nature of FDI flows?
- Would a multilateral agreement fulfil the development goals envisaged by developing countries?

If there is a need at all for a multilateral investment framework, then it could take the form of a voluntary code on investment laws which could be adopted by countries under the auspices of the United Nations.

An NGO view

Nick Mabey

Introduction

The World Wide Fund for Nature (WWF) has worked on the MAI since June 1996. We have produced between 12 and 14 papers and we have had the dubious honour of being both praised and dismissed by sitting ministers of state in the United Kingdom, though the government of course retains a firm, united front on the issue!

The MAI has changed the intellectual and political climate for debate on macroeconomic policy. This is partly because the negotiations spanned the financial crisis, the causes of which were deeply entwined with some of the capital liberalization issues in the MAI and the IMF. Liberalization can never again be considered in isolation from other issues. The idea that the sanctity of the WTO, or of any body that deals with economics, can be preserved while environmental or other issues are addressed in another forum is never going to become reality. Investment affects everything and it is much more invasive than trade. This was not appreciated by the MAI negotiators when they started. Civil society and other government departments can no longer be excluded. It is no longer acceptable to try to bounce developing countries into an agreement they have not negotiated. This was the biggest point of principle against the MAI. When WWF started lobbying on the MAI we were told it was not about developing countries, and just before it collapsed the head of OECD said it *was* for developing countries. That kind of *volte face* spreads distrust and undermines both the UN system and the trust between North and South that we need if we are to move forward.

As to an 'Environment Investment Agreement', if you look at the European Union and its environmental harmonization, there is a pretty strong case that has to be disproved by the other side for why environment should not be considered integrally inside an investment agreement.

A conflict of world views

The MAI generated such opposition because there was a fundamental clash between two different world views. On the one hand there was the world view of the trade and investment experts (though not so much of some of the companies). There was a very strong ideological strand in their debate and the chairman of the negotiations exemplified that strand. But there was also a second world view, which is not this economic view. This is the vision of sustainable development and human rights to which every government has signed up. It is the new world view.

The architects of the MAI said: ‘We know what the objective was of the MAI; it was to get a high quality agreement.’ As one developing-country delegate said in one of the outreach sessions, ‘What is high quality for you may not be high quality for us.’ What does ‘high quality’ mean? This is a central question.

The economic world view

What does the economic world look like to the intelligent, high-powered people negotiating the MAI? It is a world where free flows of capital produce greater efficiency – a simple economic argument. At a simplistic level, this is difficult to disagree with, but remember the assumptions on which that argument is based – the assumptions that the world is static, that everything is homogeneous, that there is one form of private capital. When you study this model at college, there is no social capital; there is no education; there is no environment. There is no evolution in technology which occurs inside the investment process and through learning-by-doing. In this model, companies are purely price-driven in the way they relocate: they are not looking at market growth; they are not looking at loss leaders; they are not looking at building up networks. This model does not consider equity. It considers that all trade-offs are possible between environment, between people and economic growth, and it is concerned only with nation-states. In fact, this model pretty much drops every single piece of new economic theory that has appeared in the last 20 years on the issues of growth, industrial location, industrial specialization and development. It represents an old set of theories.

If you take this view of the world, the only environmental problem you come up with is the game theorist's 'prisoner's dilemma': that countries will outbid each other by lowering standards over labour and environment in order to attract investment, and that this is 'non-optimal'. This is why there is the 'no lowering of standards' clause in the MAI; it flows directly from that logic. So the policy recommendations are to raise domestic standards and coordinate action on incentives. If you take this view of the world, you end up thinking that the MAI is a very bland agreement: it does not really do a lot; it is 'just' an investment architecture, and you simply have to fiddle at the edges to deal with other issues.

This 'first-best policy' perspective does not even approach the realities of liberalization. It is intellectually dishonest and factually incorrect. Show me a first-best world, and I will give you a first-best policy. But the assumptions of the model that underlie the MAI are false and they will always be false. This is where the tension arises.

The sustainable world view

Second, there is the world view of the massed hordes, caricatured as barbarians at the gates, out there on the Internet. How do we see the world? We see increasing negative environmental trends – 1.3 billion people in poverty; two-thirds of the poor living in water-stressed countries; soil being eroded, and 60 per cent of fisheries under threat, with fish being the primary source of protein of 950 million people. These are all affected by investment. A great deal of investment goes into natural resource areas.

We also see economic growth predicted to increase by three or four times over the next 25 years at the same time as the population will at least double. That is a lot of pressure on a world that is already going down a very slippery environmental slope – and it is the poor who will suffer from this. Climate change will affect the poor, not the rich – the rich are those who caused it. Therefore, we see a dynamic world full of resource-using industries; we see resources going from the South to the North; we see the poor being pushed into the most polluted and marginal areas; and we see a lot of unequal distribution, especially since 95 per cent of investment comes from OECD countries – the ones who are negotiating the agreement.

In this world, there are some new rules that go beyond the old-world aim of capital efficiency. There is uncertainty and irreversible environmental and social damage which is coded in the precautionary principle – a key principle left out of the MAI. There is also the question of equity: who suffers damage, and who gets benefits? If you trade environmental quality against getting a factory built, or a resource-using investment made, it is usually the same people who do not benefit from the economic growth who suffer the environmental damage. The 'polluter pays' principle was another principle from Rio that was left out of an OECD agreement, although in many ways it is the OECD's principle. The issues of equity and compensation have to be addressed. It is interesting that, compared with the deal-making culture of the WTO, environmental agreements are about assigning responsibility and not about doing deals – which is much harder for countries to accept.

If you consider that a country like the UK has been responsible for a vastly disproportionate amount of emissions of CO_2 over its lifetime as a country (given that we industrialized first), you can see that we owe a debt to the rest of the world, because our pollution has formed the foundation of our capital stock and our current wealth. So environmental agreements are very bound up, in the new world, with distribution of resources and equal access to the global commons. These are concepts that are completely missing from the 'efficient' world of the MAI.

The rights of non-state actors were codified at the Rio Earth Summit. People have the right to be heard independently of their nation-state; they have the right to have some access. This was not addressed in the MAI. The whole complex area of the indirect impacts of investment – migration, urbanization, changes in structures, breakdown of social groups, leading in turn to more environmental damage – was not even on the agenda in the MAI. That is the world in which most of us are working and how we see the impact of investment.

There are ecological limits to what we do and there are human rights limits to what we do, and these cannot be traded off against economic growth. There are limits to trade-offs and these limits are made up of environmental, political and cultural rights. In this complex, contingent and difficult world you have to consider every case and see what happens when you open up markets and let investors in. Does it increase development, does it reduce poverty, does it hurt the environment? This is not a case for promoting protectionism: it is a case for a little more reality, a little less high-level assumptions and a little more looking at what is really going on, including giving governments the capacity to see what is going on.

International investment frameworks must enable environmental protection. They are not a panacea. We never said we wanted to cure the world's environmental problems with the MAI, though this was yet another caricature of the environmental groups' position. We just wanted to make sure that the MAI supported the efforts we are all pursuing at national and subnational levels. But it did not: it stopped them; it chilled them. As well as not producing a positive agenda, the MAI limited our ability to go down a positive road. Performance requirements, for example, can affect recycling, technology transfer, local community management – all the projects WWF undertakes abroad. They can prevent the capturing of resource rents, thereby reducing incentives for sustainable management.

Subsidiarity

It really comes down to the subsidiarity principle. The MAI was in favour of investor protection. But investor protection was not an issue for any company I talked to during the negotiations. The agenda of investor protection is an old agenda, and I do not believe that people have seen it as a major agenda since the 1970s. The MAI was in favour of liberalization. But countries are liberalizing anyway, and in the studies that we have looked at, and in the countries we have visited, it does not appear that liberalization is connected to capital flows. The MAI was the wrong place to push liberalization. Liberalization and the opening of markets should be decided by national actors. National actors may want to make sure that someone else cannot reverse these decisions later to gain credibility, but that is very different from having an instrument that sees rolling back regulation, and rolling back barriers, as its main aim.

The MAI was in favour of performance requirements. Every country wants foreign investment, and if there is a barrier to that investment, one of two reasons is likely to lie behind it: either a policy interest or a vested interest. Should an international instrument be used as a means of getting rid of national vested interests? The answer from most MAI negotiators to whom I have spoken was 'yes': they believe that governments are stupid, and especially developing-country governments. This is not a caricature: this is precisely what came from the mouths of the MAI negotiators. They do not believe that governments can look at foreign investment and say, 'What is the best deal I can do? Do I put some performance requirements on them; do I give them an obligation to hire domestic workers, to feed in domestic suppliers; do I make them export so I get some hard currency; do I not let them in, or do I let them in for a certain amount of time and then close up to other firms so as to let the incomers build up a base in my country?' All these are tools that have been used before. The MAI said, 'No, you are stupid, you cannot make those strategic choices.' Why limit a country's ability to bargain with an incoming investor? The only reasons are to strengthen the investor's power, or because you think the government is stupid.

Why make sure that there is foreign access to privatizations in the first wave? This is a very important part of the MAI, but is not very much discussed. It is a key American company objective to get access to lots of privatizations in the first wave. But we all know that privatizations are undersold. Every single privatization in the UK was sold at a knock-down price. National citizens paid for those companies; they have the right to preferential access in the first round.

An MAI for sustainable development

There were lots of suggestions for changing the MAI. WWF came up with many different ideas, and from March 1997 we made very strong recommendations that were never considered. The OECD produced recommendations; UNCTAD produced recommendations on a development-friendly investment agreement – they were never discussed. The OECD was always defensive; it was never looking at what positive role it could play.

The MAI was clearly a very bad piece of economic policy. But where do we go from here? If you want a new objective, then that objective is sustainable development. WWF has many ideas as to how that could be promoted inside investment agreements. These include requirements for environmental assessment, and a code of conduct linked to investor protection so that you get protection from the international system only if you follow the international system's rules. That is pretty reasonable, and it happens in national countries. Liability should flow with profits back to the home country: that is an important principle, a remedy of last resort but something we would like. There should be more emphasis on the positives: supporting ethical business, supporting good-practice businesses by giving them preferential access to guaranteed loans and trade promotion. Let us give people out there a carrot to move in the right direction. We are not interested in dealing with a bad agreement; we want to deal with a good agreement.

In conclusion, the areas we need agreement on generally cover the things that weren't in the MAI. I am not sure that the MAI had any economic use at all, apart from increasing the bargaining power of incoming investors. Politically, rights and responsibilities have to be linked together, because you cannot get rules on responsibility for companies without giving them something in return. WWF can work on some creative institutional lobbying in some different institutions, but the politics do not allow us to move in entirely separate and unconnected tracks. If investment is simply passed over to the WTO and there is no fundamental rethink, there will just be NGO opposition again. NGOs want to see some thinking about objectives and some thinking about how people negotiate.

Finally, my favourite quote from a leader in *The Financial Times*: 'One lesson for international negotiations from the MAI fiasco – this is not how to do it!'

Part V
Summary of conference discussions

Halina Ward

Introduction

This section contains a short overview of the discussions that followed each of the presentations at the Chatham House conference on 'Trade, Investment and the Environment' in October 1998. The conference itself was attended by some 150 people, an international mix drawn from government, industry, international institutions, non-governmental organizations and the academic world. Chatham House was particularly pleased that sponsorship made possible the participation of a number of developing-country experts who would not otherwise have been able to attend.

The discussion sections of the conference clearly reflected the high level of expertise in the audience, and a search for 'solutions' rather than a simple exploration of the issues. For the most part, the discussion was 'on the record'. Here, however, the aim is to present some of the key themes and ideas, without identifying individual questioners. The summaries of presentations are my own, and have not been reviewed by their authors. The structure of the original conference is retained.

Day one

Brian Wilson MP, UK Minister for Trade, opened the conference with a keynote address (see Part I). The opportunity to question a trade minister on environment and development issues was clearly welcomed by many. What could be done to ensure that the proposed WTO High Level Meeting was different from discussions in the Committee on Trade and Environment (CTE), which had helped to air many of the issues, but had not reached consensus? And, in the light of the lack of developing country participation in the MAI, could redefining the objectives of investment liberalization help to build consensus among less developed countries, and between developed and developing countries? Mr Wilson's emphasis lay on the value of consensus and dialogue built on trust as a key to progress.

Session 1: Background: changing patterns of trade and investment

This session included two presentations. Dr Damien Geradin of the University of Liège sketched out the broad contours of the relationship between trade and environment in terms of the relationship between environmental regulation, competitiveness and the WTO rules. From the (UK) DFID, David Batt followed with a paper on the development dimension of trade and investment issues. Mr Batt introduced the 'win–win' theme, and stressed the need to 'join up government' on these issues by ensuring coherence and consistency across government departments. The ensuing discussion introduced what was to become one of the principal themes of the conference: although the countries of the North are seen as the champions of environmental protection, they do not meet their own responsibilities. How can this mismatch be addressed?

The distinction between 'developed' and 'developing' countries has always been a key element of any discussion on the relationship between trade and environment, as such discussions are frequently polarized along 'North–South' lines. But one participant asked whether in the trade arena the distinction between 'developed and developing' countries was really so sharp. The idea of working towards 'win–win' solutions through a 'convergence' of interests takes on a rather different perspective from a starting point that suggests that 'we are all developing countries'.

Some more detailed questions picked up on the 'win–win' theme of David Batt's paper. Could reductions in subsidies in agriculture and fisheries offer valuable 'win–win' opportunities? Agriculture was identified as an area with particular potential, the more so since negotiations on agriculture are scheduled to begin independently of any decision on a 'comprehensive' Millennium Round.

Session 2: Trade and environment – the key debates

Session 2 of the conference, on 'Trade and Environment – the Key Debates', presented perspectives on three related areas of the trade and environment debate: Building Markets for Sustainable Trade; Multilateral Environmental Agreements (MEAs) and Trade; and Process and Production Methods (PPMs) and Trade.

Much of the section devoted to Building Markets for Sustainable Trade homed in on the practical impact of environment rules and standards on the ground in the real world of trade. Given the controversial nature of the idea of 'squeezing unsustainable trade out of the system', why not focus instead on how to stimulate trade through market incentives?

A variety of perspectives was offered by the speakers. Nick Robins (IIED) put forward some positive case studies, but stressed that these should not be considered representative of the current situation on the ground: a continuing lack of trust and inadequate information and access to standard-setting processes present developing-country producers with real obstacles.

Moses Adigbli's paper exemplified this more sceptical view from a developing-country timber industry perspective. For example, he questioned whether some forest certification schemes are sufficiently sensitive to the concerns of developing-country producers. In his view, *all* authenticated national forest certification schemes should be equally accepted in the marketplace – in contrast to the situation in the UK, where an important buyer's group recognizes only one certification scheme: that of the Forest Stewardship Council (FSC). But others highlighted both the potential role of buyers' groups as an interim step towards scaling up the role of consumers, and the role of procurement policy in changing consumption patterns. The related issues of 'whose ethics' and 'who are the stakeholders' for the purposes of labelling schemes were addressed in discussions too; once again, the importance of consensus-building was emphasized.

David Wheeler of The Body Shop asked: 'What are the accelerators and decelerators for good business practice?' He highlighted some of the problems of voluntary labelling and certification standards, including a lack of penetration in the marketplace, the levels of investment required to meet their requirements, and the idea that they could be a distraction from another 'good', namely active corporate disclosure. He underlined the potential business benefits of an approach based on a policy of 'active engagement' with external stakeholders, but argued that labelling schemes themselves were unlikely to lead to much progress. What was needed from policy-makers was more mandated corporate disclosure (including possibly environmental or social disclosure attached to stock exchange listing requirements), and mandatory labelling on crucial environmental and social issues. In discussion, one speaker countered with a note of caution on mandatory certification and labelling – it could simply lead to control being handed over from producers (e.g. farmers in the case of organic certification) to bureaucrats. An alternative approach to the problem of 'label proliferation' was raised in discussion: if too many labels in the marketplace simply confuse consumers, why not seek to develop international standards?

Multilateral environmental agreements

The texts of presentations by Michel Potier (OECD), Duncan Brack (RIIA) and Reinhard Quick (VCI) are included in this volume. At the conference, additional papers by Michael Grubb (RIIA, on the trade implications of the Kyoto Protocol and the Climate Change Convention) and Veena Jha (UN consultant) were also presented.

During the discussions, one theme concerned the role of multilateral environmental agreements (MEAs) as a driver of industrial innovation. The Montreal Protocol was pointed up as an effective agreement in part because it had done just that, and more quickly than had been anticipated. The discussion concerning the Kyoto Protocol represented a new area of concern: for example, would emissions trading be covered by the General Agreement on Trade in Services, and how would the Subsidies Agreement apply to initial allocations of permits? These remained areas for further study.

If the Kyoto Protocol represents one emerging area of MEA/WTO concern, another relates to MEAs that might emerge in the future. Could an increase in trade-restrictive 'take-back' schemes (for example for old television sets) have an impact on MEAs such as the Basel Convention in the future, as one participant suggested? Or might it, as another speculated, lead to a push for a freestanding 'green international take-back scheme'?

Better coordination between ministries at the national level is often seen as a key to better integration of trade and environment. But the danger of ineffective coordination becoming a 'chill factor' on the negotiation of MEAs was highlighted – for example, where some countries had argued for the incorporation of a GATT 'savings clause' in the MEA.

Finally, the issues of 'hierarchy' between different legal systems were also explored. What role could the International Court of Justice (ICJ) play as an integrating force? The WTO's dispute settlement system is relying more and more on general principles of international law: has the time come when one could foresee the WTO's Appellate Body referring a case to the ICJ? No clear answer emerged, though there was some support for the principle that this should be permissible.

Process and production methods

This section included three different perspectives on this issue: Konrad von Moltke focused on re-interpreting 'like products'; Charles Arden-Clarke (WWF International) considered the impact of the *Shrimp/Turtle* Appellate Body report for the future of the PPMs debate; and René Vossenaar (UNCTAD) assessed issues relating to PPMs from a development perspective.

During the discussion session, a number of speakers considered the significance of PPMs, both politically in the trade arena and as an environmental regulation. If this most controversial issue was not yet at the centre of the political debate, was that perhaps because any attempt to develop rules of general application now could lead to a solution that was worse than the problem?

The discussion on 'sustainable trade' was taken up again in this session. There was some support for the idea that this notion of 'sustainable trade' should lie at the heart of any resolution of the relationship between trade and the environment as a whole, and of the PPMs issue in paticular. Industrialized countries in the North were often seen as the *demandeurs* on trade and environment, without recognizing that, in order to achieve something, it would be necessary for them to put something on the table. Developing countries wanted market access. Consequently, the idea of 'sustainable trade' offered real potential for a 'meeting of minds'. As such, it should be viewed as a key issue in political as well as academic circles. But one speaker underlined that 'market access' for developing countries was about more than just sustainable trade and should not be confused with it. Market access, furthermore, should be addressed first.

What were the key elements of 'sustainable trade'? There was perhaps a tendency at the conference to focus on the environmental side rather at the expense of the social, said one participant. There was a broad recognition that the notion of 'sustainable trade' would need to be reflected in a social dimension too, covering for example labour conditions. But it was recognized that the challenges of addressing the social dimension alongside the environmental added considerable complexity to the debate.

Linked to the 'sustainable trade' discussion was an emerging idea that there should be an 'environmental' or 'sustainability' assessment of further trade liberalization. This could ultimately mean that negotiators would be required to prove that liberalization would produce social and environmental benefits.

Concluding keynote address: John Gummer

Day one of the conference concluded with a keynote presentation by John Gummer (see Part I).

Mr Gummer's presentation led to discussion of the proper scope of the WTO's responsibility and of its place in a system of global governance. Did calls for the WTO to address social cultural issues, for example, simply suggest that the WTO had become a victim of its own success, or should more be made of the reference to sustainable development in the WTO's Preamble?

Was there indeed a need for a 'world governing system'? For some, the idea carried dangers, including an implication of absolutism. Others focused on the notion of 'subsidiarity' – that issues should be dealt with at the most appropriate level, and that some issues call for a global governance system. On the other hand, Mr Gummer stressed that subsidiarity should be seen as a 'bottom-up' concept. From a top-down perspective, subsidiarity 'always stops at your level'. Calling for a global governance structure could be going too far. But for many participants, what *was* needed was an equally powerful body alongside the WTO on the side of environment and, more than that, sustainable development. The cultural dimension of trade also needed attention – i.e. protecting the 'biodiversity of humanity'. Yet here, one man's culture could be another man's protectionism.

Day two

Session 3: Environment and investment

Session 3 opened with a focus on investment and the role of transnational corporations. To what extent could the activities of private actors improve environmental standards? Do transnational corporations 'leapfrog' environmentally sound technologies to the developing world or outsource dirty technologies? Can environmental regulation be 'win–win'? What role can or should transnational corporations play in multilateral negotiations? Three speakers addressed these and related issues: Tom Burke (see Part I), Veena Jha, with a particular focus on the experience in India (see Part II); and David Owen, with a particular focus on the water sector (Part IV).

For NGOs, a key issue in the discussion session was the links between deregulation and a move towards enhanced private-sector power. One participant put forward some minimum preconditions that would need to be met before her organization could accept that activities of transnational corporations could lead to improved environmental standards: these included recognition of the development priorities of host countries; acceptance of community and national ownership of natural resources; acceptance of labour and human rights; and a recognition that resources are finite.

Still on the NGO side, one participant said that it was becoming clear from a strategic perspective that NGOs would need to consider more closely the role of transnational corporations in international negotiations. One related area for consideration was the hypothesis that it was in the interests of transnational corporations to promote the creation of a forum in which trade and environment could be integrated, given their interest in the convergence of the two regimes. An obstacle lies not so much with companies as with a lack of political will to deliver up the sovereignty necessary to create a global environment organization. The WTO is as powerful as it is precisely because it has been accompanied by a transfer of sovereignty of a scale that would not be feasible on the environment side.

What of the related possibility of some degree of convergence between 'government' and 'public' politics, for example over GMOs? How could this impact on transnational corporations? Such convergence around future conflict over GMOs might not prove to be on terms sought by corporate elites. There is a real danger, said one speaker, that both the economy and the environment could be undermined precisely because of the enormous lack of integration between them.

Keynote address: 'The GATT at 50: New Challenges'

This session was followed by a keynote address from Renato Ruggiero, then Director-General of the WTO (see Part I). The discussion focused on three issues. The first was once more the feasibility of establishing a global environmental organization: a need was highlighted to ensure that this was linked to parallel progress on the development side, where for example there had been moves to seek 'bound' duty-free access for least-developed-country exports, which so far had not made much progress. The second was transparency and participation in WTO dispute settlement proceedings. While the WTO's lack of transparency continued to concern participants, the *Shrimp/Turtle* decision was hailed by one speaker as the culmination of a clear line of action to say that each dispute settlement panel is autonomous and may organize its own work as it thinks necessary – including through consideration of non-governmental representations. Third, on the prospects for a High Level Meeting, Mr Ruggiero characterized this as an opportunity for an 'open heart dialogue'. He stressed the potential for the meeting to ease the relationship between trade and environment at national level.

Environmental regulation and international investment agreements

This session included four presentations on the lessons that could be learned from the experience with the failed MAI. Dr Kristian Ehinger of Volkswagen began from an industry perspective, followed by Pradeep Mehta (CUTS, India) from a developing-country NGO perspective; Jan Huner of the Netherlands Ministry of Economic Affairs, who had worked alongside the Dutch chair of the MAI Negotiating Group; and finally Nick Mabey of WWF from an environment NGO perspective. A short discussion session followed. All agreed that mistakes had been made. For some, these lay in the fundamentals of the MAI. One speaker regretted that the MAI had not been treated as an opportunity to start afresh – instead, established concepts from bilateral investment agreements had formed its core. For others, the objectives had been sound, but the large number of exceptions tended to go against those objectives.

Session 4: Conflict resolution and dispute settlement

This session incorporated two presentations. Professor Thomas Cottier of the University of Bern began by asking why tensions between trade and environment might be increasing. Because, he answered, trade policy had become 'the number one instrument of foreign policy'. He considered WTO cases relating to environment policy, and wondered whether the emerging case law relating to biotechnology disputes suggested that the SPS Agreement offers more leeway than the concept of 'like products' in the GATT and TBT Agreements. The GATS offers far more scope than the GATT to condition 'national treatment' obligations on environmental grounds, and he hoped that potential should be fully explored. Ultimately, environmental impacts might be associated mainly with services rather than with goods.

On the issue of unilateral versus multilateral measures, the reality was that, without the dialectics of 'unilateral measures and multilateral pressures', multilateral standards would not emerge. In this area in particular, Professor Cottier saw a tension between traditional concepts of public international law – very much defended by developing countries – and a concern to protect the global commons. Might it be possible to start defining and building a consensus on the values, items and goods that belong to the idea of the 'global commons'? Much could be done through dispute settlement to resolve the tension between trade and environment, but panels could not be expected to do everything. There was a need to prepare the thinking.

James Cameron (FIELD and Baker and Mckenzie) focused on the operation of the WTO dispute settlement system, and the implications of the *Shrimp/Turtle* report for future non-governmental involvement in dispute settlement processes. A theme in the discussion concerned the 'unilateral–multilateral' relationship. In some areas, such as animal welfare, the multilateral approach was not realistic because of a lack of multilateral (as distinct from bilateral or plurilateral) political will. What then? For the time being, there seemed little cause for optimism that unilateral measures might find favour with the WTO, though there might be scope for exploring the idea of a labelling approach some more, or for looking more closely at the possibility of using tariffs as a way of shaping policies. On a related issue, how could the balance needed to protect the weak from arbitrary exercise of power by the strong most effectively work in relation to unilateral measures? And how should the WTO deal with multilaterally inspired domestic action, with those measures that somehow fall between MEAs and domestic regulation which concerns only a country's own jurisdiction? For Cameron, this was a key area for consideration in the future.

On *amicus* briefs (see James Cameron's paper, pp. 203–208), there was some discussion of the implications of the *Shrimp/Turtle* report. James Cameron stressed the value of *amicus* briefs as a means of invigorating the process, particularly in the early days of a system.

Should the WTO system incorporate a permanent arbitrator or court? Some participants thought it should. Professor Cottier put forward a number of additional suggestions for reform, starting with the consultation phase of dispute settlement proceedings. In his view this should be reinforced, with an obligation upon parties to a dispute to consult before starting formal panel proceedings. Cottier suggested that the WTO's Appellate Body should also have a 'remand power' to allow it to send cases back to panels to avoid repetition of the situation that had arisen in the *Beef Hormones* case, when the Appellate Body changed the burden of proof, but wasn't able to send the case back to be heard again through this new lense. Finally, he suggested that perhaps an official voice to represent the WTO Secretariat in dispute settlement proceedings could be a useful idea.

Final panel discussion

The final session of the conference consisted of a panel discussion on 'the future' of the trade–investment–environment debate. It consisted of a series of short panel presentations (from Charles Arden-Clarke (WWF International), Gary Sampson (WTO Secretariat – see Part I), Magda Shahin (Ministry of Foreign Affairs, Egypt – see Part III) and David Wakeford (ICI – see Part I), followed by a longer discussion and questions from the floor.

Discussion returned to the debate on whether there should be a Global Environment Organization. Once again, much discussion focused on the appropriate scope of the WTO's responsibility. Charles Arden-Clarke spoke of 'mainstreaming' the environment into all of the WTO's activities. Others took a cautious approach: that this should not mean changing the rules unless the changes were in line with the WTO's competence, which is limited to trade. One speaker stressed that the arguments in favour of making existing environmental organizations more effective or creating a global environmental organization should not stand in the way of ensuring that the WTO better accommodates environmental interests in the trade policy that it applies. For one NGO speaker, too, lobbying for a global environment organization was not considered an effective use of his organization's limited resources, which were currently targeted at working within the existing structures. In any event, returning to the earlier theme of 'global governance', one participant doubted whether even a global environmental organization would be sufficient to achieve the necessary integration.

Once again, the idea came up that after *Shrimp/Turtle* perhaps WTO dispute settlement had achieved what was needed and there was no need to change the WTO rules. The 'slippery slope' argument – implicit in many presentations throughout the conference – was reiterated: beyond trade and trade-related aspects, the WTO should not be made an organization that looks at different interests from labour to good governance. But participants were also reminded of the 'chill factor' that could result from a failure properly to integrate trade and environment, or, as a result, from trade officials becoming involved in international environmental negotiations.

There was criticism of the Committee on Trade and Environment. Had it gone far enough or even outlived its usefulness? In some areas perhaps, one participant suggested, the CTE had already done as much work as it could be expected to do. If this work had not delivered a 'solution', perhaps that was because there was nowhere to go on these issues.

Could the Millennium Round prove to be the 'terminal round' for the WTO? Could a failure sufficiently to accommodate environment and sustainable development concerns lead to its demise? Or does it in reality work rather well? One participant emphasized that, for example, in terms of all the requests for consultations initiated under the WTO, only a very small number had anything to do with environment.

Discussion returned to the 'win–win' theme and its implications. For one speaker, there was a need to focus more on the dynamics of trade in the marketplace – on the dialectic between companies in their supply chains and associated policy moves, not simply on the dialectic between 'unilateral' and 'multilateral'. As to the implications of 'win–win' solutions for the Millennium Round, one government participant highlighted three areas 'ripe for the picking' in terms of win–win solutions: (1) the elimination of fisheries subsidies, an area where considerable work had already been done; (2) the General Agreement on Trade in Services, where there could be a very clear and direct link between improved market access and environmental gains; and (3) the elimination of export subsidies in agriculture, to put an end to the current signals for overproduction, trade distortion and land use with negative impacts. The conceptual thinking on the 'win–win' theme had already been done. The challenge now was to identify the key areas for reform – to enable developing countries to say 'yes' to genuinely 'win–win' solutions.

Index